The Senior's Guide to Metabolism

Publisher's Note

The editors of FC&A have taken careful measures to ensure the accuracy and usefulness of the information in this book. While every attempt was made to assure accuracy, some Web sites, addresses, telephone numbers, and other information may have changed since printing.

This book is intended for general information only. It does not constitute medical advice or practice. We cannot guarantee the safety or effectiveness of any treatment or advice mentioned. Readers are urged to consult with their health care professionals and get their approval before undertaking therapies suggested by information in this book, keeping in mind that errors in the text may occur as in all publications and that new findings may supersede older information.

Do not let your hearts be troubled. Trust in God; trust also in me.
John 14:1

FC&A Medical Publishing®
103 Clover Green
Peachtree City, GA 30269

Produced by the staff of FC&A

ISBN 978-1-935574-09-5

Table of Contents

Belly fat: easy ways to slenderize and energize

5 surprising things that slow your metabolism

What you eat may not be to blame for your big belly. Metabolism tends to slow with age, and, as it does, your waistline expands. Fortunately, gaining weight does not have to be a normal part of aging. You just need to know how to rev up your metabolic machine.

Metabolism is the process your body uses to turn food into energy it can use. Your basal metabolism is the minimum amount of energy, or calories, the body needs to:

- breathe, grow and repair cells, and adjust hormone levels.

- maintain your body temperature.

- keep the muscles in your heart and intestine working.

Basal metabolism accounts for about two-thirds of the calories you burn every day. Most of the rest goes toward physical activity and digesting food.

Everyone's metabolism is different. The bigger you are, the more calories you burn even when resting. Ditto the more muscle you have.

Men generally have faster metabolisms than women because they tend to have more muscle and less fat.

You aren't stuck with the same metabolic rate your whole life. It changes — sometimes for the worst. Check out these five secret reasons your belly is getting bigger when your meals are not.

Aging. You tend to gain fat and lose muscle as you get older, a combination guaranteed to dampen your calorie-burning power.

Menopause. It isn't fair, but the shift in hormones that happens during menopause naturally puts the breaks on your metabolism, beginning three to four years before menopause even hits. Your body starts storing more calories as fat instead of burning them for fuel. Plus, it changes where it stores that fat, shifting it to your belly.

Sitting. Basal metabolism only accounts for some of the calories you burn every day. Physical activities account for a lot, too. The more you move around, the more calories you burn. If you slow down, then so will your metabolism.

Watching television. Compared to reading, sewing, writing, or playing board games, research suggests your metabolism is slowest while watching TV.

Extreme dieting. The body constantly tries to balance the energy it takes in with the energy it puts out. When you cut back on food too severely, as you would during a "starvation" diet, your body reacts by conserving calories. This, in turn, slows down your metabolic processes.

If your metabolism is in "slo-mo," here are the four best ways to put it in "fast forward." Do these now to start making that belly disappear.

- Lay off the television. Read, play games, work a puzzle, or chat with a friend when you want to relax.

- Fight age-related muscle loss with muscle-building activities, like lifting light weights.

- Count those calories. Women who underwent menopause in one study saw their metabolism slow, but they gained very little weight. Their secret — they compensated for the slowdown by eating fewer calories.

- Get off the couch. Remember, basal metabolism only accounts for some of the calories you burn. Physical activity, even as simple as chores and gardening, make up another hefty portion. Plus, exercise speeds up your metabolism during the workout and up to several hours afterward.

Hidden cause of weight gain

An expanding waistline, low energy, and slow metabolism are not necessarily a normal part of aging. Hypothyroidism, a condition where your thyroid gland doesn't produce enough thyroid hormone, can also cause these problems.

It's a rare but treatable disease. See your doctor if you notice these strange-but-true signs. Your body may be trying to tell you something.

- thinning eyebrows
- unintentional weight gain
- thin, brittle hair or fingernails
- hoarseness
- puffy face, hands, and feet
- thickening of your skin
- being more sensitive to cold
- loss of taste and smell

Say goodbye to your big belly

The secret to keeping your arteries young, fit, and flexible? Banish the belly fat. That's right — that little "paunch" is actually destroying your arteries by pumping out chemicals that fire up internal inflammation. A beltline bulge is not only unsightly, it can also lead to heart disease, diabetes, cancer, and other diseases related to inflammation.

You see, it's not just how much fat you carry around, but where you carry it. Belly fat is particularly dangerous. For one thing, it's linked to atherosclerosis, or plaque buildup in your arteries, while other types of fat are not. It's also a major reason overweight people develop heart disease. Abdominal fat pumps out inflammatory compounds, many more than fat from other areas. But the inflammation doesn't stay in your belly. It spreads to the whole body.

Studies show that obese people with belly fat tend to suffer from hard-to-treat insulin resistance, high blood pressure, and a greater chance of developing blood clots near their heart — conditions that set the stage for heart disease and the metabolic syndrome. Inflammation even ups your risk for other diseases, including diabetes, colon cancer, and dementia.

Even people who aren't overweight are at risk. Normal-weight women who had big waistlines also had higher levels of "bad" LDL cholesterol, triglycerides, blood sugar, and blood pressure. Overall, they were more likely to die from any cause, including heart disease and cancer, than women with trimmer waists. In all, belly fat directly affects your risk of:

- atherosclerosis
- cancer
- diabetes
- dementia
- insulin resistance

- high blood pressure
- heart disease
- frailty
- metabolic syndrome

But there is good news. The most dangerous fat in your body is actually the easiest to lose. Belly fat is often the first to go when you start shedding pounds. Whether you slim down through diet, exercise, or both, the effect is the same — your inflammation levels drop. As your belly melts away, you'll start to clear your arteries, control your blood sugar, protect your heart, regain lost energy, and more.

3 easy ways to tell if you're overweight

Figure out whether you need to lose weight before you start any ambitious diet plans.

Measure your waist. The circumference of your waist measures belly fat, the most dangerous kind of body fat. This makes it a good way to "measure" your risk of future health problems, like heart attack, diabetes, and stroke.

Find the tops of your hip bones. Wrap a tape measure around your waist there. It should be snug but not pinching your skin. Breathe out, then take your measurement. Your waistline should be smaller than 35 inches in women or 40 inches in men. A larger waistline is an indication of abdominal obesity.

Find your BMI. Body Mass Index, or BMI, estimates body fat, based on your height and weight. The Centers for Disease Control will calculate your BMI for free at the Web site *www.cdc.gov/healthyweight/assessing/bmi*. Generally, a BMI between 18.5 and 24.9 means you are a normal weight, 25 to 29.9 overweight, and over 30 obese.

Figure your maximum weight. The Maximum Weight Limit (MWL) is the highest amount you should weigh, based on your gender and height. Find your MWL and compare it to your current weight. If you're over the MWL, you know it's time to slim down.

The baseline for men is 5-feet 9-inches tall and 175 pounds. Add 5 pounds to that weight for every inch taller you are than the baseline, or subtract 5 pounds for every inch shorter. If you're a 5-foot 11-inch man, add 10 pounds to the total to get a Maximum Weight Limit of 185 pounds.

The baseline for women is 5-feet tall and 125 pounds. Add 4.5 pounds for every inch taller you are, or subtract 4.5 pounds for every inch shorter. So if you are a 5-foot 4-inch woman, add 18 pounds. Your Maximum Weight Limit is 143 pounds.

Keep in mind, the MWL is not your ideal weight. It's the heaviest you should weigh for your height and gender.

Question & Answer

Is it true that skinny people live longer than overweight people?

Don't confuse a specific weight with being "healthy." Having a few extra pounds on your hips, thighs, or arms isn't a worry, and it may even be healthier than being stick thin. In one study, overweight people had a smaller chance of dying from anything, while underweight people were more likely to die from non-heart or non-cancer illnesses.

But overweight is not the same as obese. Overweight means weighing too much; obese means packing too much fat. Research shows that obesity makes you more likely to die from heart problems, diabetes, kidney disease, and certain cancers. Focus on building muscle and reducing fat, then get ready for a longer life.

3 rules for winning the flab fight

Losing weight isn't rocket science, so stop letting it intimidate you. Instead of tying yourself into knots with complicated weight-loss plans, simply follow these three foolproof rules to win the war on flab.

Stop looking for food excitement. Food is for nourishment, not entertainment or therapy. Fran, a member of the weight-loss program Jenny Craig, agrees. "We have turned food into everything from a social connector, to an expression of love, to an antidepressant. We look to food to keep us happy and uplifted. That's part of the addiction."

If you really want to lose weight, she says, you may have to change your relationship with eating. Realize that it's not about the food. "It's about finding a different source to fuel excitement in your life — like a new activity, a date night with your spouse, an outdoor walk, a new vegetable to try, or connecting with an old friend."

Don't diet. Toss out this term. Erase it from your vocabulary. "Dieting" implies that the changes you make are short-term, and that you will be able to return to the way you used to eat once you reach your goal-weight. Not true. Do that, and you'll simply regain all the weight you lost.

Instead of thinking of it as a diet, think of it as a change in lifestyle. It sounds more permanent — and pleasant — than dieting. Make simple, easy changes in how you live, so you are more likely to stick with them. Institute them slowly so you don't get overwhelmed and discouraged.

Remember to move. Studies show that counting calories and watching what you eat will, indeed, lead to weight loss, but you'll shed pounds faster by adding a little exercise to the mix. Staying active will also help you keep the weight off once you lose it.

How to pick your perfect 'goal' weight

Aiming for a specific goal can motivate you, but don't pull one out of your hat. Some simple guidelines will help you decide how many pounds to shed and boost your chances of success.

Don't get hooked on a number. Instead, aim to lose 10 to 15 percent of your current weight. Dropping just 5 to 10 percent can cut your heart disease risk, raise your "good" HDL cholesterol levels, and lower your blood pressure, blood sugar, and triglycerides.

Take it slow. Be patient. The weight won't come off overnight. Try to lose that 10 percent over the course of six months. Then spend the next six months maintaining your new weight. If you keep it off, you can reevaluate whether you need to shed more pounds and, if so, move back into weight-loss mode.

Be realistic. Maybe that doesn't sound like enough. You may think you ought to aim higher, or lose it faster. Remember the tortoise and the hare? Slow and steady will win this race, too. Research shows that overweight people often have unrealistic expectations. In one study:

- dieters wanted to lose, on average, one-third of their body weight. That's three times the realistic goal of 10 percent.

- even people who lost a whopping 37 pounds were disappointed in themselves.

- those who dropped an amazing 55 pounds said their weight loss was merely "acceptable," but not great.

Unrealistic goals like these will sabotage your weight loss and make success hard to come by. People generally think they can lose a lot of weight too quickly, and they underestimate how much work they will have to do to reach their extreme goals. Then, when they don't succeed, they become depressed and give up altogether.

Get slim the healthy way. Experts recommend trying to shed 1/2 to 2 pounds per week. It may sound slow, but you are more likely to keep it off at this rate, and less likely to develop health problems like gallstones, fatigue, and hair loss that accompany rapid weight loss.

For most people, cutting 300 to 500 calories a day through diet and exercise will result in losing 10 percent of your body weight in six months, at a safe, healthy rate of 1/2 to 1 pound a week.

SimpleSOLUTION

Your scale says one thing, but your doctor's says another. Who is right? Follow these steps to get your real weight.

- Get on the scale first thing in the morning, after emptying your bladder but before having coffee or breakfast. Barefoot is best. If you want to wear clothes, make sure they are lightweight.

- Consider a digital scale. A leading consumer group found that digital scales were more accurate and easier to read than the old analog kind.

- Be consistent. Use the same scale every time you weigh yourself. Always weigh in at the same time of day, and wear similar lightweight clothing.

Foolproof formula for a slimmer you

Forget about following confusing diets. The real key to weight loss lies in how many calories you eat, and how many you burn.

Calories are a way of measuring the amount of energy in food. To lose that spare tire around your middle, you need to do two things:

• figure out how many calories you need every day to stay at your current weight.

• aim to get fewer calories than that.

The amount of calories someone needs to maintain their weight varies based on their gender, weight, and activity level. This simple chart gives you a good estimate.

Gender/Age	Calories needed		
	Sedentary	Moderately active	Active
Women, 51-70	1,600	1,800	2,000-2,200
Women, 71 and older	1,600	1,800	2,000
Men, 51-70	2,000-2,200	2,200-2,400	2,600-2,800
Men, 71 and older	2,000	2,200	2,400-2,600

These are general numbers. To figure out your specific caloric needs, simply multiply your weight by:

• 15, if you get at least 30 minutes of moderate or intense physical activity ever day.

• 12 calories, if you don't get this much activity daily.

This number gives you a baseline. You'll have to eat fewer calories than this if you want to lose weight. To drop 1 pound a week, you need to get about 500 fewer calories daily. To drop 2 pounds a week, you'll need about 1,000 fewer a day.

That's tough to do through diet alone. Your best bet — cut half of those calories from food, and burn the other half through physical activity like a daily walk. Exercise will help you shed more fat than dieting, and the combination will save you from having to follow a super-strict eating plan.

However you choose to do it, make sure you don't cut calories too harshly. Women should not eat fewer than 1,200 calories a day, and men no fewer than 1,500 calories daily, unless you are under a doctor's supervision. Otherwise, you may not meet your body's nutritional needs.

Power through the plateau

Almost every dieter hits a plateau where the scales don't budge for weeks, no matter how little you eat or how much you exercise. Experts say it's natural to plateau after six months of shedding fat, but the slowdown doesn't have to last.

As you lose weight, your basal metabolism actually slows down. The smaller you get, the fewer calories your body needs to perform basic functions. Plus, your body is super-efficient — it eventually adapts to using less energy.

After six months, it's also easy to start slacking off. Maybe you aren't sticking to your eating guidelines as closely as you did at first. Rewarding your success with too many treats can cancel out your efforts.

Reevaluate your goals. Do you actually need to lose more weight? Talk to your doctor, remeasure your waist circumference, or compare your current weight to your Maximum Weight Limit to decide.

Take a break. Consider giving your body a rest from actively losing weight, and switch to maintaining your new trimmer figure, instead. Try staying at your new, lower weight for six months before you return to active dieting.

Add another element. You have to lop 3,500 calories a week from your diet in order to lose 1 pound. It's tough to cut back that much on what you eat, especially if you have already limited your diet and lost a significant amount of weight. So add exercise to the mix. An aerobic workout like brisk walking can help you burn more calories and power through the plateau.

Throw your body a curve ball. Change up your exercise plan every once in a while. The challenge will keep both your mind and body sharp and prevent boredom and injuries. Rotate in new kinds of workouts, including aerobic, strength-training, balance, and flexibility.

Increase your odds of living a long, healthy life

Eating right is not always enough, especially if an illness like heart disease runs in your family. Luckily, Marian found other ways to beat the odds.

"I'm an active 62-year-old, but a family history of heart disease and high cholesterol convinced me that I needed more exercise.

"After I tried walking on a treadmill at a nearby community center, I knew I'd be happier outside. So I got a step counter and started walking in my neighborhood.

"I've seen purple tulips bloom in spring and red dogwood leaves drop in the fall. I always come home with more energy for the rest of my day."

7 secrets to staying slim for life

Losing weight is only half the battle. Keeping it off is the real trick. One group of people has managed to do just that, and they are sharing their secrets with you.

The National Weight Control Registry consists of more than 5,000 folks who have lost 30 pounds or more and kept it off for over a year. In fact, Registry members on average have shed 66 pounds and kept it off for 5.5 years. Researchers started the Registry to figure out how people who succeed at losing weight and keeping it off manage this impressive feat, and to share those tricks with the rest of the world. Here are their top seven secrets for getting slim and staying that way.

Eat breakfast every day. More than 75 percent of Registry members eat breakfast every morning. Consider a high-fiber breakfast like oatmeal, quite possibly the best breakfast food ever. Research shows it can help lower cholesterol and protect against weight gain, high blood pressure, and type 2 diabetes.

Step on the scale often. Nearly half of the members weigh in at least once a day. Three out of four weigh themselves at least once a week. Keeping an eagle-eye on your weight once you're in the maintenance phase can help you spot increases while still small. Catch your creeping waistline early will save you from having to shed lots of weight all over again.

Stay active. An incredible nine out of 10 Registry members exercise, averaging an hour a day of moderately intense activity. Most walk to keep fit, but some lift weights or bicycle.

The reason is clear. Physical activity can help you lose weight, but it becomes absolutely crucial in keeping it off long-term. One study followed people who had lost weight by dieting and were trying to keep it off for one year. Some did aerobics, some lifted weights, and others did no exercise. Non-exercisers gained back 25 percent of their belly fat, while exercisers who didn't keep up with their workouts regained a whopping 38 percent of their belly fat. Those who continued to do aerobics or strength training for just 80 minutes a week regained none.

Turn off the TV. Registry members don't watch much television. Three out of five clock fewer than 10 hours of TV time a week, much less than most Americans. Trimming back on TV leaves you more time for doing something active, like gardening or puttering in a workshop, and less time for mindlessly munching while sitting on the sofa.

Be consistent. They also don't splurge on eating. The most successful Registry members:

- eat the same smart, healthy way on weekends and holidays as they do during the week.

- continue to count calories and fat grams even after reaching their goal weight so they don't gain it back.

- enjoy mostly homemade meals, eat out fewer than three times a week, and rarely do fast food.

Learn to cope. People who use food to cope with stressful situations or negative emotions are more likely to regain any weight they lose. So are people who base their self-image on their weight and body shape. If you know you're prone to these problems, seek out the help of friends or a counselor for support. Improving your self-image, learning to manage stress, and developing coping skills for hard times will help your waistline, too.

Hang in there. You need to be vigilant to keep the weight off, especially in the beginning. But the most successful Registry members say it gets easier over time.

The ultimate secret to sticking with a diet — pick one that feels easy to follow. Women who thought their diet was complicated were much more likely to give up, one study found.

In some cases, a complex diet gives you more flexibility in what you eat. However, Jutta Mata, a professor at Stanford University, warns that people should look at several diet plans before deciding on one. Consider how many rules each has and how many things you'll have to remember to do or avoid while following it.

"If they find it very difficult, the likelihood that they will prematurely give up the diet is higher, and they should try to find a different plan."

4 amazing fat-fighting foods

When it comes to losing the weight around your middle, it's often not how much you eat, but what you eat. Try these four amazing foods to help you melt that fat away.

Eggs. No one would call this a "diet food," but overweight people who ate this 35-cent meal of two scrambled eggs regularly for breakfast lost more weight and inches than those who ate a bagel breakfast — plus they had more energy throughout the day.

Both meals packed the same number of calories, but only the eggs helped people lose weight. Despite their natural cholesterol, eating eggs five days a week for eight weeks did not raise people's cholesterol or triglyceride levels.

The slimming effects of eggs only worked for people who cut calories elsewhere. Those who ate eggs without dieting didn't see the same benefit.

Grapefruit. It's a weight-loss stunner. Grapefruits really are great diet foods. Eating this one kind of fruit before meals stimulates weight loss — even if you do nothing else. Eating half a grapefruit before each meal for three months helped obese people lose three more pounds than those not eating the fruit and improved insulin resistance. Grapefruit juice aided weight loss, too, though not as much.

The nutrient naringenin may be part of the answer. It tells your body to stop storing fat in the liver and to burn it instead. This citrus compound may:

- keep the liver from pumping out very-low-density cholesterol (VLDL), the worst kind.

- improve insulin sensitivity and blood sugar tolerance.

- prevent weight gain, even with a fat-filled diet.

Check with your doctor before stocking up on grapefruit, however. This fruit and its juice affect how the body processes certain medications, including statin drugs. Ask your doctor or pharmacist whether it could interfere with any medicines you are taking.

Lentils. This Biblical food can be a saving grace today. Lentils' high protein content actually triggers your body to release a hunger-squashing hormone called PYY, so you eat less and feel full. Not to mention, they're super low in fat and cholesterol, making them a healthier source of protein than many animal foods. Plus, lentils can help you lower your cholesterol, avoid cancer, dodge diabetes, and protect your eyesight.

- These legumes have a low glycemic index (GI) which helped dieters not only lose weight but also slash cholesterol.

- Their combination of folate, fiber, and phytochemicals fight several types of cancer, including breast, colon, pancreatic, and laryngeal cancers.

- Lentils are rich in both soluble fiber and resistant starch. Foods with both may protect against type 2 diabetes and help people with this disease better manage their blood sugar.

- Low-GI foods like lentils may guard your eyes against macular degeneration by helping control blood sugar. Chronically high blood sugar can damage the delicate tissue in the eye, setting the stage for vision problems.

Blueberries. These tiny fruits prevented weight gain and belly fat buildup in an animal study, in part by changing the genes that control how your body processes fat and sugar. This could improve insulin sensitivity in people and keep them from packing on fat. Blueberries may also help you feel fuller and eat less.

4 foods that secretly sabotage your diet

The very same foods you're eating to help you lose weight could be undermining your efforts. They masquerade as "health" or "diet" foods, but they may trigger your body to put on more pounds.

Diet drinks. You sip them for their sweet taste and zero calories, but drinking diet beverages made with artificial sweeteners may backfire. Researchers followed more than 3,500 people in San Antonio for nine years. Those who got the most artificial sweeteners from food and drinks saw their BMIs surge nearly 50 percent more than people who didn't eat the sugar substitutes. Experts have a few theories.

- Real sugar tends to make you feel full and satisfied. Artificial sweeteners, however, may prompt you to eat more fat and protein. In the study, people who drank artificially sweetened beverages also began getting more of their daily calories from fat, particularly saturated fat.

- You may underestimate how many calories you're getting from "lite" products. If you splurge and spend the calories you "saved" elsewhere, you may end up eating more than you bargained for.

- Switching to artificial sweeteners may truly help you cut your daily calories. This, in turn, can slow your metabolism, making you more likely to gain weight. Eating real sugar while you cut calories actually helps offset that metabolic slowdown.

- The artificial sweetener aspartame may be toxic to the part of the brain that senses when you are full, setting you up for obesity.

Fat-free products. Less fat does not mean fewer calories. Manufacturers often add sugar to make up for the flavor lost from fat. As a result, low-fat and fat-free foods can have just as many, if not more, calories as their regular versions.

Unfortunately, you may not realize it. Many people think they can eat as much of a reduced-fat food as they want without gaining weight, but calories are what count. Compare the Nutrition Facts labels on reduced-fat foods with their regular counterparts. Make sure you're really getting a healthier product with fewer calories.

Sweetened yogurts. They pose as a dieter's best friend because of their calcium and vitamin D, but yogurts sweetened with high-fructose corn syrup (HFCS) could really be the enemy.

Other sugars, like glucose, dampen your appetite. Fructose increases it. What's worse, your body turns more fructose than glucose into fat, and does it faster. Being overweight may actually ramp up this fattening process.

Some surprising foods rely on HFCS for added sweetness, including some fruit juices, high-fiber cereals, ketchup, breads, salad dressings, baked beans, canned goods, and regular soda — but not all do. Check the ingredient lists and look for brands that shun this sweetener.

Soups made with MSG. Enjoying a bowl of broth-based soup before a main meal can help you drop weight without feeling hungry. Soups fill you up with fewer calories, helping you eat less overall — unless that soup is seasoned with monosodium glutamate (MSG).

A Chinese study found that the more MSG people ate, the more likely they were to be overweight. Researchers think MSG may damage the part of the brain that controls appetite, as well as disrupt your hormones in a way that promotes obesity. Check the ingredient list on foods to spot products made with this seasoning.

Simple**SOLUTION**

Not all juices are waistline-friendly. Here are some easy ways to separate the good from the bad and the just plain ugly.

- Look for those made with "100% juice."
- Check the ingredient list, and avoid juices with any form of added sugar.
- Compare the Nutrition Facts panels, and pick the brand with the most nutrients and least sugar per glass.
- Beware of "juice cocktails" and "punches." They may not contain 100-percent fruit juice.

Citrus juices, especially pink grapefruit and orange juice, seem to pack the most nutrients per calorie. If you love apple juice, buy the cloudy kind. It boasts more disease-fighting antioxidants than clear apple juice.

Outsmart snack cravings

Beat snack attacks and hungry rumbles with some savvy planning and a little psychology.

Eat more often. Don't skip meals or go too long without eating. Try to eat three small meals and three snacks a day. By eating small amounts more often, you'll feel less hungry and be less tempted to give in to junk food cravings.

Skip snacks at TV-time. It's easy to overeat while watching your favorite shows because so many commercials urge you to indulge. Prime time television can really lead you astray, since nighttime snacks, like ice cream, chips, and cookies, are typically packed with fat and calories. If you get hungry in the evenings, eat something small but filling — an apple or half a serving of whole grain cereal.

Keep a food diary. It doesn't have to be elaborate. Simply jot down what you eat and when you eat it. Research shows the very act of writing it down can help you eat less. Keeping a food diary doubled people's weight loss in one study. It combats mindless snacking and can help you spot bad eating patterns.

Avoid banning foods. A zero-tolerance policy can backfire if you slip up. One little mistake can prompt you to abandon your plan, overeat, and ultimately fail to lose weight. Instead of outlawing your favorite foods, choose healthier versions.

Take chocolate for example. Research shows dark chocolate fills you up more than milk chocolate and better satisfies your craving for sweet, salty, or high-fat foods. Don't ban chocolate altogether. Simply savor some dark rather than milk chocolate when the craving strikes.

Stay prepared. It's not a calorie counter, and it's not a pill. It's a snack. Don't leave home without one. Carry one with you every day, and this secret weapon will protect you from obesity. A stash of fruit or nuts can save you from the fast food drive through when you're on the go.

Lots of healthy foods come in convenient snack sizes small enough to fit in a purse. Consider individually wrapped dried plums, the next super food of the fruit world. Cheap and sweet, they may be the ideal weight loss snack. These tasty fruits are bursting with the sweetness of candy, yet can really help you trim belly fat. They're also proven to have amazing disease-fighting power.

- High-fiber foods, like dried plums, get digested more slowly, making you feel full from fewer calories. It's no coincidence that people who eat fiber-rich foods also tend to have healthier body weights.

- Studies show dried plums can both prevent and reverse bone loss, helping ward off osteoporosis.

- Antioxidant compounds in plums may stunt the growth of colon cancer cells.

Nuts are no snack-slackers, either. Just two tablespoons of nuts can help you shrink dangerous belly fat. People who munched on two tablespoons of mixed nuts every day for a year shrank their waistlines more than people who didn't eat nuts.

Top 3 foods that boost metabolism

It's true. Some foods really can jump-start your metabolism and help you burn more calories naturally.

Green tea. Let green tea rev up your metabolism. Its potent combination of caffeine and compounds called catechins could help you shed weight and keep it off. Researchers say the tea helps your body burn more calories while resting and burn more fat overall. People in one study lost more weight over three months and burned an extra 44 calories a day sipping green tea than those who skipped the beverage. It also seems to:

- decrease your heart disease risk.

- slash your heart attack risk almost in half.

- cut cholesterol levels and block your gut from absorbing cholesterol from food.

- boost your insulin sensitivity, help regulate your blood sugar levels, and maybe even heal the damaged pancreas cells that produce insulin.

Sipping seven cups a day can help you get slim and stay that way. Keep in mind, green tea contains caffeine, although less than coffee or black tea, and adding milk to it weakens its insulin-regulating ability. It can also block your absorption of iron. Drink it with lemon or between meals to minimize this effect.

Chili peppers. Scientists have discovered that foods high in capsaicin, the spicy substance in chili peppers, could help you eat less and burn more energy. Capsaicin seems to interact with the gene TRPV1 in your body to speed up your metabolism and keep you from packing on fat. So slice up some hot peppers or add a dash of chili pepper to your dish and get ready to "burn" away those extra pounds.

Water. The simple act of drinking water can help you shed weight. In one study, people watched their metabolism increase 30 percent after drinking two cups of water, a boost that lasted more than an hour. Experts think that drinking an extra 1.5 liters, or a little more than six cups, of water daily could help you burn 48 calories more each day. It may not sound like much, but the numbers add up fast. That's an extra 17,000 calories in one year, or 5.3 pounds of body fat.

Be fat savvy to fight flab

Not all fats are bad. Some can actually help you lose weight by making you feel full and acting as natural appetite suppressants. The fat in food causes your stomach to empty more slowly and gives you that satisfying "full" sense after meals. The trick is picking foods filled with the right kind, and eating them in healthy amounts.

Make your own appetite suppressant. Just eat almonds, pecans, olive oil, avocados, and sunflower seeds, a few delectable foods rich in monounsaturated fatty acids (MUFAs). One type of MUFA called oleic acid causes a chemical reaction that stops your belly from feeling hungry. It triggers your small intestine to churn out the hunger-fighting compound OEA. This trips the switch that tells your digestive tract it's full. The result — less hunger for longer periods of time, which can help stop snack cravings.

This funny-named nutrient can also literally block fat from building up around your belly, without reducing calories. People with diabetes were put on one of two diets — high in carbs or high in MUFAs. Surprisingly, the carbohydrate eaters gained fat around their middle, while MUFA eaters didn't.

Learn to love fatty fish. Salmon and canola oils are excellent sources of another healthy fat, known as polyunsaturated fatty acids (PUFAs). Two types of PUFAs, DHA and EPA, may supercharge your weight-loss efforts if you eat them as part of a calorie-cutting diet. Men who added fish or fish oil to their calorie-cutting regimen lost more weight over one month than men who didn't. Experts say PUFAs may speed metabolism and shed flab by revving up brown fat, a special type of body fat that can burn loads of calories.

Steer clear of saturated fat. Foods loaded with saturated fat, such as ice cream and hamburgers, actually prompt you to overeat everything else. Researchers found that a type of saturated fat called palmitic acid found in beef, butter, cheese, and milk travels to the brain and affects your appetite. After eating it, your brain tells your body to ignore leptin and insulin, the hormones that tell you when to stop eating. Worse, the effect can last up to three days.

Saturated fat also interacts with your genes, making some people much more likely to gain belly fat than others when they eat it.

Ban the biggest cause of big bellies. Bigger bellies are guaranteed if you keep eating trans fat. It adds more fat to your belly and moves fat you already have to your abdomen. Plus, it seriously boosts your heart disease risk, contributes to type 2 diabetes, lowers your "good" HDL cholesterol, and raises your "bad" LDL cholesterol and triglycerides. In fact, trans fat increases your chances of becoming obese even more than saturated fat.

About 70 percent of the trans fat you eat probably comes from store-bought baked goods, such as crackers, muffins, and cookies, and fried foods in restaurants. You can avoid unhealthy fats by following a few simple rules.

- Read food labels. Check the Nutrition Facts panel on food labels for the amount of trans fat and saturated fat per serving.

- Don't fall for "0 grams trans fat" claims. Foods can claim to have 0 grams of trans fat if they have less than half a gram per serving. Unfortunately, a serving may be smaller than the amount you normally eat. Get a few servings, and you could unwittingly eat a couple of grams of trans fat.

- Buy whole, fresh foods instead of prepackaged ones. Processed foods are more likely to pack trans fat, especially baked and fried goodies.

Reap the benefits of baby fat

Keeping your baby fat may be the key to staying slim. Babies have lots of so-called "brown" fat to help them stay warm. While white fat cells are filled with fat, brown fat cells are packed with mitochondria, tiny power generators that grab fats and sugar from your bloodstream and burn them for fuel. In adults, brown fat can actually burn calories and kick your weight-loss program into high gear.

Although scientists thought brown fat disappeared later in life, a recent study shows adults may still have some of this good fat, and researchers are working on ways to help it fight obesity.

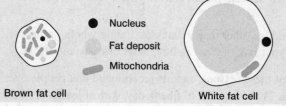

Nucleus

Fat deposit

Mitochondria

Brown fat cell   White fat cell

Bust belly fat with tasty carbs

Discover the secrets of natural "good carbs" that the diet-peddlers hope you never find out. Some high-carb foods, like whole grains, actually help you reduce belly fat.

Seniors 60 to 80 years old who ate the most whole grains had the lowest BMI and the least body fat, particularly in their midsection. Whole-grain cereals had the biggest effect. In a separate study, people who were told to get all their daily grains from whole grains for three months also lost weight, shrank their waistlines, tamed inflammation, and shed body fat, especially belly fat, compared to people who ate refined grains, like white bread.

These power-packed carbs do more than blast away big bellies. They also help:

- keep your blood sugar stable. Replacing refined grains with whole grains may slash your diabetes risk and improve blood sugar levels. Their fiber content slows your body's absorption of nutrients, including carbohydrates. By evening out blood sugar spikes, whole grains improve insulin sensitivity.

- protect your eyesight in old age. Cereal fibers that boast a low glycemic index (GI), such as oatmeal, seem to reduce the risk of age-related macular degeneration. By leveling out the spikes in your blood sugar, whole-grain cereals may end up protecting the delicate retinal cells in your eyes.

- dodge other major illnesses. Eating whole-grain foods slashes your risk of heart failure, heart disease, and stroke.

For all of these reasons, experts recommend that people over the age of 50 eat 21 to 30 grams of fiber a day, with at least half of that coming from whole-grain foods.

QUICK*fix*

Adding more dairy to your daily menu could help speed weight loss and burn more fat. Research shows people tend to lose more weight if they up their dairy or calcium intake, while moderately trimming calories elsewhere. In fact, getting three servings of milk, yogurt, or cheese daily enhance weight and fat loss in people who also cut calories, especially if they weren't getting enough dairy in their diets to begin with.

Dairy products, and specifically the mineral calcium, may block your body's absorption of fat in food. Calcium may also help your body burn more fat, but only if you cut back on calories, too.

Surprising weapon in the war on fat

Want to lose fat while doing nothing? Look no further than resistant starch, a carbohydrate that digests slowly and ferments in your gut. Eat a meal containing resistant starch just once a day, and your body will burn nearly 25 percent more fat, automatically. People who ate a meal where resistant starch made up just 5 percent of the total carbohydrates boosted their body's fat-burning power almost 25 percent.

You could get similar results by replacing some of the starchy foods you normally eat with those containing resistant starch. Simply swap refined grains for whole ones, hot pasta for cold pasta, baked potatoes for cold potatoes, or a ripe banana for a green banana. Legumes, such as white beans and lentils, are also great sources.

Aside from burning fat, foods rich in resistant starch can help control your hunger for hours and hours to help you lose weight. Plus, they'll help regulate your blood sugar and nurture your immune system.

- These fermentable carbs boost levels of gut hormones that quell appetite.

- Foods containing resistant starch tend to have fewer calories, ounce for ounce, than other foods, so you can eat more of them and worry less about your waistline.

- They also tend to have a lower glycemic index, which improves both your blood sugar and insulin levels, and helps suppress your appetite.

- Resistant starch acts like a prebiotic in your digestive tract, feeding and promoting the growth of friendly bacteria that help support your immune system.

Animals fed a diet fortified with resistant starch weighed the same as those on regular diets, but they had less body fat, particularly belly fat, and a better balance between their blood sugar and insulin levels. Plus, the resistant starch diet seemed to fill them up and be more satisfying than the diet filled with regular, easily digestible starch.

Pumpernickel and rye breads are packed with resistant starch. So are barley, corn flakes, muesli, and puffed wheat cereals. Manufacturers have caught on to the craze by fortifying some breads, cereals, pastas, and nutrition bars with Hi-maize, a type of resistant starch. Other types of resistant starch may appear in a food's Ingredients list as "resistant cornstarch," "corn starch," or "maltodextrin."

The dangers of 'cleansing' diets

Some detox diets require fasting. Others are all-juice diets or ban meat, wheat, dairy, sugar, and so on. Many push fruits, vegetables, beans, nuts, and seeds, which can make them seem healthy.

The methods may differ, but all detox diets claim the same thing — toxins in the environment build up inside your body and need to be flushed out periodically through a special diet. The people pushing the diets blame toxic buildup for everything from headaches and fatigue to nausea and other health problems.

Health professionals say your body does not need help purifying itself if you eat a diet filled with fruits, vegetables, fiber, and plenty of water. No scientific evidence proves detox diets will clear out toxins faster, make you healthier, or give you more energy. They may help you drop weight quickly, but the pounds you lose will be water and muscle, not fat. Most people regain the weight shortly after stopping the diet.

That said, some detox advice can be healthy. For instance, drinking more water, cutting back on caffeine, and loading up on fruits and vegetables is a smart idea. Limiting salt can decrease bloating and lower your blood pressure. Reducing your intake of added sugar and processed foods can help you cut calories.

Don't fall for colon cleansing, fasting, or liquid diets. Avoid special "detoxifying" supplements, too. These usually contain laxatives that can lead to dehydration, nutrient imbalances, and digestive problems. People with diabetes, heart disease, and other chronic conditions should not attempt a detox program.

Question & Answer

Why is it easier to gain weight than to lose it?

For one thing, it's much easier to take in calories than burn them. A slice of coffee cake serves up 570 calories. A 154-pound person would have to walk briskly for two hours to work off the same amount.

It doesn't help that your body works against you. Your metabolism slows with age and menopause, so you burn fewer calories while resting than you did in your youth. And if you become less active with age, you'll burn even fewer calories..

Discover the ultimate slim-down secret

The kind of diet you're on may not matter in the end, as long as it's one you can stick with. That's because calories are the key to losing weight.

A major study pitted several popular diets, including low-carb, low-fat, and high-protein diets, against each other. The types of food people ate on each one differed, but everyone cut their daily calories by the same amount. After two years, everyone had lost about the same amount of weight — regardless of their diet. The moral of this story — the amount of calories you trim may matter more than the type of diet you choose.

That said, different diets may work better for different people, based on your health problems and personal preferences. For instance, if you love carbohydrates, a low-carb, Atkins-style diet may not work well for you. Choose a plan that doesn't go against your natural preferences, so you'll stick with it. Then go after your new eating plan with enthusiasm and persistence — but be patient.

People only lose an average of 4 to 9 pounds on any diet, but even modest weight loss makes a difference. Shedding those few pounds can prevent or treat diseases like diabetes, as well as improve cholesterol, blood sugar, and inflammation.

SimpleSOLUTION

Eating smaller meals throughout the day may melt off more pounds, more easily. Instead of eating a light breakfast and lunch, then a big dinner at night, have four to five smaller meals and snacks throughout the day. Your body makes more insulin after a big, high-calorie meal than after a small, low-calorie one. Those high insulin levels actually prompt your body to store more fat and increase your appetite.

Be sure to eat breakfast to stave off hunger and munching. Plan your meals and snacks during the times you know you tend to get hungry, so you aren't tempted to grab something fatty, sugary, and convenient in a jam.

Added benefits of a low-fat diet

It's one of the best-studied ways to lose weight, and the one recommended by most major health authorities. Low-fat diets focus on counting fat grams rather than calories, with the goal to get no more than 30 percent of your calories from fat each day. Some, like the Ornish plan, aim even lower and cap the total fat at no more than 10 percent of your daily calories.

Fat packs more calories than any other nutrient. Trimming even a small amount from your diet can cut a substantial number of calories, more than if you trimmed the same amount of carbs or protein. Ultimately, calories are the key to weight loss or gain.

Low-fat diets may work particularly well for people concerned about their heart health. Cutting fat helps lower cholesterol, which in turn protects against heart attacks and strokes. This diet also focuses on avoiding trans fats and saturated fats, which contribute to heart disease and diabetes. Keep these tips in mind if you decide to try this diet.

- Going low-fat does not mean you can load up on carbohydrates. You'll still need to avoid the temptation of calorie-packed, sugar-filled carbohydrates.

- Low-fat versions of your favorite foods may not be waistline friendly. Sure, they may contain less fat than the regular version, but they may boast just as many or more calories, thanks to added sugar.

- Cutting fat too low can keep you from getting enough nutrients from food, since your body needs some fat to absorb certain nutrients. Allow yourself a little healthy, unsaturated fat, like olive oil and canola oil.

Fat contains nine calories per gram. Figuring out how much fat you can eat every day is easy. Let's say you want to limit fat to 30 percent of your daily calories. Multiply your calorie goal by 0.3, then divide that by 9 to get the maximum grams of fat you can eat daily.

Question & Answer

Is obesity contagious?

Yes, but not because it's contagious like an illness. Obesity tends to spread among friends, spouses, and families. Thirty years of study show a person is:

- 57 percent more likely to become obese if a friend does.
- 71 percent more likely if that friend is a best friend.
- 40 percent more likely to become obese if a sibling does.
- 37 percent more likely if their spouse becomes obese.

Gaining weight may become more acceptable if the people around you do it, too. The good news? Weight loss is also contagious. A person's chances of slimming down shoot up 57 percent if a friend loses weight. So grab a buddy and get started.

Drop pounds fast with a low-carb diet

High-protein, low-carbohydrate diets, such as Atkins, are all the rage, and science is finding they aren't so bad after all. But before you get too excited, they aren't safe for everyone, either.

These types of eating plans focus on cutting out carbs and getting more protein. Unlike some diets, they can be simple to follow, which may help you to stick with them. Low-carb plans come in two varieties.

- the Zone-style, which replaces some carbohydrates with protein but still limits the amount of fat you eat

- the Atkins-style, which replaces even more carbs with protein but lets you eat as much fat as you want

The combination of lots of protein and few carbs seems to force your body to burn fat rather than glucose, or blood sugar, for energy. Plus, protein keeps you feeling fuller and more satisfied. Men may do particularly well on them. According to one study, men on a low-carb diet ate fewer calories and felt less hungry than men on a more moderate-carbohydrate diet.

You may lose weight faster in the first six to 12 months than you would on other types of diets. After about a year, however, people often lose the same amount of weight on calorie- or fat-cutting diets as on a carb-cutting one.

Like other weight-loss plans, high-protein, low-carb diets may help your heart. They seem to lower triglycerides, raise your "good" HDL cholesterol, and may help lower blood pressure. "Bad" LDL cholesterol levels tend to remain the same or rise slightly, particularly under the strict Atkins eating plan. Atkins-style low-carb diets can also cause a condition called ketosis, which is especially dangerous for people with heart disease, diabetes, or kidney problems.

Not everyone should consider this kind of eating plan. Think twice if you're at risk for any of these conditions.

Kidney problems. High-protein diets put extra stress on your kidneys and liver, which can cause or aggravate kidney stones. It can also speed up the progression of kidney disease in people who have the illness or have diabetes, even if they only stay on the diet for a short time.

Diabetes. Research shows low-carb diets don't necessarily boost your diabetes risk, especially if you get your fat and protein from vegetable sources. But people who already have type 2 diabetes, metabolic syndrome, or obesity should talk to their doctor before trying this kind of diet, because of potential kidney problems.

Osteoporosis. Atkins, in particular, may cause your body to lose a lot of calcium through urine, raising your risk of both kidney stones and osteoporosis.

Nutritional deficiencies. Some high-protein, low-carb diets limit the complex carbs you eat, not just the simple ones. That's a bad thing. Many healthy foods, such as fruits and vegetables, are packed with complex carbs. Avoiding them can lead to vitamin and mineral deficiencies, among other health problems.

Short-term studies suggest these diets do not increase your heart disease risk, but experts still worry about the long-term effects of too much protein and saturated fat and too few fruits, vegetables, and whole grains. Experts only recommend following a high-protein, low-carb diet on a short-term basis and under your doctor's supervision.

Right diet boosts your mood

Low-carb diets may lift your mood more than low-fat diets over the short-term. After all, they don't limit your calories, and they do help you feel fuller and more satisfied.

Long-term, however, high-carb diets may boost your mood the most. Carbohydrates raise your level of the feel-good brain chemical serotonin. Fat and protein actually lower it. Studies link low levels of serotonin to depression and anxiety.

Love carbs and still lose weight

Low-glycemic index diets aren't just for people with diabetes anymore. Popular plans including The Zone and Sugar Busters use them to help you get trim while eating healthy.

There are two ways to measure the effect food has on your blood sugar.

- The glycemic index (GI) measures how fast an individual food makes your blood sugar rise after eating it. Foods with a low GI, like fruit, lentils, whole grains, and soybeans, digest slowly, making your blood sugar rise slowly, too.

- The glycemic load (GL) goes a step further and takes serving size into account. Some foods that have a high GI value, like watermelon, actually have a low GL, because the serving size you'd typically eat won't make much difference in your blood sugar.

Both low-GI and low-GL diets still let you enjoy carbohydrates. On a low-GI diet, you only change the type of carbs you eat, not how much. With a low-GL diet, you change both the type and amount of carbs you eat.

Low-GI foods help stabilize your insulin levels because the carbohydrates in them digest slowly. This, in turn, staves off hunger, leaves you feeling more satisfied, and helps you eat less. With less excess insulin floating around your bloodstream, your body may also burn more fat for fuel instead of carbs, especially if you combine a low-GI diet with exercise. Some research suggests a low-GL diet that focuses on eating low-GI foods and some fat may help you shed more body fat and keep it off better than a traditional low-fat diet.

These plans may be easier to follow long-term than low-carb or low-fat diets because they don't put a total ban on any foods. They may work particularly well if you have certain conditions.

Diabetes. Eating low-GI foods can help you shed pounds without risking dangerous bouts of low blood sugar, and without raising your bad LDL cholesterol the way low-carb diets can do. It may also improve insulin sensitivity in people with diabetes.

Metabolic syndrome. People with metabolic syndrome shrank their waist and lowered their blood pressure more if they followed a low-GL eating plan than a low-fat plan. People without metabolic syndrome seemed to fare better on the low-fat diet.

High triglycerides. A low-GL plan that emphasized proteins and low-GI carbs worked twice as well as a low-fat diet, but only in people with high triglycerides.

Don't try to guess a food's GI based on its Nutrition Facts label. Some foods may surprise you. Most "whole-grain" breads, breakfast cereals, and other processed cereal products have high GIs. Use handy GI and GL food lists to guide you to the right choices. You can search for the GI and GL of specific foods for free at the Web site *www.glycemicindex.com.*

Conquer a big belly the Mediterranean way

Italians, Spaniards, and Greeks are renowned for their good food, but they don't seem to pack on the pounds like people in America. That's partly because they enjoy what's known as a Mediterranean diet, the same way they have eaten for centuries. In the traditional Mediterranean diet, you:

- build meals around plants, not meats.

- only eat small portions of meat and chicken with your meals.

- eat large servings of whole grains, fresh fruits, vegetables, nuts, and legumes.

- aim for foods naturally rich in fiber, nutrients, and antioxidants.

- eat plenty of fish and other seafood full of healthy omega-3 fats.

- prepare foods using extra virgin olive oil.

- cook and season foods simply, without rich sauces or gravies.

- avoid red meat, eggs, butter, sweets, and other desserts, or only eat them in small amounts.

This healthy way of eating is more than a lifestyle. Eating this way can help you get slim, too. People who switched to a typical Mediterranean eating plan — rich in vegetables and low in red meat, with poultry and fish replacing beef and lamb at meals — lost more weight than those following a low-fat diet. Two years after the study started, the Mediterranean dieters had shed an average of 10 pounds each, lowered their blood pressure, shrank their waistlines, boosted their "good" HDL cholesterol, and dampened inflammation throughout their bodies.

Plus, they didn't have to drastically cut back on fat. One-third of their calories came from fat, which included a handful of nuts and two to three tablespoons of olive oil every day.

The Mediterranean diet holds some special advantages for people at risk of these diseases.

Diabetes. You'll get lots of monounsaturated fatty acids (MUFAs) on this eating plan, thanks to its emphasis on nuts and olive oil. These fats may improve insulin sensitivity and, therefore, blood sugar and insulin levels. In the same study, people with diabetes saw their fasting blood sugar improve on the Mediterranean plan, but not on the low-fat or low-carb diets.

Heart disease. Research has proven that the Mediterranean diet improves risk factors associated with heart disease. It has also been linked to a longer life span and a lower risk of cancer.

Keep in mind, this eating plan allows you to enjoy many carbohydrate-rich foods. Be sure to choose those with a low glycemic index. Since the diet limits red meat, guard against iron deficiency by loading up on foods rich in vitamin C, like red bell peppers and citrus fruits, to help your body absorb iron. Finally, consider taking a calcium supplement to maintain your bones, since the Mediterranean way of eating tends to limit dairy products.

SimpleSOLUTION

Counting calories can be hard when you're cooking from scratch. Home-cooked meals tend to have fewer calories than restaurant or prepackaged products, but it's still a good idea to know what goes in your mouth.

- Head to the bookstore and buy a healthy-eating cookbook that includes the nutritional information for each recipe.

- Measure high-calorie ingredients, like the oil for stir-fry, instead of pouring it directly into the pan.

- Experiment with spices and herbs. They flavor meals with far fewer calories than butter and oil.

- Use Internet calculators to find out how many calories are in different foods. Try the U.S. Department of Agriculture's free food lookup at *www.myfoodapedia.gov*.

Can't-miss plan for shrinking your waist

One diet that can help you blast belly fat without worrying about carbs or counting fat grams is the low-calorie diet. With this type of diet, the only things you cut are calories.

Numerous studies show you can drop more pounds by controlling your calories and eating moderate amounts of fat than by following a low-fat diet. The results are impressive. People on a low-calorie plan lost inches around their middle, lowered their triglycerides, and put a damper on inflammatory compounds linked to diabetes, kidney failure, and plaque buildup in their arteries.

Cutting back on calories does not have to mean starvation. You can easily shave hundreds of calories from your daily total just by making a few simple changes.

- Swap sugary juices, sodas, energy drinks, and fancy coffees for unsweetened tea or water. A can of regular soda contains 136 calories, while a cup of black tea only has two.

- Remove the skin from your chicken breast before eating it, and you'll save another 60 calories. Trim the fat from steak to cut 40 more.

- Top raw veggies with salsa instead of ranch dressing, and you'll eat 70 fewer calories per tablespoon.

Low-calorie diets let you eat somewhere between 800 and 1,999 calories a day, depending on how many calories your body needs to function. To decide how much to cut, you first need to figure out about how many calories your body needs every day. See *Foolproof formula for a slimmer you* earlier in this chapter. Then keep these tips in mind.

- The more calories you cut, the harder it may be to stick to your plan. In one study, people who tried to get just 800 calories a day really struggled. Experts suggest taking a moderate approach to trimming calories.

- Eating fewer calories can actually slow your metabolism. Your body learns to conserve energy as it gets used to working with less. This helps explain why weight loss tends to plateau after six to 12 months of dieting. You can prevent this slowdown by getting regular exercise while following your eating plan.

- Don't cut calories to fewer than 1,100 a day, unless you are being supervised by a doctor or nutrition expert. Go any lower, and you may not get enough nutrients.

- You don't have to count fat grams while following a low-cal diet, but you may want to. Fat packs more calories than any other nutrient. You can cut a lot of calories by trimming a little fat.

Counting calories is generally safe for everyone, as long as you don't go too low. In fact, this type of diet may work especially well if you have diabetes or high blood pressure. People with diabetes who take insulin will need to closely monitor their blood sugar.

Go vegan to get slim

People who don't eat meat may have the right idea when it comes to keeping trim and healthy. Switching to a vegan diet helped people in one study lose twice as much weight after one year as people who went on a typical, cholesterol-lowering diet of grains, fruits, vegetables, and lean meat. Plus, the vegetarians had kept off three times as much weight two years later.

Being a vegetarian can mean different things, depending on how strictly you follow this way of eating.

- Vegan is the strictest form of vegetarian. They don't eat any animal products — no meat, fish, dairy, or eggs.

- Lacto-vegetarians are less strict. They eat dairy but no meat, fish, or eggs.

- Lacto-ovo-vegetarians are even more laid back, eating dairy and eggs but no meat or fish.

- Pesco-vegetarians are the least strict, eating fish, dairy, and eggs but no meat.

The stricter a vegetarian you are, the lower your BMI, a measure of how much fat you have in your body. Generally, lower is better. Vegans had the lowest BMI and risk of type 2 diabetes in one study.

Experts think vegetarians may weigh less because they mostly eat foods with low energy density. These foods may take up lots of room on your plate, but they have few calories. Eating a lot of food low in calories makes the vegan diet surprisingly easy to follow.

Tweaking what you eat and cutting out meat and animal products is a quick way to trim calories and drop a few sizes without feeling as though you're starving yourself. You'll also load up on disease-fighting nutrients, including fiber, magnesium, potassium, vitamin C, vitamin E, and folate, as well as carotenoids, flavonoids, and other plant compounds. Despite all this goodness, vegetarians face some special nutritional needs.

Protein. Protein is made up of compounds called amino acids. Meat usually contains all of the amino acids you need. Most plant foods, on the other hand, are missing a few. Luckily, they aren't missing the same ones, so you can get complete protein by mixing and matching. Eat a variety of vegetables, starches, and beans throughout the day to meet your body's protein needs.

Omega-3 fatty acids. Vegetarian diets tend to be low in EPA and DHA, two omega-3 fats found in fish. To make up for that, you can take DHA supplements and eat plenty of walnuts, flaxseed, canola oil, or soy foods.

Iron. Your body has a harder time absorbing iron from plant foods than from animal foods, like red meat. Iron from leavened bread and fermented foods, such as soy-based miso and tempeh, may be easier to absorb. Vitamin C helps, too. Be sure to eat citrus fruits and vegetables chock-full of vitamin C.

Calcium. You can still get this mineral even if you cut out dairy products. Aside from supplements, fruit juices fortified with calcium, bok choy, broccoli, collards, kale, and Chinese cabbage are all rich in calcium.

Vitamin D. Vitamin-D deficiency can be a real danger for vegans. Look for fortified soy and rice milk, orange juice, and breakfast cereal. Consider a supplement if you can't get enough vitamin D from these sources.

Vitamin B12. Only animal foods contain this crucial nutrient. Lacto-ovo-vegetarians can get B12 from dairy foods and eggs if eaten regularly. Stricter vegetarians should consider rice and soy milk, breakfast cereal, and fake meat fortified with vitamin B12, or supplements.

New twist on the Atkins diet

A new version of the Atkins diet might be a healthier and safer way to lose weight. The "Eco-Atkins" plan replaces the meat, eggs, and dairy of Atkins with vegetable sources of protein, such as soy, nuts, and gluten. It also allows you to eat a few more carbohydrates a day and, unlike the original Atkins diet, limits your calories.

People on the Eco-Atkins plan lost about the same amount of weight as those on a high-carb vegetarian diet. In addition, the Eco group saw a bigger drop in triglycerides and bad LDL cholesterol and improved the ratio of good HDL cholesterol to total cholesterol.

7 ways to spot fad diets that don't work

Fad diets like the Blood Type diet, the Cabbage Soup diet, and the Fat Flush all have one thing in common — they make big, pound-shedding promises they probably can't keep. Some fads are even downright dangerous. Beware of any diet plan that:

- claims you will lose weight fast, at a rate of more than 1 or 2 pounds a week.

- promises you can shed pounds and keep them off even while enjoying unhealthy fatty foods or never having to exercise.

- bases its claims and results on before-and-after photos and testimonials, instead of hard science.

- totally bans certain nutrients or entire food groups, like carbs, sugar, or fats. None of these are bad in moderation, and they're found in plenty of healthy foods. Plus, avoiding them entirely can lead to overwhelming cravings that can blow your diet.

- tells you to skip meals or replace them with special drinks or food bars. The nutrition in these products cannot replace a balanced meal.

- works by drastically cutting your calories, as with starvation diets. These plans try to take the weight off fast, but you end up dropping water weight, not fat, and regaining it when you stop the diet. In fact, starvation diets actually slow your metabolism.

- charges for expensive seminars, supplements, herbs, or prepackaged meals you supposedly "need" for the plan to work properly.

More reasons to go organic

Some people suspect that the pesticides on produce and the growth hormones in meat and dairy throw a wrench in your metabolism and contribute to obesity.

Scientists are still on the fence about these claims, but the Environmental Protection Agency is now studying pesticides to see what, if any, danger they pose to your body. The final verdict may take years, but buying organic can give you peace of mind now.

Organic produce tends to have significantly fewer traces of pesticides than regular produce. As for meat, the U.S. Department of Agriculture bans farmers from feeding growth hormones to "organic" cattle, sheep, and dairy cows.

Going organic can help you trim your waist for another reason, too. It's expensive. Farmers produce these foods on a smaller scale and put more work into them. Not surprisingly, you can get good deals if you shop smart. Buy organic fruits and vegetables in season to snag them at around the same price as regular produce.

Tips to stop holiday weight gain

Holiday eating can do more than blow your diet. It's the main reason people gain weight as they get older, according to research from the National Institutes of Health (NIH).

The average person gains just over 1 pound a year, much of that during the winter holidays. People who are already overweight may gain up to 5 pounds. Unfortunately, most people don't lose that weight over the course of the year.

As you know, the feasting period doesn't last just one day. It goes on for about six weeks, from Thanksgiving into the New Year. Finding ways to avoid putting on pounds during the holidays can help put a stop to your expanding waistline.

Stay active. The holidays are busy times, but don't slack off your daily walks or workouts. One of the biggest predictors of weight gain in the NIH study was whether people stayed active. Those who were less active over the holidays gained more weight.

Fitting in a workout is easy. Park farther from stores when you do your holiday shopping. At the mall, aim for a brisk pace rather than a leisurely stroll.

Don't go to events hungry. Eat a healthy snack beforehand. In the NIH study, being hungry also predicted how much weight people would gain. Those who said they were hungry over the holidays gained the most weight.

Downsize portions, especially at buffets. Take a small scoop of your favorite foods rather than loading your plate with everything. Make yourself wait 20 minutes before going back for seconds.

Avoid fast food. Resist the convenience of fast food while running holiday errands. Plan ahead and pack a sandwich and snacks to take with you. Right before the holidays hit, prepare and freeze some healthy meals to pop in your microwave after a busy day.

Don't try to "diet." Aim to maintain your current weight during the holidays, not lose more. Otherwise, you are setting yourself up for failure.

Make a healthy dish. Bring a low-calorie dish to holiday potlucks, or another food you know you can safely eat. Other guests are sure to appreciate it, and you are guaranteed one thing you can enjoy guilt-free.

Give holiday recipes a healthy makeover

Dieting doesn't mean giving up your favorite holiday dishes. It means making smart substitutions, swapping out the fattening ingredients for ones that are easy on your waistline.

Instead of	Try
bread crumbs for breading	unprocessed bran flakes mixed with oatmeal or oat flour, then crushed
buttermilk, 1 cup	15 Tbsp. skim milk plus 2 Tbsp. lemon juice
cream cheese	Neufchatel or light cream cheese
heavy cream	equal parts half & half and fat-free evaporated milk; for soups or casseroles, evaporated skim milk
oil (for baking)	equal parts unsweetened apple sauce and oil
oil (for cooking)	leave out or reduce by 1/2 or 2/3
sour cream	fat-free plain yogurt
whipping cream	fat-free whipped topping or chilled, evaporated skim milk
white flour	oat flour, soy flour, or 100-percent whole-wheat flour
white sugar	1 tsp. mashed banana per 1 Tbsp. sugar being replaced

NEAT way to rev up your metabolism

Burn up to 500 extra calories a day — without breaking into a sweat — and lose all the weight you want, including that stubborn belly fat. Just tap into NEAT, the metabolism-revving secret of those who stay slim.

Nonexercise activity thermogenesis (NEAT) is a fancy way of describing all the things you do every day that aren't considered exercise — like going to work, playing the piano, and doing dishes. NEAT moves like these don't burn a lot of calories on their own, but the numbers add up over the course of a day.

Lean people tend to do more NEAT activities than overweight people. When researchers studied this, they discovered that obese people sat, on average, 2.5 hours more each day than thin people. Simply filling this "down" time with movement, such as standing, walking, or fidgeting, may be enough to put the brakes on a growing waistline.

People in this study could have burned 350 more calories a day if they had spent those 2.5 hours standing or doing other NEAT activities. At that rate, they could have dropped as much as 33 pounds in one year, all without changing what they ate. Want to shift your weight loss into overdrive? Burn 500 extra calories a day by spending three hours doing NEAT things like pulling weeds, riding your bicycle, or painting a room rather than three hours watching television.

NEAT doesn't have to mean chores. Experts urge you to pick activities you enjoy. That way, getting off the couch becomes something you want to do every day. Dance around your house while listening to music, go for a stroll with a friend, prune your flowers, or anything else that involves standing or moving.

Here's a look at how many calories an average 154-pound person will burn doing these NEAT activities for 30 minutes.

Activity	Calories burned
light gardening or yard work	165
dancing	165
golf (walking and carrying your clubs)	165
walking	140

Fitness plan for beginners

It's never too late to become more active, and it's guaranteed to help you shed extra pounds. Older adults reap the benefits of being physical into their 80s, according to a new study.

- People age 70 were almost half as likely to die over the next eight years if they were active.

- People age 85 were nearly four times more likely to die over the next three years if they were not active.

- Starting to exercise even late in life, between ages 70 and 85, still gave people an edge in living longer.

- People who were active at age 78 were more likely to remain independent at age 85.

- Physical activity increased people's survival rate at any age, and the oldest people in the study benefited the most.

- Active seniors were less likely to fall, break a bone, or suffer from chronic joint or muscle pain.

Ease yourself into more activity with something simple — like walking. Spend five minutes in the beginning warming up your muscles so you don't injure them. Do something light, like walking at a stroll. Gradually pick up the pace until you're moving at a brisk clip. Cool down at the end of your walk the same way, by slowing your pace, and gently stretch your muscles for a few minutes. Remember to sip water before, during, and after any workout.

You may not be able to move very far or fast in the beginning. That's OK. It's best to take things slowly. Begin with low-intensity exercises.

If you haven't been active for a long time, start out doing just five or 10 minutes at a time. You will gradually build strength and stamina.

Keep challenging yourself as your body gets stronger. Focus on being active for longer periods of time. Make 30 minutes your goal. Once you achieve that, raise the bar by walking faster, or uphill.

In the end, you want to spend 30 minutes a day, five days a week doing a moderately intense aerobic activity, like brisk walking. The good news is, you don't have to do it all at once. Experts say you can break that 30 minutes of exercise into bite-size blocks. Go for a 10-minute walk in the morning, another one in the afternoon, and one in the evening. It doesn't matter when you get your workout, as long as you do at least 10 minutes at a time.

QUICK*fix*

The first few months of any new habit are crucial. If you can stick with some form of physical activity for six months, there's a good chance it will last the rest of your life. Make exercise fun and motivating.

- Hang a mirror next to at-home exercise equipment, so you can see the positive changes in your body.
- Watch TV while you work out. Tune into your favorite shows, pop in a rented movie, or catch up on programs you recorded.
- Read something fun, like a travel magazine or your favorite author, while on the treadmill.
- Use the library. Check out music, movies, and audio books to keep you company while getting in shape.

Rethink exercise

Staying active is just as important as eating healthy, but you don't have to run marathons or bike 20 miles. Take it from Pat, 56 years old and an avid gardener. "I know some people think gardening isn't really exercise, but I'm here to say, 'Are they kidding?'

"Working in my garden means bending and lifting, moving and stretching, not to mention digging and hauling! Anyone who's ever had a garden knows that shoveling compost, lifting 40-pound bags of mulch, transplanting seedlings, dividing plants, and pulling weeds are serious physical activities.

"There's always something to do, from spring planting and weeding to fall raking and cleanup. It keeps a body moving!"

Amish secret to staying slim

Can't resist that extra dessert? Learn from the Amish. Their diet is rich in fatty foods and sweets, yet they have fewer weight problems than most other people.

Chalk it up to an active lifestyle. Without televisions to keep them glued to the couch, Amish men average an amazing 18,400 steps a day and women 14,200 steps daily. Most people, on the other hand, walk only 9,400 steps a day.

The Amish don't slow down with age, either. Amish seniors tend to take just as many steps as the younger folks. Most other seniors drop to around 7,000 daily steps in their golden years.

These humble people aren't naturally slim. Some are genetically prone to obesity, just like many people. The difference — all this activity offsets their natural predisposition to gain weight. Experts say the Amish prove that being active can help you stay trim, even if your genes make you prone to obesity.

Walking as much as possible is a great way to be more like the Amish. A daily walk will help:

- melt away belly fat. Aerobic exercises, like brisk walking, are the best kind for shedding pounds. Brazilians who walked just 30 minutes a day five days a week successfully shrank their waistlines and trimmed body fat.

- drop your blood sugar. The Brazilian walking program also lowered people's fasting blood sugar.

- clear your arteries. People with blocked blood vessels in their legs, called peripheral arterial disease, who walked on a treadmill three times a week improved blood flow through their arteries, reduced their risk of heart problems, and were able to walk farther over time.

- invigorate you with more energy than you ever thought possible. Spending 20 minutes taking an easy walk can rev up your nervous system and make you feel energized. It did for people complaining of fatigue in a study at the University of Georgia.

Boost your chances for better health and successful weight loss with these timely tips.

Set a step goal. Aiming for a specific goal motivated people to walk more, even if they weren't able to meet that goal. Experts suggest shooting for 10,000 steps a day to stay fit.

Wear a pedometer. This inexpensive device will help you track how many steps you take and monitor your progress. People in one study walked 2,500 more steps daily when they wore a pedometer. At that rate, this little device could help you drop an extra 5 pounds a year.

Take a dog. Seniors who walk their dogs regularly remain more mobile as they age. Pooches provide great motivation, and, unlike human companions, a dog will never try to talk you out of your daily walk.

Speed up and slow down. Try switching up your speed. Walk fast three days a week and slow on two days. Obese women who did this for four months trimmed more inches off their waists; lost more weight overall; and shed twice as much fat, five times more belly fat, and three times more thigh fat, compared to women who only walked at one speed.

SimpleSOLUTION

You've hit a plateau in your diet and exercise regimen, and you can't seem to get past it. You may be tempted to eat even less, but don't. You should never go below 1,200 calories a day. If you do, your body goes into starvation mode, and your metabolism slows down to save energy.

That means if you're burning 400 calories during daily exercise, you need to increase your calorie total to 1,600 a day to offset it. The key is to choose nutrient-packed foods like fruits and vegetables along with some protein.

Lose weight in bed or on the couch

It's not what you think — these simple, no-sweat exercises boost your body's metabolism, so you actually burn more calories, even when you sleep. Strengthening, or resistance, exercises can rev up your metabolism, burn belly fat, protect your bones, and preserve your independence as you age.

Burn more calories. People who have more muscle also have a faster metabolism. Muscle tissue burns more calories than fat tissue, even while you rest. By building muscle, strength training can boost your metabolism as much as 15 percent, so you burn more calories than ever.

Blast away belly fat. Lifting weights twice a week is proven to fight the fat around your middle — helping you stay thinner and healthier — for life. It slowed or prevented women from packing on belly fat, in one recent study.

Stay independent. What's the single biggest cause of your body's deterioration as you age? Surprise, it's muscle loss. But there's still something you can do. Resistance exercises can keep building muscle strength and mass, plus improve your mobility, into your 90s.

Just ask the 14 seniors who spent six months on a strength-training program. By the end, they were noticeably stronger and even catching up to their younger counterparts. The training also reversed age-related changes at the most basic level, the genes inside their muscle cells.

Build stronger bones. Women can lose 1 to 2 percent of bone mass each year after menopause, but strength training actually makes your bones denser and stronger. Research also shows that building muscle reduces the risk of fracture in women ages 50 to 70.

- Don't let lifting weights intimidate you. You don't need to be a muscle-bound athlete to reap the benefits. Start with light weights, only 1 or 2 pounds, or with no weights at all, depending on your physical condition. Try lifting and lowering the weight eight times in a row. If you can't, then it's too heavy. Lifting weights that are too heavy can injure the very muscles you want to strengthen.

- Gradually add more weight. You need to keep challenging your muscles to get the most from your workout. Slowly build up the number of times you can lift it (repetitions) and how many groups of repetitions you can do in a row (set). Once you can easily do two sets of 10 to 15 repetitions, increase the weight to an amount you can only lift eight times.

- Maximize your muscle-building with good form. Lift the weight slowly while breathing out, and lower it even more slowly while breathing in. Lowering the weight should take about twice as long as raising it. Make your movements smooth and steady, not jerky.

- Avoid exercising the same muscles two days in a row. They need a break, so switch off. Work on strengthening your upper body on Monday, Wednesday, and Friday and your lower body on Tuesday, Thursday, and Saturday.

Restaurant self-defense

You may get more than you bargained for when eating out — more calories, that is. A new study reveals that restaurant food packs nearly 20 percent more calories on average than they claim on the menu. Some meals contain twice the calories.

Oversized portions are part of the problem. Bigger servings mean more calories. What's more, the nutritional information may only count the entrée, not side items. In five restaurants, the sides contained more calories than the entrée itself, doubling the meal's calorie content.

That spells diet disaster. Your best bet is to eat out sparingly while trying to lose weight. When you do go out, you may want to assume your meal contains more calories than it claims.

Clever ways to guard against injury

Choosing the proper shoes can make or break your exercise routine. If you plan to do one type of activity often, like walking or playing tennis, buy shoes specifically made for that activity. Whatever kind you buy, look for a pair with:

* flat, nonskid soles.

* good heel support.

* plenty of room for your toes.

* a cushioned arch that's not too high or thick.

* Velcro fasteners, if your fingers have trouble tying the laces.

Try on several pairs. The perfect pair should feel comfortable right from the start. A good fit is especially important if you suffer from diabetes or arthritis. Replace your shoes when:

* the tread on the bottom gets worn down.

* your feet feel tired, particularly in the arches, after wearing the shoes.

* your hips, knees, or shins hurt after an activity.

Plenty of people suffer from foot pain that keeps them sidelined and sedentary. Foot experts say a few easy fixes can turn your shoes into allies against pain. A specialty shoe store known as a pedorthic shop can craft custom-made insoles, or orthotics, to ease problems caused by high arches, bunions, or arthritis. Heel lifts may help hip pain, while heel cups can aid foot pain, heel pain, and plantar fasciitis.

Get fit while sitting

You can build muscle and burn fat from just about anywhere — even a chair. That's great news if you're in a wheelchair or simply can't walk very far.

Talk to your doctor first to make sure it's safe for you to exercise and whether there are any movements you shouldn't do. Once you get the all-clear, you can practice five simple moves that will help you do everything from carry groceries to back out of tricky parking spaces with ease. Work your way up to doing two sets of 10 to 15 repetitions for each exercise.

Side arm raise. This movement strengthens your shoulders to make lifting things like groceries easier. Sit in an armless chair with your feet flat on the floor, shoulder-width apart. Place your arms at your sides, holding light weights if you're able, and breathe in. Then breathe out as you slowly raise both arms straight out to your sides until your hands are at shoulder height. Breathe in again as you gently lower your arms.

Seated row. For this exercise, you'll need a long resistance band, which resembles a giant rubber band. This movement strengthens your upper back, shoulders, and neck to make everyday chores, such as vacuuming and raking, easier on your body.

Sit in an armless chair with your feet flat on the floor, shoulder-width apart. Place the center of the resistance band under your feet, and hold the ends with your hands. Turn your palms inward and breathe in. Pull up and back slowly as you breathe out until your hands are at your hips. Hold the pose for one second, then slowly lower your hands.

Chair dip. You don't need any special equipment for this one, just a chair with armrests. The chair dip strengthens your arm muscles to help you get out of a chair.

Sit with your feet flat on the floor, shoulder-width apart. Lean a little forward but keep your back and shoulders straight — no stooping. Breathe in as you grab the chair arms at your sides. Breathe out and slowly push your body off the chair. Don't stand up completely. Instead, hold the pose for one second, and gradually lower yourself back down.

Leg straightening. This move may seem too simple, but it will go a long way toward building thigh muscle and easing knee arthritis.

Sit with your back against the back of the chair, with only the toes and balls of your feet touching the floor. Place a rolled up towel under one thigh at the edge of the chair and breathe in. Slowly raise that foot, as you breathe out, until the leg is straight, but don't lock your knee. Flex your foot by pointing your toes to the ceiling, then gently lower your leg back to the floor. Repeat with your other leg. Once this exercise becomes easy, add ankle weights to keep building those muscles.

Back twist. The simplest things seem to get harder with age, like swinging a golf club or turning to look behind you when backing out of a parking space. This exercise will help. Check with your doctor first if you have had hip or back surgery.

Sit toward the edge of a chair with armrests, as upright as possible. Make sure your feet are flat on the floor, shoulder-width apart. Slowly twist at your waist until you face left. Your hips should keep facing forward, not turn with you.

Turn your head to the left. Put your left hand on the left armrest and your right hand on your left thigh. Gently twist as far to the left as you can without hurting yourself. Hold the position for 10 to 30 seconds, then repeat the same move to your right. Unlike the other exercises, you should do this one at least four times on each side.

Energy **BOOSTER**

Video games can help you lose weight, not gain it, if you play the right kind. The new generation of games, like Nintendo's Wii games, are made to get you up and moving.

Go bowling, golfing, or playing tennis without leaving your home. They're a fun way to boost your energy levels and burn calories at the same time. Researchers found that people playing the Wii Boxing game burned 148 more calories per hour than if they sat on the couch and watched TV or played more traditional video games.

The bottom line — squeezing in an hour of Wii every day, alone or with a playing partner, can be a fun way to rev up weight loss.

Slimming supplements for a flatter tummy

A handful of nutrients may help your body burn more fat and gain the muscle you need.

CLA. Conjugated linoleic acid (CLA) may help rev up your metabolism, melt away the body fat you have, and prevent you from putting on more.

Experts think it works by stopping your body from storing excess calories as fat and forcing it to burn more fat for fuel. Whatever the reason, research suggests this supplement could help people drop almost a pound of fat for every four weeks they take it. Unfortunately, the effect seems to wear off after six months.

Some formulations of CLA may be safer and more effective than others. Look for a product with a combination of the cis-9, trans-11 isomer and the trans-10, cis-12 isomer. Not every label will list this information, but it should list how much CLA is in it. Check the Supplement Facts ingredient list to make sure it contains at least 75 percent CLA.

Arginine. Your body needs this amino acid to make nitric oxide (NO) and other important compounds. Both arginine and NO help burn fat and stop its storage.

Experts think this nutrient affects the way your body uses energy, pouring more of it into building muscle and storing less of it as fat. Rats given arginine gained less belly fat but more muscle, as well as more "good" brown fat, the kind that actually burns calories.

L-carnitine. Your body needs this nutrient to process energy and turn it into a form your body can use. Not surprisingly, you seem to need more of it when struggling with metabolic problems, like diabetes and obesity. A carnitine shortage can cause mitochondria, the tiny power plants in your cells, to break down.

In animals, taking carnitine supplements for eight weeks reversed these mitochondrial problems. And in people, 66 seniors over the age of 100 built more muscle, developed more physical and mental energy, lost more fat, scored higher on thinking tests, and were better able to walk after they took 2 grams of L-carnitine once a day for six months.

Resveratrol. This natural compound found in grapes and red wine may help treat obesity. In lab studies, resveratrol stopped fat cells from multiplying, kept young fat cells from growing into full-fledged ones, and triggered these cells to die.

You can get it naturally from foods or in supplements. Either way, pair it with another plant compound, quercetin, to maximize its fat-fighting power. Some products, such as Resvinatrol Complete, combine these two compounds into one supplement.

The dangers of diet pills

It's tempting to turn to a pill to magically melt off unwanted pounds, but buyer beware. The Federal Drug Administration recently recalled 72 weight loss products because they contained undeclared drugs, sometimes in doses far higher than the maximum safe limit.

Even so-called "natural" ingredients can endanger your health. The weight loss herbs fen-phen and ephedra have both been banned for causing serious health problems — from strokes and heart attacks to irregular heartbeats and seizures.

Be wary of diet products that make outrageous promises. If it sounds too good to be true, it probably is. Ask your doctor about the safest way for you to lose weight.

Safe & steady blood sugar for nonstop energy

7 hidden signs of diabetes

One in four people have prediabetes, but only 4 percent of them know it. For the other 96 percent, diabetes sneaks up silently, a truly quiet killer. Don't get taken by surprise. Be on the lookout for these seven signs.

Red, swollen, tender gums. Nine out of 10 people with gum disease are at high risk for diabetes, compared to six out of 10 without gum disease. Brush daily, see your dentist regularly for cleanings, and get tested for diabetes if you find out you have gum disease.

High blood pressure. Women with high blood pressure were more than twice as likely to develop diabetes over 10 years as women with normal blood pressure. Even women with only slightly high, but still normal, blood pressure faced a greater risk, as did women whose blood pressure crept upward over time.

Don't wait. Talk to your doctor about diabetes testing if your blood pressure is high or on the high end of normal. Then learn powerful ways to lower it in *Natural remedies that pump up your heart*.

Digestive problems. People with diabetes are more likely to suffer upper gastrointestinal problems, such as heartburn, acid reflux, and chest pain that's not caused by heart disease. Indigestion can be a subtle sign, too.

If you have bloating, uncomfortable fullness, nausea, vomiting, or ulcer-like pain that wakes you up but goes away when you eat, see your doctor about diabetes testing.

Thirst. Sugar builds up in your blood when you have diabetes. As the amount of sugar in your blood rises, it spills into your urine. Your kidneys excrete more water to dilute it. This creates large volumes of urine, sending you to the bathroom more often and making you abnormally thirsty as your body struggles to stay hydrated. Calories get flushed out along with the extra urine, leading to weight loss and leaving you unusually hungry. These symptoms may come on slowly, so it pays to stay aware.

Mental confusion and fatigue. Stresses like a severe infection, stroke, or heart attack can send blood sugar through the roof in people with diabetes. These super-high sugar levels can cause a condition known as hyperosmolar nonketotic syndrome, where the excess sugar and sodium in the blood sucks water out of cells.

It's a serious condition marked by confusion, drowsiness, a dry parched mouth, warm dry skin, hunger, and nausea or vomiting. Call your doctor or an ambulance immediately if you notice these symptoms.

Slow-healing wounds. High blood sugar keeps your immune system from fighting off infections the way it should, so any infections you get tend to be more severe. Over time, high blood sugar also narrows your blood vessels, reducing blood flow. This poor circulation prevents wounds from healing well.

Be on the lookout for wounds that won't heal or more infections than normal. Women, in particular, may develop more bladder and vaginal infections.

Numbness, tingling, or burning pain. These sensations in your hands or feet may signal nerve damage caused by diabetes. In fact, for some people they are the first noticeable signs of this disease. High blood sugar and poor circulation can eventually damage the nerves in your extremities, leading to diabetic neuropathy. Take these symptoms seriously and see your doctor. It's never too late to start treating diabetes.

SimpleSOLUTION

An exciting new test can predict your chance of developing diabetes over the next five years, giving you a head start on fighting it. The PreDx Diabetes Risk Test measures certain proteins and other substances in your blood that are linked to diabetes, then scores your risk on a scale of 1 to 10.

Your doctor can order this test from Tethys Bioscience by calling 888-697-7339 or visiting the Web site *www.predxdiabetes.com*. Be warned — your health insurance or Medicare may not cover it. Find out the cost before you sign up.

Don't want to pay? The American Diabetes Association offers a free diabetes risk assessment online at *www.diabetes.org* or by phone at 800-DIABETES. Simply answer a few questions about your weight, age, family history, and other characteristics.

Top 5 ways to prevent type 2 diabetes

The best offense is a good defense, and that applies to diabetes. Following just five pieces of advice can save you from expensive drugs and insulin injections, plus help you live a longer, healthier life.

Shed pounds. Being obese is a huge contributor to type 2 diabetes, but you don't have to drop a lot of weight to drop your risk. Losing just 5 to 10 percent of your weight — 10 to 20 pounds for a 200-pound person — helps lower blood sugar, plus improve your blood pressure, triglycerides, and good HDL cholesterol, all risk factors for heart disease.

A study published in the prestigious journal *Lancet* showed people dropped their diabetes risk an incredible 16 percent for every 2.2 pounds they lost. At that rate, shedding 10 pounds would slash your risk by 73 percent.

Catch more zzz's. Too little sleep may lower your levels of leptin, a hormone that makes you feel full, and raise your levels of ghrelin, a hunger hormone, a recipe for weight gain. On top of that, not getting enough sleep, especially deep sleep, can throw off your blood sugar and insulin levels.

Don't stay up late watching television, and talk to your doctor if you think you have sleep apnea, a potentially deadly sleep disorder. See the *Sounder sleep puts new life into your days* chapter for more advice on getting a good night's rest.

Stay active. Even a little activity can help beat back diabetes. Walking the equivalent of 30 to 45 minutes a day, five days a week kept obese animals from developing diabetes, including those on a high-fat diet.

Belly fat pumps out compounds that cause inflammation, upping the risk for both heart disease and diabetes. This little bit of exercise did the opposite in this study, bringing down inflammation, improving insulin sensitivity, and cutting fat buildup in the liver — all without a change in diet.

According to Jeffrey Woods, University of Illinois professor and study author, "Even if you struggle with dieting, we believe you can still reduce the likelihood of obesity-related inflammatory diseases, such as type 2 diabetes and heart disease, by adding a modest amount of exercise to your life."

Take care of your teeth. Brushing your teeth may actually help prevent diabetes. Women who rarely brushed were more than twice as likely to have diabetes, compared to people who brushed after each meal. Men faced higher risks, as well. These people also tended to have higher blood pressure, higher triglycerides, and lower HDL cholesterol.

People with inflamed gums have more inflammatory compounds in the rest of their body, and that inflammation contributes to the development of diabetes, high blood pressure, and heart disease.

Stop smoking. A German study showed that seniors who smoked were almost three times more likely to develop diabetes as those who had never smoked. The outcome was worse for smokers with prediabetes, who were eight times more likely to end up with the full-blown disease.

Inhaling secondhand smoke is bad, too. It raised the risk of diabetes 2.5 times in people who had never smoked, and 4.4 times in never-smokers who had prediabetes. Talk to your doctor about medicines and products designed to help you kick the habit.

Question & Answer

What's the difference between diabetes and prediabetes?

In prediabetes, your blood sugar is higher than normal, but not high enough to qualify as full-blown diabetes. Most people who have prediabetes develop type 2 diabetes within 10 years, unless they change their lifestyle.

Diagnosis cutoffs (in milligrams per deciliter)

	Fasting glucose test	Glucose tolerance test
Prediabetes	100 to 125 mg/dL	140 to 199 mg/dL
Diabetes	above 125 mg/dL	above 199 mg/dL

Be aware that even if your lab results point to prediabetes, your doctor may not call it that. He may say you have "impaired fasting glucose" or "impaired glucose tolerance." These terms are doctor-speak for prediabetes, so don't shrug them off.

Escape disease with these superheroes

The ultimate anti-diabetes treatment may be sitting in your refrigerator right now — foods and beverages that have a proven track record of warding off diabetes.

Love those leafy greens. Broccoli, brussels sprouts, kale, collards, spinach, and other leafy green vegetables are loaded with vitamin K. In one study, people who got the most vitamin K from either food or supplements were more sensitive to the action of insulin and had better blood sugar balance. In another study, taking a small amount of vitamin K each day for three years slowed the progression of insulin resistance in older men.

Vitamin K helps build the bone protein osteocalcin. This same protein may give a boost to the pancreas cells that make insulin. Vitamin K also squashes inflammation, which may improve insulin sensitivity and blood sugar levels.

The amount of vitamin K people took in the second study — 500 micrograms — is easy to get from food. Just one cup of boiled spinach delivers twice that amount.

Take time for tea and coffee. A major review of 18 studies involving more than 450,000 people found that every cup of coffee people drank each day cut their diabetes risk by 7 percent. It may not sound like much, but it adds up fast. Decaffeinated coffee and tea offered similar protection. Drinking three to four cups of tea each day trimmed the risk by one-fifth, while the same amount of decaf coffee lowered it by one-third.

Caffeine may not matter, but the time of day you take your break might. A separate study suggested coffee only offered protection if people drank it during lunch. Coffee with milk didn't seem to boast any benefits. Keep in mind that caffeinated coffee has been linked to bone loss in elderly women, as well as higher levels of homocysteine, cholesterol, and blood pressure.

Don't forget dairy. Its winning combination of vitamin D, calcium, and magnesium could slash your diabetes risk.

- Magnesium deficiency is linked to high insulin levels, glucose intolerance, and insulin resistance, a recipe for type 2 diabetes. Getting more of this mineral may help, but only if it comes from animal and dairy sources, not plants.

- Cells need calcium to help them use insulin. In one study, women who got the most calcium every day trimmed their diabetes risk by one-fourth.

- People with the lowest levels of vitamin D in their blood seem more likely to have insulin resistance. Getting more of this incredible vitamin may reverse this condition. Women who took 4,000 IU of vitamin D daily, twice what the National Institutes of Health says is safe, saw their insulin sensitivity improve and fasting insulin drop after six months.

Most people, especially seniors, do not get enough calcium and vitamin D each day. Fortify yourself with good food sources, like low-fat dairy, and ask your doctor if you should take supplements.

Learn about the lychee. It's an exotic, strawberry-looking fruit grown mostly in China, but you can find it now in Florida, California, and Hawaii, as well. Good thing, because lychees are rich in antioxidants that may derail metabolic problems. In a small study, people who took lychee supplements shrunk their waistline, shed belly fat, and improved their insulin resistance.

Lychees look like grapes on the inside, but they pack a much bigger antioxidant punch. French scientists rank this unusual fruit second only to strawberries in the amount of polyphenols it provides, beating out grapes, cherries, apricots, and figs. Experts say these antioxidants silence the genes involved in insulin resistance and quiet inflammation linked to metabolism problems.

Enjoy them fresh, or peel and pit them, then stuff with cottage cheese or pecans. Cut them in half and bake on top of ham during the final hour of cooking. You can even eat dried lychees like raisins. Just avoid canned fruit packed in sugary syrup.

5 foods to avoid to dodge type 2

You are what you eat. And, unfortunately, some foods are more likely than others to increase your risk of diabetes. The good news — they're easy to avoid, and doing so can slash your chances of getting this disease.

Toss the cheesecake. The saturated fat in this and other foods sends your immune system into fighting mode. Immune cells mistake these fats for foreign invaders. As a result, they start pumping out inflammation-causing compounds linked to diabetes.

Mice with healthy immune systems who ate a high-fat diet developed glucose intolerance and insulin resistance, precursors to diabetes. Mice whose immune cells ignored the fat, however, were able to eat fatty foods with less inflammation and without blood sugar problems. Scientists are using this knowledge to develop new therapies to fight diabetes.

Forget french fries. Eating french fries leads to a greater risk of type 2 diabetes and insulin resistance. Experts finger trans fat as the major culprit. Like saturated fat, it seems to boost the inflammatory compounds in your body.

The Nurses' Health Study showed the more trans fat people ate, the more likely they were to develop diabetes. Animal studies have shown that trans fat can cause insulin resistance and harm the way your body naturally handles blood sugar.

Steer clear of white bread. Several studies show eating foods made with refined grains, like white bread, boost your insulin resistance and harm blood sugar control. In one study, older adults who ate the most refined grains had the highest fasting blood sugar.

Eating carbohydrates that digest easily and get absorbed quickly into your bloodstream, like refined grains, may lead to a bigger rise in insulin after eating. This may cause the insulin-making cells in your pancreas to burn out faster.

Switch to whole-grain versions of your favorite carbohydrates. Here's what to look for:

- products labeled "100-percent whole grain."

- whole wheat, whole rye, oatmeal, barley, wheat berries, or brown rice as the first ingredient listed.

- whole-grain breads that have at least 2 grams of fiber per serving.

Skip fruit drinks. They can be chock-full of added fructose. This sugar has a low glycemic index, so experts once thought it safe for people with diabetes. Now they say it may be risky.

In animals, eating large amounts of fructose on a regular basis leads to insulin resistance, obesity, type 2 diabetes, and high blood pressure. Humans fare much the same. Overweight people gained more belly fat from drinking beverages sweetened with fructose than with another sugar, glucose. Fructose also boosted their fasting blood sugar and made them less sensitive to the actions of insulin.

Fruit drinks, soft drinks, baked goods, condiments, syrups, and candies are major sources of added fructose. Check ingredient lists and avoid products with this type of sugar.

Pass on pepperoni. You've probably heard that red meat is bad for you, but the real culprit may be processed meats — think hot dogs, bacon, sausage, deli meats, and pepperoni or any meat smoked, salted, cured, or chemically preserved.

Harvard researchers discovered that eating processed meat, but not unprocessed red meat, upped people's risk for diabetes by 19 percent and heart disease by 42 percent. Finnish researchers saw similar results. Over 12 years, eating processed meats raised the type 2 diabetes risk 37 percent among the study participants. Red meat and poultry did not.

Put the brakes on prediabetes

You're more than twice as likely to get fatal heart disease if you have prediabetes, yet doctors often don't treat this condition or even explain it. You can keep prediabetes from developing into full-blown type 2 with a few life-saving facts.

Shed a few pounds. No need to lose a lot of weight. Dropping just 10 to 15 pounds for a 200-pound person can be enough to stop prediabetes from becoming type 2. People in the major Diabetes Prevention Program (DPP) study did it. They started with prediabetes and a set of goals — lose weight, eat less fat, and be more active. They only lost an average of 12 pounds, but it made a huge difference, slashing their diabetes risk by more than half.

Get on your feet. The best way to lose weight and keep it off is by adding exercise to any diet plan. Plus, physical activity cuts your risk for diabetes, heart disease, and some cancers.

- Start out slow and easy. Simply do something you enjoy three or four days a week that involves movement. Take a walk in your neighborhood, go window shopping at the mall, or play ball with your grandchildren. Don't worry yet about how long you do it.

- Set goals in week two. Aim for 60 minutes of activity, like brisk walking. You can break it into bite-size pieces, such as a 10-minute walk six days a week, if necessary.

- Bump it up. Try doing 90 minutes total during the third week. Add a few more minutes each week until you reach a total of two and a half hours of activity over the course of seven days.

Keep a diary. The researchers behind the DPP call this the most important part of changing your behavior. Write down everything you eat and drink each day while trying to lose weight. This will help you keep track of what and how much you eat, and how your eating habits change over time. The same goes for any physical activity you do.

- Be honest and write down what you really eat.

- Be accurate. Count the slices of cheese and mayonnaise on your sandwich, for instance.

- Make a note as soon as you eat something, so you don't forget.

- Write down any activity you did and how long you did it. Don't count breaks.

- Note the distance, if it's something measurable, like walking.

- Only write down activities you do for at least 10 minutes. Less doesn't count.

Trim the fat from food. Instead of cutting calories, the DPP had people limit fat. Not only is too much fat linked to high cholesterol, heart attack, and diabetes, but trimming fat from your diet may be just as effective as counting calories.

Fat contains more calories than carbohydrates or protein, so cutting just a little has a big impact. You could lose 1 to 2 pounds a week just by limiting fat to 25 percent of your daily calories. Women who kept fat calories to less than 20 percent of their total shed an average of 7 pounds in one year, without actually trying to lose weight.

Learn to manage stress. Many people turn to food or become less active and withdrawn when under stress. Developing other ways to cope can help put a stop to these self-destructive behaviors. In the DPP, counselors taught people to get a grip on stress by:

- learning to say no.

- allowing others to help carry the load of housework, yardwork, laundry, and errands.

- setting realistic goals, for weight loss among other things, instead of aiming for perfection.

- turning to friends and others who support their health goals.

- starting new habits when stress hits, such as going for a walk instead of munching.

- taking 10-minute timeouts to do something, other than eating, that made them feel good, like a foot massage, hot bath, or reading a book or magazine.

- taking a deep breath, counting to five, and breathing out slowly, letting muscles go loose.

Ditch negative thoughts. The mind can be your biggest enemy. Negative thoughts hit you with a double-whammy. They can make you stop caring and veer off the plan, then make you feel worse about yourself when you do stray. The DPP taught people three steps to stop these mental goblins.

- Recognize when you are having a negative thought.

- Imagine shouting "Stop" to yourself, and picture a big, red Stop sign.

- Talk back to yourself with a positive thought.

The road to beating diabetes can be challenging, but the results are worth it. Don't put it off. Take control of your health and your future, and your body will thank you with a longer life.

6 foods that fight diabetes

Living in a fog of fatigue? Blood sugar imbalances may be to blame. Luckily, these six anti-fatigue foods can help. Some are common, some newly discovered, but all will help you perk up and have more energy by balancing your blood sugar and guarding against diabetes.

Vinegar. Science has shown vinegar improves insulin sensitivity, but now experts say it may stop after-meal spikes in your blood sugar, too.

Ten men with type 1 diabetes drank a vinegar-water mixture or plain water five minutes before eating a carbohydrate-packed meal. The men drinking the vinegar mixture cut their rise in blood sugar by almost 20 percent, compared to those drinking the water. Researchers say as little as 2 tablespoons of vinegar with a meal can help dampen spikes and improve your blood sugar.

Lemon juice has a similar effect. You can lower your blood sugar level by adding this tangy juice to your foods.

The acid in vinegar and lemon juice slows your digestion, so your body absorbs the sugar in foods more slowly.

White button mushrooms. Surprisingly, these tiny funguses are filled with nutrients that may fight diabetes and heart disease. They're packed with fiber; vitamins C, D, B12, and folate; and powerful antioxidants called polyphenols.

In animals with diabetes, eating button mushrooms slashed blood sugar and triglycerides. And in animals with high cholesterol, they also cut total and bad LDL cholesterol while boosting good HDL cholesterol.

Soy. While soy supplements may not protect you against diabetes, eating fermented soybean foods might. Soy contains proteins and compounds known as isoflavones that may help manage blood sugar. Getting these compounds as supplements did not help people in one study. However, fermenting soybeans alters these nutrients, possibly for the better.

Research suggests eating fermented soybean products improves insulin resistance and helps the body secrete more insulin, a combination that could slow the progression of diabetes.

Coriander seeds. Feeding an extract made from the seeds to diabetic animals lowered their blood sugar and helped the few working beta cells they had left produce more insulin.

Coriander seeds have a mild flavor. Use them as a base for homemade curry powder or to flavor marinades and soup stocks. They lose their aroma quickly after grinding, so buy the whole seeds, put them in a pepper mill, and grind as needed.

Black tea. Green tea gets most of the attention, but black tea may better treat high blood sugar. It's rich in a compound that slows the digestion of starches, resulting in a smaller rise in blood sugar after a meal. It also had the most antioxidant power to squash damaging free radical compounds.

Walnuts. The idea that a handful of these could crush diabetes sounds nuts, but it may be true. Overweight people with diabetes who ate 1 ounce of nuts every day slashed their fasting insulin levels in the first three months.

Thank the healthy fats known as PUFAs (polyunsaturated fatty acids). The fats you eat end up in your muscle tissue. More PUFAs in muscle leads to more insulin receptors on muscle cells and better insulin action in your body. These fats may make for a healthier heart, too. Eating 2 ounces of walnuts daily in another study boosted blood vessel health in people with diabetes.

Question & Answer

Can diabetes be cured?

Yes, in some cases. A pancreas transplant can cure type 1 diabetes, but you will need to take immune-suppressing drugs for the rest of your life. Still, if the transplant takes, you will no longer have the disease.

You can manage type 2 diabetes with diet, exercise, and medicine, but the only "cure" so far seems to be gastric surgery in some morbidly obese people. Surgically induced weight loss cured diabetes in three out of four people in one review of studies. Blood sugar and insulin levels improve within days of the surgery, even before weight loss begins.

Not everyone is a good candidate for this type of procedure. Discuss your options with your doctor.

Heal yourself with whole-grain foods

Not all bread is bad for you. Those made with whole grains can actually improve your blood sugar control. The fiber in these foods helps your pancreas secrete more insulin and makes your cells more receptive to it. Plus, a high-fiber diet may lower blood sugar and cholesterol naturally in people with type 2 diabetes. Find a good fit with these whole-grain options.

Whole white wheat. It's white, but it isn't refined. White wheat is the albino version of red wheat, from which most flour is made. Unlike refined white flour, whole white wheat flour still packs the nutrient-rich parts of the grain — the bran, germ, and endosperm. Plus, it boasts a milder flavor than regular whole wheat, making it better for baking.

King Arthur, Farmer Direct Foods, and Hodgson Mill all sell whole white wheat flour. Some ready-to-eat foods are made with this whole wheat, too, such as Pepperidge Farm, Nature's Own, Cobblestone Mill, and Wonder breads; Dr. Kracker crackers; and Arrowhead Mills Organic Bulgur Wheat.

White rye. Instead of sharply spiking your blood sugar, rye bread causes a gradual rise and fall, which means less demand for insulin from tired pancreas cells. White rye flour also delivers more soluble fiber than whole-wheat breads.

Compared to other breads, rye triggered lower blood sugar responses and boosted insulin levels in one study. White rye flour worked best, even better than rye bran and whole-wheat flours.

Sourdough. In overweight people, eating sourdough bread triggered a smaller rise in blood sugar than whole-wheat and whole-wheat barley breads. In fact, it may have boosted their insulin sensitivity a whopping 25 percent.

Sourdough contains natural acids that make it digest more slowly than other breads. These same acids may also block the gut from absorbing some of the starch in the bread.

Buckwheat. This humble flour may help keep a lid on blood sugar after meals, thanks to the compound D-chiro-inositol. Eating cookies made with buckwheat flour lowered blood sugar in people with diabetes, while buckwheat extract slashed blood sugar 20 percent in diabetic animals.

If you love pasta, try Japanese soba noodles, which are made from buckwheat. Or make a stack of homemade flapjacks from buckwheat flour instead of white.

Natural recipe for cleaning out arteries

Diabetes puts you at high risk for heart disease and heart attacks, but never fear. Research shows you can avoid — even reverse — the often deadly complications, even if you already have diabetes.

In atherosclerosis, a fatty deposit called plaque builds up inside your artery walls, causing them to narrow. When this happens to the arteries that supply blood and oxygen to your heart, it's called coronary heart disease (CHD), or coronary artery disease (CAD). CHD is a common complication of diabetes, as well as a deadly one, leading to heart attack, heart failure, angina, and death.

It's serious, but it isn't a death sentence. People in one study reversed CHD by making a few basic changes in their lives. They:

- switched to a very low-fat vegetarian diet, where fat accounted for fewer than 10 percent of their daily calories.

- avoided simple sugars and focused on eating complex carbo-hydrates and unprocessed foods.

- learned to manage stress through training, with the goal of practicing stress management for one hour each day.

- began doing more aerobic exercises, mostly walking, for a total of three hours a week.

- stopped smoking.

Those who didn't make these changes saw their CHD worsen over five years and suffered twice as many heart problems, including heart attacks and heart-related death, and the need for angioplasty, bypass surgery, and hospitalization.

People who did make the changes dropped their LDL cholesterol an amazing 40 percent in just one year, lost 24 pounds the first year, and kept off more than half of that weight over the next five years. Age and severity of CHD did not make a difference. Only sticking to the program seemed to matter. Those who did improved the most.

Later research showed that people with diabetes also reaped big benefits from these changes. After only three months, they had slashed their CHD risk factors, including weight, body fat, and LDL cholesterol. Plus, they saw big improvements in their overall quality of life. Three out of four people with diabetes who stuck with the program were able to avoid CHD-related surgery for at least three years.

Talk to your diabetes team about how to make these changes in your daily life. They can help you draw up a realistic plan and give you the support and encouragement you need to stay with it.

Count on carbs to control diabetes

Lots of people think they can't eat carbohydrates — sugars and starchy foods — if they have diabetes. Not true. The American Diabetes Association (ADA) says carbs should still account for most of your daily calories. They provide most of the energy your body needs to function, plus are major sources of vitamins, minerals, fiber, and other nutrients.

It is helpful to track how much carbohydrate you eat at each meal, especially if you take insulin. The ADA recommends that people with diabetes begin by counting carbs. This system allows you to eat a wide variety of foods and is easier to follow than exchange plans.

Counting carbs can give you tighter control over your blood sugar, and by keeping your blood sugar and insulin levels steady, you'll stay energized and lose weight.

Set your goal. Different people can handle different amounts of carbohydrate, based on how active they are; what medicines they take; and their age, weight, and height, among other things.

The ADA suggests starting with 45 to 60 grams (g) of carbohydrate at each meal. Track your blood sugar carefully and adjust your carb allowance based on how your body reacts. Be sure at least 25 of those carb grams come in the form of fiber.

Talk with your doctor, registered dietitian, or diabetes healthcare team. They can help you figure out the right amount for you.

Find the carb content. There are two main ways to figure the amount of carbohydrate in a food.

- Prepackaged foods tell you on the label. Check the Nutrition Facts panel under Total Carbohydrate to get the grams of carb per serving. Then check the serving size at the top. If you eat more than one serving, you'll need to increase the number of carbs you count.

- Fresh food can be tricky, but a few rules of thumb make it easy. In general, one serving of fruit or starchy food packs around 15 g of carbohydrate, dairy 12 g, vegetables 5 g, and meat or fats, such as butter, 0 g. Keep in mind, these are general numbers. For the specific carb content of foods, look to Web sites like *www.carb-counter.org*.

Discover "discount" foods. Fiber is a type of carbohydrate, but your body doesn't digest it the way it does sugar and starches. So if a food contains 5 or more grams of fiber per serving, you score a carb discount. Divide the number of fiber grams in half and subtract that from the total carbohydrate content to find the number of carb grams you should count.

Sugar substitutes earn you a similar discount. The reduced-calorie sweeteners xylitol, sorbitol, mannitol, maltitol, and isomalt found in sugar-free candy, gum, and desserts still count toward your carbohydrate totals, but the same math applies to them. If a serving contains more than 5 g of these sweeteners, use the same formula to find your discounted carb count.

Balance your blood sugar. Counting carbohydrates can also help level out highs and lows in your blood sugar. Test your sugar before a meal. If it's low, you can bring it back in line by eating a few extra grams of carb. If it's high, cut back a little. Discuss this strategy in more detail with your doctor or dietitian to avoid dangerous swings in blood sugar.

Experts recommend eating the same amount of carbs at each meal for tight blood sugar control. Sometimes, you may want to eat more carbs than usual. Just remember if you do, your blood sugar will go higher than normal, and vice versa when you eat fewer. Be sure to adjust your insulin accordingly when you alter your eating pattern.

Carb-counting myth busted

Foods like meat and cheese have few, if any, carbs to count. "I thought since they were 'free' I could eat as much of them as I wanted. My wife said otherwise," remembers Arthur. "We argued over it for awhile, then I finally asked my doctor."

His doctor explained that even a food with few carbohydrates can still be bad for you. Foods soaked in saturated fat, trans fat, sodium, cholesterol, or empty calories don't do your heart any favors.

"Am I ever glad I asked. My doc set me straight. Now I count carbs, but I also keep an eye on the fat, sodium, and other things. I feel better, and I know I'll live longer."

No-hassle way to plan healthy meals

It's almost too easy. With the Plate Method, you can manage diabetes without the hassle of counting carbs, fat grams, or calories. It may even help you lose weight.

It doesn't give you a list of things you can and cannot eat. Instead, it focuses on eating all foods in the right proportions. The key is portion size. The amount of food you put on your plate should be determined by the number of calories you need each day.

You don't have to buy special plates. Simply use the ones you already have — but measure them first. This method won't do much good if you eat off large platters. Experts recommend using lunch and dinner plates 9 inches across, and a slightly smaller plate for breakfast.

Start by drawing an imaginary line down the center of your plate. On one side of that line, draw another line, dividing the section in half again.

- For breakfast, fill half the plate with starchy foods, such as whole-grain toast, high-fiber cereal, oatmeal, grits, hominy, or cream of wheat. Load one of the small sections with fruit and the other with protein, like Canadian bacon or eggs. Enjoy a glass of milk on the side, if you like.

- For lunch and dinner, fill half the plate with nonstarchy vegetables, such as broccoli, carrots, salad, cabbage, green beans, salsa, or cucumbers. Load one small section with a starch, like rice, pasta, tortillas, cooked beans or peas, potatoes, winter squash, or corn. Use the other quarter for healthy protein such as lean meat, chicken, fish, or low-fat cheese.

You can also add a serving of fruit on the side and a glass of low-fat milk. If you don't drink milk, you can have a very small serving of carbohydrate, like a small dinner roll or cup of low-fat yogurt.

Simple tips to lower GI

The glycemic index (GI) and glycemic load (GL) measure how fast foods raise your blood sugar after eating them, and they can fine-tune your control over diabetes.

Foods with a low GI, like fruit, lentils, whole grains, and soybeans, digest slowly, so your blood sugar rises slowly, too. Those with a high GI — bread, white potatoes, and pasta — digest quickly, making your blood sugar spike sharply.

Glycemic load takes serving size into account. Some foods with a high GI, such as watermelon, actually have a low GL, because you wouldn't eat a big enough serving for them to impact your blood sugar much.

While the GI and GL can be useful, they can also be hard to follow. That's why the American Diabetes Association suggests you focus on some sort of carb-counting first. Then you can fine-tune your blood sugar control further with the GI and GL.

You can look up the GI of specific foods on Web sites such as *www.glycemicindex.com*. Lower the glycemic index of your high-GI favorites with these kitchen tricks.

- Chill boiled potatoes and serve cold. Chilling them increases their resistant starch, which has less effect on blood sugar.

- Add a dash of vinegar, lime, or lemon juice. The acid in them slows digestion, so sugars get absorbed into your blood much more slowly.

- Parboil rice. Pressure-cooking rice instead of steaming it slashed the GI by 30 percent in a Danish study.

- Avoid overcooking pasta. Al dente, or slightly firm, pasta has a lower glycemic index than the mushy kind.

- Boil, don't bake, your yams. Baked and roasted yams, potatoes, and plantains tend to have a higher glycemic index than boiled versions.

Simple**SOLUTION**

Track your carbs on the go with clever devices you can carry anywhere.

The Track3 by Coheso is a small, handheld gadget that counts carbohydrates and calories, tracks medication, and doubles as a diet and exercise journal. It sells for $80 at www.coheso.com or by calling 877-750-2300.

If you own an iPod, iPhone, Palm Pilot, or other handheld helper, you can purchase an app — a small computer program — for a fraction of that. The Track3 app costs around $6 through iTunes. Just load it and you're ready to go.

The Diabetes Pilot works on more devices, including handheld computers (PDAs), iPhones, iPod Touch, and Windows Mobile phones. It tracks your carbs, calories, fat, protein, fiber, sodium, and cholesterol, along with blood sugar and blood pressure readings, insulin and other medications, exercise, and more. Download it at www.diabetespilot.com.

3 safe, simple ways to lose weight

Losing that flabby belly is one way to bring your blood sugar back in line, but not all diets are safe for people with diabetes. These three are. Research proves they can help you shed pounds while managing your blood sugar.

Mediterranean plan. More than 200 overweight people newly diagnosed with type 2 diabetes tried one of two eating plans — a traditional low-fat diet or a Mediterranean diet. Those following the Mediterranean plan were less likely to need diabetes medication four years later. Plus, they lost more weight and saw bigger improvements in their blood sugar.

The Mediterranean meal plan was rich in vegetables and whole grains but low on red meat. People ate poultry and fish, instead. It also allowed people to eat a sizable amount of fat every day, mostly in the form of two to four tablespoons of olive oil.

Both groups lost weight, although the Mediterranean dieters lost more. But weight loss didn't account for the bigger benefits. Experts think olive oil did. It's loaded with healthy monounsaturated fats, which may improve insulin sensitivity. Try it on salads with balsamic vinegar, and drizzle it on steamed vegetables in place of butter.

Vegan diet. Switching to a low-fat, plant-based vegan diet may outdo the standard eating advice offered by the American Diabetes Association. Nearly half of people with type 2 diabetes who went vegan were able to cut back on their diabetes medications after about six months.

While both eating plans improved diabetes and cut cholesterol, vegans saw greater benefits. They lost 14 pounds compared to the ADA group's 7 pounds and had a bigger drop in their LDL cholesterol.

Eating vegan means skipping animal foods, such as meat, poultry, dairy, eggs, and fish, and relying solely on plant foods. For that reason, these diets tend to be low in fat. As a result, vegans in this study were allowed to eat as much food as they wanted. The ADA-dieters, however, had to tighten their belts and cut a serious amount of calories.

Vegans in this study took 100 micrograms of vitamin B12 every other day. If you try this plan, you'll probably need B12-fortified food or supplements, since the nutrient is naturally found only in animal products.

Diet Plate. New evidence suggests you can lose weight and improve blood sugar without changing what you eat. Experts say most cases of type 2 diabetes are directly caused by obesity. As portion sizes have grown in restaurants and at home, so have waistlines.

Watching your portions could help you reverse your own growing waistline, even if you take insulin. Researchers gave people with diabetes either special plates to help them figure portion sizes, or nutrition advice. Plate-users who took insulin were more likely to lose 5 percent of their body weight than people getting dietary advice.

Five percent is a magic number, because dropping as little as 5 percent of your weight slashes your risk for obesity-related cancer, heart attack, and death. And while plate-users were able to cut back their diabetes medications, other people needed more medicine over time. That could add up to serious savings at the drugstore.

You can order the plates used in this study from the Web site *www.dietplate.us* or by phone at 866-822-9664.

Naturally sweet way to beat diabetes

Natural sweeteners aren't necessarily off limits if you have diabetes. Just be savvy about which ones you choose and how you use them.

Most foods with added sugar are sweetened with refined sugar and corn syrup, which have almost no vitamins, minerals, or healthy phytochemicals. Other natural sweeteners do.

A recent study, for instance, found that 1 ounce of date sugar or one tablespoon of blackstrap molasses pack almost as many antioxidants as a whole cup of blueberries or a small glass of red wine. Dark molasses, barley and brown rice malt syrup, dark brown sugar, and maple syrup weren't far behind.

Honey boasted more antioxidants than refined sugar, too, and some research suggests it may help lower blood sugar. In one study, 25 people with type 2 diabetes gradually swapped natural, unprocessed honey for other sweeteners in their daily diets over the course of eight weeks.

They made no other dietary changes, but those eating honey lost weight; raised their good HDL cholesterol; and lowered their triglycerides, total cholesterol, and LDL cholesterol. The credit probably goes to the minerals and antioxidants in natural honey. People who use this sweetener tend to have more vitamin C, beta carotene, and other antioxidants in their blood, some of the same compounds in green tea believed to boost weight loss.

Use honey with caution, however. The honey-eaters in this study may have seen some healthy changes, but their HbA1c levels also went up, which is your average level of blood sugar over the previous few months. Talk to your doctor or dietician before making a major adjustment like this to your meal plan.

Remember, too, that honey contains carbohydrates and calories — slightly more than white, granulated sugar. One teaspoon of honey should count for 4.5 carbohydrates and 21 calories when you plan your meals.

Guilt-free plan to satisfy your sweet tooth

Artificial sweeteners taste sweet as sugar but boast low or no carbs or calories, making them perfect for people with diabetes.

You'll often find reduced-calorie sweeteners, or sugar alcohols, in "sugar free" and "no sugar added" foods, like candy, gum, ice cream, cookies, and pudding. These include mannitol, sorbitol, xylitol, lactitol, erythritol, and maltitol, as well as isomalt and hydrogenated starch hydrolysates. They contain about half the calories and carbs of regular sugar, but they still count toward your daily total. To count their carbs:

- check the Nutrition Facts panel on the food's label.

- divide the amount of sugar alcohol carbs in half if one serving of food contains more than 5 grams of sugar alcohols.

- subtract that from the total grams of carbohydrates in one serving.

- count this number toward your carb allowance.

Reduced-calorie sweeteners do raise your blood sugar, just not as much as regular sugars or starches. How much they affect blood sugar varies from person to person, so monitor yours carefully until you know how you react.

Low-calorie sweeteners, on the other hand, don't affect your blood sugar at all because they contain no carbohydrate. Low-calorie sweeteners, such as Aspartame (NutraSweet, Equal), saccharin (Sweet'N Low, Sugar Twin), sucralose (Splenda), and acesulfame potassium (Sweet One, Swiss Sweet, Sunett), are popular in diet sodas, baked goods, light yogurt, and candy.

Aspartame has been linked to headaches and migraines in some people. If you notice these symptoms, try switching to sucralose. People with the genetic disease phenylketonuria (PKU) should avoid aspartame.

Otherwise, artificial sweeteners seem to be safe for people who have diabetes, with a few precautions. Foods made with them can still be loaded with fat, carbohydrates, and calories. Sugar-free baked goods, in particular, tend to be packed with saturated and trans fat.

Read nutrition labels carefully before digging in. Compare sugar-free items to their regular counterparts to see if you're actually getting a healthier product. You can cook and bake your own recipes with reduced- and low-calorie sweeteners, too.

- Use acesulfame potassium (Sweet One) for both cooking and baking alongside granulated sugar. It's 200 times sweeter than sugar, so you will need less of it. Substitute six packets (1 gram each) for each quarter cup of sugar.

- Add aspartame to puddings, no-bake pies, and other dishes after cooking. It breaks down in high heat, so don't use it in cookies or cakes. For best results, substitute six, 1-gram packets for each quarter cup of sugar.

- Keep an eye on the oven. Recipes made with sucralose (Splenda) tend to bake faster than with sugar. Substitute sucralose cup for cup for sugar.

- Cook with saccharin, but don't substitute it for more than half the sugar in a recipe. Use six, 1-gram packets for each quarter cup of sugar.

QUICK *fix*

Heating pads and electric blankets pose a special risk for people with diabetes. Some people with diabetes lose feeling in their arms or legs. If that happens, you may not be able to tell if a blanket gets too hot. You could be burned without knowing it. Because diabetes hampers your body's healing, that's a serious problem. You can use an electric blanket safely if you turn it on to heat the bed, then turn it off before you crawl under the covers. Don't leave the blanket on while in bed, and don't use heating pads.

Kitchen cures for troubling symptoms

Hypoglycemia, or low blood sugar, can catch you by surprise. You might feel shaky, dizzy, or sweaty, and you may be hungry or have a headache. Other common signs include sudden moodiness or confusion, pale skin, tingling around your mouth, and clumsy or jerky movements.

If you feel these symptoms, use your meter to check your blood sugar. If it's below 70 milligrams per deciliter (mg/dL), act fast to bring your blood sugar back to normal. It's simple. Just eat something that contains 15 to 20 grams (g) of carbohydrates. Good choices include snacks like fruit juice, hard candy, or crackers. Stay away from chocolate or cookies, since these treats have too much fat to raise your blood sugar quickly. You can also buy glucose tablets or gel to have on hand.

These items in your pantry have about 15 g sugar.

- 1/2 cup fruit juice or nondiet soda

- 4 or 5 saltines

- 2 tablespoons raisins

- 4 teaspoons sugar

- 1 tablespoon honey

Always carry some form of sugar with you. After you treat your low blood sugar, wait 15 minutes and check your blood sugar again. If it's still below 70 mg/dL, have another serving of carbohydrate. Be sure to eat your regular meals and snacks after the hypoglycemia passes to keep your blood sugar in the normal range.

Question & Answer

Can people with diabetes eat sweet fruits, like strawberries and pineapple?

Absolutely. It's true. Fruits contain natural sugars like fructose, but they are also chock-full of vitamins, minerals, and fiber. Just be sure to count the carbohydrates in fruit toward your total if you use carb-counting to manage diabetes.

Some fruits, particularly dried ones, pack more carbohydrate than others. No problem — simply eat a smaller portion. These sweet snacks each contain about 15 carbs. Enjoy.

- half a medium banana
- half a cup of cubed mango
- one and one-quarter cup of whole strawberries
- three-quarters cup of cubed pineapple

Hidden cause of unstable blood sugar

A little-known stomach problem could be the real reason your blood sugar bounces out of control.

One out of every 10 people with diabetes may also suffer from gastroparesis, a condition where your stomach takes longer than normal to move food into your small intestine. The delay can give you nausea and heartburn, make you feel full sooner than usual, and cause vomiting. You may also feel bloated, lose weight, and have trouble maintaining stable blood sugar. Diabetes-related nerve damage is often the culprit, but high blood sugar itself can gum up the works.

The symptoms aren't the real problem, inconvenient as they may be. When your stomach empties slower than normal, it totally blows your blood sugar balance. Don't ignore this problem. Talk to your doctor and try these suggestions.

Scan your medicine cabinet. A change in medications may be all you need. These drugs can make your stomach empty slowly. Discuss alternatives with your doctor.

- antacids made with aluminum hydroxide

- anticholinergic agents, used to treat a variety of disorders

- beta-adrenergic receptor agonists for asthma, bronchitis, emphysema, and other lung diseases

- calcium channel blockers for high blood pressure

- drugs containing diphenhydramine (Benadryl)

- histamine H2 antagonists for heartburn and ulcers

- interferon alfa for hepatitis and some cancers

- levodopa for Parkinson's disease

- opioid painkillers

- proton pump inhibitors for acid reflux, ulcers, and erosive esophagitis

- tricyclic antidepressants

- sucralfate (Carafate) for ulcers

Choose applesauce over apples. Foods with plenty of liquid may move through your stomach better than solid food. Drink more liquids, eat foods that are easy to digest, and purée others to aid digestion.

Eat smaller meals more often. Six small meals a day instead of three large ones take a load off your stomach. This eating schedule puts smaller amounts of food in your stomach at a time, making digestion easier and keeping you from feeling uncomfortably full.

Cut back on fat and fiber. People with diabetes are usually told to eat more fiber, not less, but it may worsen gastroparesis since it's difficult to digest. Fat and alcohol can aggravate the problem, too.

Your doctor may recommend you stop taking fiber supplements and avoid foods with lots of insoluble fiber, like oranges and broccoli.

Avoid vinegar. It can smooth out blood sugar spikes after a meal, but it also makes your stomach empty slower, something you don't need if you suffer from gastroparesis.

Your doctor can prescribe medications to ease nausea and help you digest food faster if these simple changes don't do enough.

'Silver bullet' for better health

Imagine an inexpensive pill that could slash high blood sugar, cut your risk of heart-related death, make you stronger, give you more endurance, and even build bone density. Would you take it? Who wouldn't?

That's exactly what exercise can do for you. Muscles burn both glucose and fat for fuel. Working muscles pull large amounts of glucose from your blood, which keeps the sugar from building up in your bloodstream. The more muscle you have, the more glucose you burn, and exercise builds muscle.

It also helps your body get better at using glucose and insulin. Moving muscles turn on tiny transporters that shift glucose from the blood and into cells — exactly what people with diabetes have trouble doing. Activity helps reverse insulin resistance, too, making your body more responsive to the effects of insulin. In fact, part of the reason people stop responding to insulin as they age is because they become less active.

Exercising regularly can slash your HbA1c levels. Plus, you'll reap the benefits of better blood sugar regardless of whether you lose weight.

It's great for your heart, too. Exercise is proven to lower your heart rate, blood pressure, cholesterol, and triglycerides. That's key, because diabetes makes you much more likely to develop atherosclerosis, which causes heart disease, angina, and heart attack and can lead to strokes and peripheral arterial disease in your legs.

Exercise does not have to mean pumping iron at the gym, although lifting weights does help battle diabetes. Something as simple as going for a walk will help reduce your HbA1c level.

In a Dutch study, taking a brisk, 60-minute walk three days a week for one year lowered HbA1c levels as much as using weights and fitness machines. Think of ways to ramp up activity in your everyday life.

- Get off the bus one stop early.

- Stand up and move around while talking on the phone.

- Park far away from the store and walk.

- Go window shopping.

- Take your dog — or your grandchildren — for a walk.

- Start a walking club with like-minded friends.

- Do your own yardwork instead of paying someone else, and save money, too.

QUICK*fix*

An aerobic workout, like walking, is great for controlling diabetes. Just be sure to take care of your tootsies before, during, and after.

- Use silica gel or air midsoles.
- Wear polyester or cotton-polyester socks to prevent blisters and keep your feet dry.
- Choose comfortable shoes that fit well.
- Check your feet carefully both before and after workouts for blisters, cuts, or other damage.

Stop diabetes in its earliest stages

You don't have to be a boxer to do a number on diabetes, but a smart combination of walking and lifting weights will give you an edge in defeating it.

Get your heart pumping. Just one week of moderate aerobic activity can help your body naturally control blood sugar and increase insulin response. Experts now know aerobic, or endurance exercises such as walking and bicycling, slash HbA1c levels, the major marker of blood sugar management.

New research from the University of Michigan helps explain how. Twelve older adults spent an hour each day for a week doing exercises such as walking on a treadmill and riding a stationary bicycle. By the end, their body's sensitivity to insulin had improved, and the pancreas cells that make insulin worked better.

Build those muscles. Strength training, or resistance exercises like weight lifting, improve both glucose tolerance and insulin sensitivity throughout your body. In fact, they can manage blood sugar about as effectively as aerobic exercise. Strength training builds more muscle, which helps your body use glucose. It gives you more strength, too, so you stay active and live independently longer.

Don't try lifting heavy weights if you are older or have had diabetes for a long time. Start with light weights and do more repetitions, instead. For more tips on these types of workouts, see *Lose weight in bed or on the couch* in the *Belly fat: easy ways to slenderize and energize* chapter.

Double up. You will roll back diabetes the most by doing a combination of aerobic and resistance exercises, especially if your HbA1c levels are 7.5 percent or higher.

People with type 2 who did either aerobics or weight lifting three times a week dropped their HbA1c by 0.5 percent after five and a half months. But those who did a combination of the two dropped it twice as much, a whopping 1 percent — enough to slash your risk of a major heart problem by 15 to 20 percent.

For lasting improvements in blood sugar, you need to burn about 1,000 calories a week through exercise. For a 154-pound person, that's the same as gardening for one hour a week plus walking for 30 minutes on five days.

You'll reap even bigger rewards by burning 2,000 calories a week. For a 154-pound person, that could mean gardening for two hours a week; lifting light weights for 30 minutes, three days a week; and walking for 30 minutes every day. The more you weigh, the more calories you burn doing these activities.

These goals can be challenging if you are not used to being active or have had diabetes for a long time. That's OK. Start slowly. As little as five to 10 minutes of exercise at a time will help. Gradually add a few minutes to your workouts as you grow stronger until you reach your goal. You can also break up your exercise into short spurts over the course of a day. Just be as active as you can.

Ask your doctor to refer you to an exercise physiologist or physical therapist to help you set up a safe program that is based on your health, diabetes status, and personal goals.

When and how to work out safely

People with diabetes who suffer from damage to nerves and blood vessels in their feet and eyes, heart disease or blood vessel blockages, or arthritis may need to stick with low-stress, low-impact workouts, like swimming and bicycling. Check with your doctor to find out what, if any, activities you should avoid.

Nerve damage. You will need to avoid certain exercises if you have lost sensation in your feet due to peripheral neuropathy. Try these gentle substitutes.

- swimming instead of treadmill walking

- bicycling instead of long walks

- rowing instead of jogging

- chair, arm and other non-weight-bearing exercises instead of step exercises

Heart problems. Autonomic neuropathy can boost your risk of heart problems during exercise, especially when you first start out. This condition can make it hard to regulate your body temperature, so avoid working out in hot or cold environments if you have it, and be sure to drink plenty of water.

People with diabetes are more prone to other heart problems, too. You are more likely to suffer a heart-related event while exercising if you are:

- in poor physical shape.
- over the age of 60.
- have diabetic retinopathy.

Your doctor can run tests to tell if you face a higher risk for heart events and advise you about which exercises to try and which to avoid. You may need a stress test, particularly if you have had diabetes for more than five years, are over the age of 70, or have two or more risk factors for heart disease.

Vision trouble. High blood sugar can damage the blood vessels in your eyes, leading to diabetic retinopathy. Strenuous activity such as heavy weight lifting can worsen vision problems in people with proliferative diabetic retinopathy (PDR), causing hemorrhaging in the eye or retinal detachment.

If you know you have PDR, avoid activities that involve straining (weight lifting), pounding (jogging), jarring (high-impact aerobics), and racquet sports. Instead, go swimming or walking and try stationary cycling.

People with nonproliferative diabetic retinopathy can do more activities but should still avoid power weight lifting, boxing, and heavy competitive sports or other pastimes.

SimpleSOLUTION

Some overweight women admit they avoid gyms because they feel self-conscious and intimidated. Don't let worries over how you look in short sleeves derail your efforts to beat diabetes. If you are a woman, consider an all-female fitness center, such as Curves, to ease your discomfort and encourage you to stick with it.

QUICK*fix*

Exercising when you have diabetes means taking a few extra precautions.

- Wear a medical ID bracelet or other identification that lets people know you have diabetes in case you have a low blood sugar episode. Include your name, address, and phone number; doctor's name and phone number; and a list of your medications and doses.

- Carry a blood glucose monitor with you if you plan an extra-long workout.

- Take glucose tablets, Life Savers, or other emergency sugar with you in case of low blood sugar.

- Drink water before you start exercising and stay hydrated during your workout.

- Exercise with a buddy or group. You will motivate each other, plus have someone to help you if your blood sugar bottoms out.

Guard against blood sugar swings while working out

Exercise can naturally lower your blood sugar, as working muscles suck up glucose from your blood for energy. That's a good thing 99 percent of the time. But occasionally, exercise can trigger a hypoglycemic episode. Then, before too long, blood sugar can shoot back up as your body compensates for using lots of energy. Guard against these swings with easy-to-follow advice.

Test first. Check your blood sugar before you start exercising. It needs to be between 100 and 130 mg/dL if you have type 2 diabetes. If it is less than 100 mg/dL, eat a high-carbohydrate snack, like a piece of fruit or a granola bar, before beginning. Do not exercise if it is above 300 mg/dL.

Be prepared. Carry a source of fast-acting glucose with you while working out, such as glucose tabs or hard candy.

Stay alert. Watch for signs of hypoglycemia. Stop and test your blood sugar if you feel faint, weak, or have heart palpitations or other symptoms. Eat a snack to raise your blood sugar, if needed.

Retest afterward. Check your blood sugar right after exercising and again a few hours later. It can continue dropping for several hours.

Tweak your timing. Try scheduling your workouts after a meal or snack if your blood sugar tends to bottom out after exercise. A good pre-workout snack provides 15 grams of carbohydrate, like these.

- three gingersnaps

- 2 tablespoons of raisins

- small apple or banana

- half a cup of frozen, low-fat yogurt

- one Glucerna snack bar

- six saltine crackers

- 6 ounces of light yogurt

- one-quarter cup of low-fat granola

- half an English muffin

Talk to your doctor about adjusting your diabetes medicines if your blood sugar routinely drops too low after activity.

Ask the expert. Ask your doctor what time of day is best for you to exercise. He can help you plan a schedule that balances activity, meals, and medication.

Energy **BOOSTER**

Get moving if you want to be more alert and have energy all day long. Follow these simple tips to make the most of any activity.

- Start with a warm-up, five to 10 minutes of low-intensity aerobic activity, like walking or cycling. This gets your heart and other muscles, as well as your lungs, ready for a workout.

- Stretch gently for another five to 10 minutes. Focus on the muscles you plan to exercise.

- Slow down your heart gradually after a workout with another five to 10 minutes of gentle activity.

- Drink around 16 ounces (two cups) of fluid in the two hours leading up to your workout, and continue sipping during it. Dehydration affects your blood sugar levels and heart function.

Trio of supplements help treat diabetes

These well-researched supplements may help stabilize blood sugar and ease painful complications from diabetes. Take them under your doctor's supervision. If they do lower your blood sugar, your doctor may need to adjust your diabetes medicines accordingly.

Alpha-lipoic acid. This antioxidant helps your body fight off harmful free radicals and turn glucose into the energy that powers your cells. It seems to:

- improve insulin sensitivity and blood sugar control in type 2 diabetes, but not lower HbA1c levels.

- ease the symptoms of peripheral neuropathy, such as burning, pain, numbness, and prickling sensations in your legs and feet.

- help protect against diabetes-related damage to the heart, kidneys, and small blood vessels.

Generally, people take between 200 and 400 milligrams (mg) of alpha-lipoic acid three times a day for diabetes and neuropathy.

Chromium. Insulin normally attaches to cells to make them absorb sugar from your bloodstream. In insulin resistance, this system stops working. Chromium teams up with insulin to help it unlock the "door" into cells so glucose can get in again. More than 200 people with type 2 diabetes saw significant improvements in their fasting blood sugar and HbA1c levels when taking a combination of 600 micrograms (mcg) of chromium picolinate and 2 mg of biotin.

There are different types of chromium. Your body absorbs chromium picolinate and chromium polynicotinate better than chromium chloride. Experts say taking 500 mcg of chromium twice a day should lower your HbA1c in two months. Talk to your doctor about the proper dosage for you. Most people tolerate this mineral well, but a few react to it even at low dosages. Be cautious about taking it if you suffer from depression or bipolar disorder.

Choose your brand carefully, too. An independent lab found that only two out of six brands of chromium supplements passed quality tests recently. Three of the four that failed contained dangerous amounts of hexavalent chromium, the kind linked to cancer. To find out which made the cut, visit the website *www.consumerlab.com.*

Ginseng. Two types of ginseng may offer aid for diabetes. American ginseng, or *Panax quinquefolius*, seems to lower blood sugar and help stabilize it after meals. Experts think it:

- protects the pancreas cells that make insulin from dying an early death.

- ramps up insulin production.

- reduces insulin resistance in muscle and fat tissue.

Look for a powdered root supplement that contains at least 2 percent total ginsenosides (20 mg per gram of ginseng powder), or an extract with at least 4 percent total ginsenosides (40 mg per gram).

Korean red ginseng is actually Asian ginseng *(Panax ginseng)* that has been steamed and dried, unlike unprocessed Asian "white" ginseng. People who took 2 grams of Korean red three times a day before meals saw improvement in both blood sugar and insulin regulation. Look for powdered Korean red ginseng with at least 1.5 percent total ginsenosides (15 mg per gram of ginseng) or an extract with at least 3 percent total ginsenosides (30 mg per gram).

Avoid any kind of ginseng supplement if you take antidepressants or the blood thinning drug warfarin (Coumadin).

Question & Answer

I have heard that I shouldn't take glucosamine for my arthritis because it will raise my blood sugar. Is that true?

Glucosamine is a popular joint supplement, often combined with chondroitin. In theory, it might make your diabetes medications less effective, but research so far doesn't prove this. Glucosamine has not affected insulin sensitivity or caused insulin resistance in studies involving people with diabetes.

Experts now agree the supplement is safe to try if you have diabetes. However, the Arthritis Foundation still recommends monitoring your blood sugar more closely once you start taking it.

Shrug off stress for tighter control

Getting a grip on stress takes on new importance when you have diabetes, because stress can actually send your blood sugar skyrocketing — despite your best efforts.

Some sources of stress are short-lived, like getting stuck in a traffic jam or taking a difficult test. Others last longer, such as taking care of an aging parent. People with type 1 diabetes may see their blood sugar rise in times of stress — or fall. With type 2 diabetes, stress usually makes your blood sugar rise.

Make the connection. How can you know if stress affects your blood sugar? The American Diabetes Association suggests you track it.

- Before you test your blood sugar, write down your stress level on a scale of one to 10.

- Then check your blood sugar, and write down the reading next to your stress number.

- Continue keeping track for a few weeks.

- Look for a pattern in sugar highs and lows. You may need to make a graph of both sets of numbers to see a pattern.

If your blood sugar tends to be higher when your stress is high, stress is affecting your glucose levels.

Stress impacts your blood sugar in two major ways. First, a stressful situation triggers the release of certain hormones, leading to a rise in blood sugar. Second, when your blood sugar is chronically high, your brain tries to protect itself by strengthening the barrier that keeps glucose from moving from your blood into your brain cells.

Unfortunately, when your brain needs more glucose, it responds by sending out a signal calling for more sugar — not by simply lowering the barrier. Your body reacts by pushing blood sugar levels even higher, creating a vicious cycle of high blood sugar.

And diabetes itself can be stressful with the hassles of dealing with medicine and managing your blood sugar and food intake. People under stress may drink more alcohol and exercise less. They may get busy or forget to check their blood sugar or eat balanced meals. In an extreme case, stress may even make you not care about watching your blood sugar.

Stress can have a huge impact on the course of your diabetes. In fact, some experts suspect that certain people with diabetes may not actually need medicine to lower their blood sugar. Instead, they may be able to get their blood sugar into the safe range simply with relaxation techniques.

Get off the stress roller coaster. Try these simple tricks to lower your stress levels.

- Avoid situations that cause you anxiety.

- Change the way you think about your problems. People who try to solve their problems and those who tell themselves a problem isn't a big deal are less likely to have high blood sugar.

- Choose to exercise — it helps battle stress.

- Consider learning a new relaxation technique, such as breathing exercises, progressive relaxation therapy, or biofeedback. For more information on relaxation techniques, see the *Stress busters that set you free* chapter.

- Join a diabetes support group.

- Find a counselor or therapist to help you deal with your stress.

How to pick a meter that meets your needs

Checking your blood sugar at home is central to managing diabetes. Studies prove that people who use home meters develop fewer complications from diabetes.

Testing your blood sugar regularly alerts you quickly if it gets too high or falls dangerously low. You can then figure out how certain foods and activities affect your blood sugar. In addition, knowing your number lets you treat yourself with just the right amount of insulin or other medication to adjust your blood sugar. Shop wisely for a glucose meter with the features you need.

Size. Nowadays, meters can be really tiny. That can make them easy to fit in your purse, but be sure yours is large enough to hold comfortably without dropping it.

Results output. A glucose meter gives test results on a screen or through audible output. Look for a meter screen with numbers displayed large enough for you to read easily. If you have vision problems, consider a meter that speaks results out loud.

Test strips. These items are sometimes pretty small, making them hard to handle if you have numbness or arthritis in your fingers. Look for a meter that uses larger strips or dispenses the strips for you. That way, you won't have to insert a strip each time you test. Also look for strips in easy-to-open containers.

Testing site. Typically, meters test a drop of blood from your fingertips, the most accurate site. Some meters let you check at alternate sites, such as your arm or leg. Don't use an alternate site if you struggle with bouts of low blood sugar.

Memory storage. Most meters store your test results, but some meters store more results than others — up to 400 results, for instance. On the other hand, certain meters hold on to other important information to help you track patterns in your blood sugar. This information can help you better manage your diabetes. And some meters let you download your test results onto a computer.

Cost. First, there's the price of the meter. You may be able to find rebates, and some manufacturers allow you to trade in an old meter for a deal on a new one. But your biggest cost will be for test strips — not the meter itself. Medicare or your health insurance should cover some of the cost of both the strips and the meter, but check to be sure before purchasing.

Method of coding. Some meters recognize a test strip's code automatically, while others need you to input the information. That process is known as coding. It can take several steps, and doing it wrong can skew your test results. If you are concerned, consider picking a meter that doesn't need manual coding.

Check out meters on display at your local pharmacy so you can get a feel for the model you think you want. You can also get good advice on choosing a meter from your doctor, pharmacist, or diabetes educator.

Little-known ways to avoid false readings

Your glucose meter could be giving you wrong readings, putting you at risk for dangerously low blood sugar — even coma. Most glucose meters rely on test strips that contain chemicals to measure your blood sugar. Put a drop of blood on the test strip, and a complex chemical reaction takes place. When conditions are perfect, the reading should be accurate.

But certain medicines and health conditions can interfere with the reaction, sometimes dangerously skewing your results. This is especially a problem with test strips containing the enzyme GDH-PQQ. These strips are very common, including some made by ACCU-CHEK, Freestyle, and TRUEtest.

Drug interactions. The most common drug that can affect test results is acetaminophen (Tylenol). A normal dose of acetaminophen probably won't have much effect on your reading, but everyone processes drugs at different rates. That means some people could get poor test results from even a standard dose. Acetaminophen is not the only problem. Be careful if you take one of these other supplements or drugs.

- vitamin C

- L-dopa, for Parkinson's disease

- tolazamide, a diabetes drug

Health conditions. Certain conditions and treatments can alter your body's chemistry, also skewing blood sugar test results. Be wary if you have anemia, sickle-cell disease, low blood pressure, or end-stage renal failure. Even dehydration can change your results.

Other situations. Smoking, being on peritoneal dialysis, or undergoing oxygen therapy can also interfere with accuracy. And atmospheric conditions — high altitudes, excess humidity, and extreme temperatures — can also be a problem.

Read any warnings that came with your glucose meter and test strips to see what medicines or conditions affect accuracy. That way, you will know your blood sugar readings may not be reliable at certain times. Before you treat yourself, be sure to gauge how you feel in addition to taking the reading.

SimpleSOLUTION

Summer heat can damage your insulin, affecting the amount you need to get the same effect. Keep your insulin cool in the heat of summer.

- Never leave insulin in a hot car, and keep it out of direct sunlight.
- Use ice packs or freezable gel packs to keep insulin cool in a lunch pack or small cooler. Be sure insulin doesn't touch the ice packs, since that can also damage it.
- Consider investing in a cooling wallet. These come in various sizes and can hold vials, pens, and pumps, keeping contents cool for up to two days. One popular brand is Frio, available at *www.frious.com* or from your diabetes supply company.

The latest news about intensive insulin therapy

Doctors once believed getting your HbA1c levels as low as possible was best for managing type 2 diabetes, a practice sometimes called tight glycemic control or intensive glucose control. The idea — to stave off diabetes complications by keeping HbA1c levels around 6.5 or 7 percent, closer to normal levels.

New research shows this could do more harm than good. In the ACCORD study, this strategy increased the risk of death for some people and may outweigh the benefits in those with:

- long-standing diabetes who also have heart disease or a high risk for it.

- severe or frequent bouts of hypoglycemia.

- a short life expectancy.

A separate study, the VA Diabetes Trial, found similar results. People who began intensive glucose control within 15 years of their diabetes diagnosis did gain protection, dropping their risk for heart and blood vessel incidents, such as heart attack and stroke, a whopping 40 percent.

Beginning the strict regimen later, however, did not help and was dangerous in some cases. People who began intensive glucose control 16 to 20 years after their diagnosis saw no heart protection. And heart attacks and stroke more than doubled in people who began it 20 years or more after their diabetes diagnosis.

Experts say tight glycemic control may be good for some people, like those newly diagnosed with diabetes, but it may do more harm or pose too much of a burden for others. A more realistic goal for many may be an HbA1c level between 7 and 7.5 percent. Even that may be too difficult for people whose bodies make very little insulin.

Discuss with your doctor what you can handle, what you prefer, and the potential safety and side effects of lowering your numbers. Then together, set goals personalized for you.

Surprising things that spike blood sugar

Your body's reactions can be unpredictable when you have diabetes. Don't get caught unaware by these hidden triggers of high blood sugar.

Cholesterol drugs. Certain statin drugs seem to raise fasting blood sugar. This happens to people who don't have diabetes, too. Yet, in one study, people with diabetes saw their blood sugar rise twice as much as those without the disease. Statins may cause changes in your body that block cells from absorbing sugar and stop the pancreas from releasing insulin.

Some, but not all, studies suggest these statins may increase blood sugar and HbA1c levels.

- atorvastatin (Lipitor)

- simvastatin (Zocor)

- rosuvastatin (Crestor)

Pitavastatin (Livalo) and pravastatin (Pravachol) don't seem to affect blood sugar. Some experts recommend pitavastatin, a newer drug, for cholesterol-control in people with diabetes, because it works about as well as atorvastatin without rocking blood sugar control.

Discuss the risks and benefits of these medications with your doctor, and never stop taking a statin drug on your own. Despite this side effect, strong evidence suggests statins help slash the risk of heart attack, stroke, and other heart problems in people with diabetes.

Colds and flu. Something as small as a common cold can send your blood sugar skyrocketing. Your body churns out hormones in response to stresses, like illness. These hormones tell your liver to release extra glucose into your bloodstream to give your body more energy to fight the illness.

Unfortunately, this strategy backfires when you have diabetes. The same hormones can work against insulin, actually making your cells more resistant to it. People who don't have diabetes simply make more insulin to overcome the resistance, but your pancreas may not be able to keep up with the demand if you have diabetes. The end result — more sugar builds up in your bloodstream.

You need to take special care of yourself when sick to battle dangerous swings in blood sugar.

- Never, ever skip a dose of diabetes medicine or insulin when you're ill, even if you cannot eat.

- Check your blood sugar every three to four hours, including during the night, or have someone check it for you.

- Call your doctor if your blood sugar rises above 250 mg/dL.

- Try to eat your normal daily allotment of carbohydrates during your illness.

- Rest and stay warm.

- Drink plenty of fluids. Your body flushes out more water when blood sugar is high, and you need to replace it. Get 8 ounces of caffeine-free fluid every 30 to 60 minutes. Alternate salty fluids, like broth, with low-sodium ones, like water.

Handle your feet with care

Taking good care of your feet should be an everyday event when you have diabetes. That's because your feet are at risk in two ways. First, there's nerve damage, which can keep you from feeling injury to your feet or toes. The other major problem is reduced blood flow. Circulation troubles mean any infections or wounds take longer to heal.

Here's how a small foot problem can have major consequences. Let's say you get a blister from wearing new shoes, but you don't feel any discomfort because of nerve damage. The blister may get infected if you don't take care of it. If your blood sugar is high, the extra glucose feeds bacteria to spur on the infection. Your tiny wound can then grow larger, since poor circulation gets in the way of healing. In a worst case, the infection might not heal, causing gangrene and leading to an amputation.

It sounds horrible, but this possibility is why taking care of your feet is so important if you have diabetes. When you baby your tootsies, you'll avoid serious problems.

Stay on guard. Check your feet daily for cuts, blisters, calluses, and other problems — especially if you have nerve damage or poor circulation. Ask for help or use a mirror if you have trouble seeing all angles.

Practice careful hygiene. Keep your feet clean by washing them daily in warm water. Test the water temperature with your elbow to be sure it's not too hot. Dry your feet carefully, especially between your toes. Finish off by applying lotion to areas with dry skin.

Your toenails need trimming at least once a week, and they're easiest to work with when they're soft after a bath. Don't cut them too short, and file the edges carefully with an emery board. That emery board or a pumice stone also comes in handy to gently file away corns and calluses before they cause trouble.

Don't go barefoot. Your feet need protection — even indoors. Wear slippers or shoes around the house to guard against injury. Wear socks or stockings — nothing too tight — with shoes to prevent blisters.

And pick shoes that fit your feet well. Shop for new shoes late in the day, when feet tend to be at their largest. Wear your new shoes for only a few hours daily for the first few weeks. Ask your doctor to check your feet at every diabetes checkup and do a complete foot exam every year.

Put an end to early morning sugar spikes

Don't let the "dawn phenomenon" derail your diabetes control. This early-morning rise in blood sugar typically strikes between 2 a.m. and 8 a.m. To most people, it's a mystery — why would their sugar rise before they even eat breakfast? Experts point to several possible reasons.

- hormones your body releases in the early phase of sleep, which can make your blood sugar rise
- taking too little insulin the evening before
- indulging in a carbohydrate-filled snack before bed
- taking the wrong dose of diabetes medication

Pinpointing the cause is simple. Set your alarm to wake you around 2 a.m. or 3 a.m. for several nights in a row. Get up, check your blood sugar, and write it down. Show the results to your doctor on your next visit.

Be picky about pedicures

Pampering your feet is key when you have diabetes, but a bad pedicure is bad news.

Getting a pedicure can be dangerous if the salon doesn't use sanitary practices, tools are dirty, or your pedicurist is not well trained. Even if you have diabetes, you may be able to have a pedicure if you don't have complications from the disease. But if you have an infection, ulcer, or cut on your feet or legs, or if you suffer from neuropathy — nerve damage — in your feet, then pedicures are not for you.

Pick a top salon. Do your homework to be sure your salon uses safe and clean techniques. First, see if your nail technician is licensed. Then find out what type of foot baths are used. Pipes in some baths can spread bacteria, so "pipeless" foot baths can help cut this risk.

Using individual buckets or bowls is another safe option. Also be sure the salon cleans the foot baths between customers using a hospital-grade, EPA-registered disinfectant that's made for pedicure foot baths.

Schedule a manicure at the salon so you can check out the facility and see how foot baths and tools are cleaned. Experts say tools should be cleaned after each use in an autoclave — a pressurized, heated chamber. Watch to see if your technician opens a new pack of sterilized tools after you sit down. Also be sure the salon uses stainless steel tools, which are easier to clean than porous nail files or wooden cuticle sticks.

Request special care. Let your technician know you have diabetes, and ask her to take these extra steps.

- Massage your feet gently.

- Be sure the water is warm — not hot.

- Don't clip your cuticles or file calluses, and skip the credo blade, which looks like a razor.

- Cut your toenails straight across.

- Massage lotion completely into your feet, and don't leave any between your toes.

You can help by not shaving your legs for two days before getting a pedicure. That way, you'll avoid nicks and keep skin from being irritated, both possible entry points for bacteria.

Question & Answer

Can cinnamon treat my diabetes?

It's still under debate. Several small studies suggest the spice helps control blood sugar, while several others don't. In one study, seasoning food with a little more than one teaspoon of cinnamon seemed to lower after-meal insulin levels.

Cinnamon has a long history as a diabetes-fighting spice, and it certainly contains compounds with the potential to lower blood sugar. So far, research hasn't proved it works. Cinnamon may turn out to be no more than a folk remedy, but seasoning your morning oatmeal with this delicious spice is still a good idea.

Regular dental care cuts diabetes costs

People with diabetes are more prone to teeth and gum problems. That's because high blood sugar allows bacteria in your mouth to thrive, encouraging a white, sticky film called plaque to grow on your teeth. If it's not removed, it can harden into tartar, setting the stage for chronic inflammation and infection in your mouth.

In addition, ulcers and sores in your gums act as doorways, letting inflammatory compounds and bacteria enter your bloodstream. When that happens, your body has more trouble moving glucose out of your blood, eventually leading to complications with your eyes, heart, and kidneys as well as other organs.

Diabetes weakens your body's resistance to infection, so people with poorly controlled diabetes get periodontal diseases more often. This infection of your gums and the bones that hold teeth in place leads to tooth loss — even worse if your diabetes is poorly controlled.

Slash your costs, save your health. Treating gum disease could shave 10 percent off your medical costs every month if you have diabetes. University of Michigan researchers found that people with diabetes who had dental cleanings or periodontal scalings once or twice a year had monthly medical costs that were 11 percent lower than other people. Their combined medical and drug costs were 10 percent lower. Those who got treatment even more frequently — three or four times a year — saved 12 percent. In this case, spending money actually saves money.

Take matters into your own hands. Protecting your teeth and gums starts with at-home care.

- Brush at least twice a day with a fluoride toothpaste. Better yet, brush after each meal or snack using a soft-bristled toothbrush. If arthritis keeps you from maneuvering your toothbrush easily, consider an electric toothbrush.

- Floss or use a between-teeth cleaning tool once a day.

- Ask your dentist about a germ-killing mouthwash or toothpaste.

- Control your blood sugar.

- Don't smoke, especially if you're older than age 45.

- See your dentist if your gums become red, swollen, or tender; bleed easily; or pull away from your teeth. Other reasons to head to the dentist include persistent bad breath or a bad taste in your mouth, a difference in the way your teeth fit together when you bite, or a change in the fit of your partial dentures.

Get the most from your visit. Tell your dentist about your diabetes, and schedule dental appointments and surgeries in the morning or whenever your insulin tends to be highest. If you need lots of work, such as multiple fillings, schedule it for several short appointments.

Don't forget to bring along small snacks and your diabetes medication in case your blood sugar drops. Finally, ask your dentist about antibi otics if you have frequent infections.

Special tips for surviving menopause

Menopause poses special challenges for women with diabetes, but you can handle them by arming yourself with a little information.

Hot flashes. It can be hard to tell the difference between change-of-life issues — hot flashes or excess sweats — and feelings of low blood sugar. Getting it wrong can be dangerous if you don't treat your low blood sugar thinking it's just menopause. On the other hand, you may end up eating more to treat low blood sugar, when you're actually having a hot flash.

To avoid sabotaging your blood sugar control, check it more often than usual once menopause starts.

Hormone therapy. Experts say hormone-replacement therapy (HRT) probably won't affect glycemic control. In fact, some studies suggest HRT may actually help blood sugar control, while others show it has no effect. Either way, it probably won't be a big problem. But check your blood sugar often when starting or stopping HRT or changing dosage, just in case.

Weight changes. Shifting hormones during menopause encourage your body to lose muscle and gain fat, especially around your midsection. This change can mean a higher risk for heart problems and more trouble managing your blood sugar.

That gives you more reason than ever to control your weight through physical activity.

Natural remedies that pump up your heart

4 simple ways to protect your heart

Drugs are not your only option for preventing or treating heart disease. Some lifestyle and nutrition changes are nearly as powerful as prescription drugs, while others can start improving your health in minutes.

A University of Cambridge study found that people who kept just four healthy habits slashed their risk of dying from heart disease, cancer, or any other cause during the 11-year study. When researchers compared people who practiced all four to people who practiced none, the "healthy habits" group had only a quarter as much risk of dying as the "no healthy habits" group. Other studies suggest these four habits can also help prevent diabetes and cancer. But the Cambridge study found that these simple habits are the most effective against heart disease.

Eat more fruits and veggies. The healthy habits group ate at least five servings of fruits and veggies every day, a practice that led to high levels of vitamin C in their bloodstreams. Combined with the right diet, this may be almost as effective against heart disease as some prescription medications.

- The typical American diet may be short on fruits and vegetables, but the DASH diet for high blood pressure is packed full of them. One study found that people with high blood pressure who switched to the DASH diet for eight weeks lowered their blood pressure 11 points more than people on the typical American diet. Experts say that 11-point difference is similar to what most people can expect from a prescription drug.

- In another study, people tried a diet rich in plant sterols from veggies, fruits, and vegetable oils; high in fiber from oats and barley; high in almonds and soy protein; but low in saturated fat. This reduced their "bad" LDL cholesterol by 29 percent — nearly as much as some cholesterol-lowering drugs.

Get active. If your job keeps you physically active, or if you spend 30 minutes a day taking a brisk walk, you are following the example of the healthy habits group. That is important because regular, moderate physical activity reduces the first number in your blood pressure reading by about four points and the second number by three points. Exercise also helps prevent heart disease.

Stop smoking. Quit smoking and your risk of heart trouble starts shrinking right away. Your blood pressure starts dropping just 20 minutes after quitting. After one year, your extra risk of heart disease compared to a nonsmoker is half as high as when you first quit. After five years, your stroke risk is the same as if you've never smoked. After 15 years, your heart disease risk equals that of a nonsmoker as well.

Limit alcohol. Drinking moderate amounts of alcohol has been linked to a lower risk of heart disease. But drinking too much alcohol can raise your risk of heart disease and may contribute to cancer. What's more, drinking smaller amounts of alcohol may even affect women's risk of breast cancer, so if you don't drink, don't start, say experts. If you already drink, have no more than one drink a day if you are a woman or two drinks a day if you are a man. One drink equals a 12-ounce bottle of beer, 4-ounce glass of wine, or 1 1/2-ounce shot of 80-proof spirits. They all contain the same amount of alcohol.

Deaths	Alcohol prevented	Alcohol caused
100,000		
50,000		other cardiovascular disease
		liver disease
		cancer
25,000	heart disease	pancreatitis
	stroke	overdose
	diabetes	injury

If you don't drink, don't start for your heart. Alcohol's annual death toll far outnumbers deaths prevented by alcohol.

Silent killer: what every woman should know about heart disease

Heartburn, lack of appetite, fatigue, dizziness. If you had those symptoms, would you suspect you were having a heart attack? Although women can suffer chest pain, they're more likely than men to have less common symptoms such as these.

Heart disease is the number one cause of death in women over 64 in the United States and kills nearly one third of all women worldwide. In spite of this, many people still think of it as a man's disease. That is why you may not have heard much about women's heart danger until the last few years.

Recognize danger signs. Because of the difficulty in recognizing symptoms, women tend to delay calling for emergency help. That can be a costly mistake because treatments to limit heart damage should be given within one hour of the first sign of a heart attack. Women need to be aware of the following signs.

- strong or mild pain or discomfort in the center of the chest; may last more than a few minutes or go away and come back

- pain or discomfort in the arms, back, neck, jaw, stomach, or other areas of the upper body

- shortness of breath

- nausea or vomiting

- breaking out in a cold sweat

- light-headedness

Less common heart attack signs may also include heartburn, feeling tired or weak, heart flutters, coughing, or appetite loss.

The more of these symptoms you have, the more likely the problem is a heart attack. Even if you are not sure, get medical help right away.

Prevent heart trouble. Knowing the signs of heart attack is wise, but taking steps to avoid one is even smarter. Fortunately, women have a better chance of doing that today than ever before. Based on newly available studies of women, experts recently revised their heart protection guidelines. Here is what they recommend.

- Do not smoke, and avoid secondhand smoke. If you smoke, ask your doctor to suggest a process to help you quit.

- Aim for 30 minutes of moderate physical activity — like brisk walking — most or all days of the week. Try 60 to 90 minutes daily if you need to lose or control your weight.

- Aim for a diet rich in fruits, veggies, whole grains, and high fiber foods.

- Eat fish, preferably the oily kind, at least twice a week.

- Limit calories from saturated fat to no more than 7 percent of your daily calories. *(See Q&A box for how to calculate.)*

- Limit daily cholesterol from foods to 300 milligrams (mg) a day.

- Drink no more than one alcoholic drink a day.

- Limit sodium to 2,300 mg or one teaspoon of salt in your diet each day.

- Read labels, and eat as few trans fatty acids as possible.

- Keep your waist measurement below 35 inches and your body mass index (BMI) between 18.5 and 24.9 kg/m2.

- Aim for a blood pressure reading below 120/80 mm/Hg.

- Aim for LDL cholesterol below 100 mg/DL, triglycerides below 150 mg/dL and an HDL cholesterol reading of 50 mg/DL or higher.

Question & Answer

How do I figure out how much saturated fat I can eat?

The American Heart Association recommends you get no more than 7 percent of daily calories from saturated fats. To figure that number, first check out *Foolproof formula for a slimmer you* in the *Belly fat* chapter to discover how many calories you should eat each day. Multiply that calorie number by 0.07 to compute how many of those calories should come from saturated fat. For example, 2,000 calories x 0.07 = 140 calories.

Finally, divide your saturated fat calories by nine (140/9 = 15.5). That's how many grams you can safely have each day. Check nutrition labels to see how much saturated fat each product contains.

Fight heart disease without drugs

Some doctors say you should take powerful statin drugs if your C-reactive protein (CRP) levels are high, even if you have no heart disease — but others are not so sure. CRP helps measure your inflammation levels. More CRP means more inflammation in blood vessels and greater odds of heart disease. If your doctor recommends statins because your CRP is above 1 mg/L, but you have normal cholesterol and not much risk of heart disease, ask if you can try these lifestyle changes first.

Enjoy a cup of tea. Men who drank black tea regularly reduced their CRP in six weeks, one study found.

Think farm fresh. Women who ate more fruits and veggies had lower CRP than women who ate less, one study suggests. Researchers think the antioxidants in produce help cut CRP. To eat like the study participants, enjoy more apples, cantaloupe, watermelon, grapes, bananas, onions, tomatoes, mixed vegetables, lettuce, cucumbers, and green beans.

Smooth CRP with roughage. Americans who got the most fiber from fruits, veggies, and whole grains were 63 percent less likely to have high CRP than those who got the least, research suggests. Most people only get half of the 20 to 35 grams of fiber recommended for adults. So add more fiber from oatmeal, nuts, seeds, peas, beans, apples, pears, blueberries, whole grain bread and breakfast cereals, wheat bran, and veggies like carrots, zucchini, and tomatoes.

Eat more fish. People with higher blood levels of omega-3 fatty acids had lower CRP in a recent study. Japanese research also found that people who ate more fish rich in omega-3 were less likely to have high CRP. The American Heart Association recommends older adults eat fish at least twice a week. Smaller fish like sardines will help you avoid getting too much mercury.

Sample dark chocolate. Italians who ate a single 20-gram serving of dark chocolate every three days had lower CRP than Italians who ate more dark chocolate or avoided it completely. Twenty grams is about half of a Hershey's Special Dark chocolate bar.

Get your daily vitamin C. Among people with a CRP level of 2 mg/L or greater, one study found that 1,000-mg supplement of vitamin C a day reduced CRP almost as much as statins had in previous studies. Vitamin C also lowered CRP levels between 1 and 2 mg/L. Remember, the daily recommended intake of vitamin C is 90 mg for men and 75 mg for women while the upper limit is 2,000 mg. Before you try vitamin C supplements, ask your doctor about the risks and benefits of vitamin C and the risks and benefits of statins.

Control your weight. A recent lab study suggests fat cells actually make CRP. Maybe that is why obese and overweight people have higher CRP. If you are overweight, try losing weight. Studies show CRP can drop after weight loss.

Move it to lose it. People with CRP above 2 mg/L have a higher risk of strokes and heart attacks, but research suggests physical activity can help bring CRP down.

Take an aspirin a day. Aspirin has been shown to reduce CRP, but it can be risky for some people. Talk to your doctor before you try it.

A recent illness, injury, or pulled tooth before your CRP test may cause an inaccurate CRP reading. You may also get an inaccurate reading if you have gout, rheumatoid arthritis, urinary tract infection, prostatitis, high blood pressure, diabetes, or an infection. Talk to your doctor about this to determine whether you need a second CRP test.

Question & Answer

9 natural ways to raise your 'good' cholesterol

Your cholesterol test shows your "good" artery-scrubbing high-density lipoprotein (HDL) cholesterol is low, but you're not sure how to raise your HDL naturally. Start with these tips.

Eat more tomatoes. An Israeli study found that just 10 1/2 ounces of tomato-based foods every day for a month raised HDL cholesterol by 15 percent. If you would like to try this, focus on tempting, heart-healthy dishes such as low-sodium tomato-vegetable soup or pasta with marinara sauce.

Drink cranberry juice. Overweight men raised their HDL levels by drinking 8 1/2 ounces of cranberry juice cocktail a day for four weeks. Researchers think polyphenols in the cranberries may be the key. Try replacing your daily soft drink with delicious cranberry juice for a heart-healthy HDL boost.

Make a DASH for health. The DASH diet for high blood pressure may raise HDL up to 21 percent for men or 33 percent for women.

Save sweets for treats. The more added sugars people had in their diets, the lower their HDL was likely to be, reported a recent study out of Atlanta. These added sugars include the sweeteners food manufacturers add to processed foods as well as those that restaurant and home cooks add to foods they prepare.

A Canadian study found that eating fewer servings of sugar-sweetened soft drinks, juices, and snacks was linked with higher HDL. Cutting carbohydrates also helped. Try to limit sugary drinks and added-sugar carbohydrates in your diet. One analysis suggests that limiting carbohydrates like these may raise your HDL by as much as 10 percent.

Avoid trans fats. The fewer trans fats you eat, the better your HDL levels will be. Trans fats mostly lurk in foods with partially hydrogenated oils like store-bought baked goods, fried restaurant foods, and stick margarine. When buying packaged foods, check labels to make sure the trans-fat content is 0 grams and that "partially hydrogenated" does not appear in the ingredients list.

Rev up your activity. A few months of moderate-to-vigorous aerobic exercise may kick up HDL levels as much as 25 percent in women, research suggests. Before you start an exercise program, check with your doctor. If she says you can exercise safely, find an aerobic exercise you love. Start with short periods of light exercise, and gradually work up to 30 minutes of moderate or vigorous activity most days of the week.

Lose weight. If you are overweight, you have another way to solve your cholesterol problem. For every 2 pounds of excess weight you shed, you raise your HDL by 0.5 mg/dL.

Kick the habit. Quitting smoking will help your heart in many ways, including raising your HDL by about 4 mg/dL.

Know the drinking rules. Moderate drinking can help raise HDL. That means one or two drinks per day for men and one drink a day for women. A drink is equal to one 5-ounce glass of wine or 12 ounces of beer. But if you do not drink, don't start.

If these natural measures are not enough to bring your HDL up to the optimal level of 60 mg/dL, talk to your doctor. She may recommend medications that can help.

8 ways to give your BP a helping hand

Get inaccurate blood pressure readings at your doctor's office, and you could end up on medication you do not need. Here is how you can help make sure your blood pressure is right.

Skip the coffee. Avoid coffee and any other caffeine-containing foods and beverages for at least 60 minutes before your test. Caffeine may boost your blood pressure.

Visit the bathroom. Make a stop before you leave for the doctor's office. A full bladder raises your blood pressure.

Enter the smoke-free zone. Do not smoke for at least 30 minutes before your blood pressure check.

Avoid a workout. Schedule your day so you will not do any light, moderate, or strenuous physical activity for at least a half hour before you arrive at the doctor's office.

Review your medicine cabinet. Tell your doctor about any over-the-counter (OTC) medications you took today and any you take regularly. Be sure to check the ingredients on the label before you take them.

Several OTC drugs can cause temporary or more lasting rises in blood pressure. These include:

- painkillers like acetaminophen (Tylenol), naproxen sodium (Aleve), and ibuprofen (Advil)

- cold and allergy medicines that contain decongestants like pseudoephedrine or phenylephrine

- nasal decongestant sprays that contain oxymetazoline, phenylephrine, or naphazoline

- OTC nicotine patches and gum for quitting smoking

Ask your doctor about alternatives to these products. In some cases, a different medication can get the job done just as well without affecting your blood pressure.

List your prescriptions. Make sure your doctor knows about any prescription medications you take, including those prescribed by other doctors. Examples of prescription drugs that raise your blood pressure are:

- birth control pills

- cyclosporine (Neoral, Sandimmune)

- methylprednisolone (Medrol)

- antidepressants like bupropion (Wellbutrin), venlafaxine (Effexor), desipramine (Norpramin), and phenelzine (Nardil)

Be very quiet. Do not talk while the blood pressure cuff is on your arm. If possible, sit quietly for up to five minutes before the reading is taken.

Do not cross your legs or ankles. A Turkish study discovered this alone can raise your blood pressure temporarily. Keep your feet flat on the floor.

If the blood pressure reading at your doctor's office is higher than you expected, ask to have more readings taken to determine whether the first one was a fluke. Experts recommend averaging the numbers from three readings for the most accuracy.

Lower your blood pressure 5 points in 5 minutes

You can reduce your blood pressure up to 10 points in just five minutes. Seventy-year-old Faye has done this for years. When her blood pressure is too high, Faye closes her eyes and takes several long, deep breaths. Then she visualizes a peaceful place, such as a favorite vacation spot, and tries to remember every detail about it including the sights, sounds, and smells. A few minutes later, she opens her eyes and takes her blood pressure again. It is always 5 to 10 points lower.

Aspirin risks you need to know

Popping a daily baby aspirin to fend off heart problems is a way of life for many older adults. But this simple act could be a disaster waiting to happen for some people who combine aspirin with other painkillers. For others, simply taking aspirin alone may raise their risk of stroke and serious complications.

Watch for dangerous combinations. Blood clots can cause heart attacks and strokes, and aspirin's blood-thinning power helps prevent those clots. Unfortunately, recent studies suggest naproxen, ibuprofen, and celecoxib interfere with baby aspirin's blood-thinning ability. So if you take painkillers like Naprosyn, Motrin, or Celebrex along with aspirin, you may be more vulnerable to a stroke or heart attack than you thought. This may be particularly dangerous if you are at high risk for a second heart attack or have unstable angina.

To ease this problem, some experts suggest you take ibuprofen or naproxen either eight hours before or 30 minutes after taking aspirin. You may also need to take baby aspirin one hour before celecoxib. But more research is needed, so talk to your doctor to learn the latest.

Determine your chances of bleeding. People without heart disease should think twice about getting on the aspirin bandwagon, doctors say. Aspirin can increase men's risk of a hemorrhagic stroke from heavy bleeding in the brain. It can also raise both men's and women's risk for serious — or even deadly — bleeding in the digestive tract. Your danger of serious, aspirin-caused stomach bleeding triples at age 60 and more than quadruples at age 70.

That is why you probably should not take a daily aspirin if you are generally healthy, have never been diagnosed with heart disease or related conditions, have never had a heart attack or stroke, and have no risk factors for heart disease or stroke.

The U.S. Preventive Services Task Force recommends a daily baby aspirin to reduce heart attack risk in men age 45 to 79 or to reduce stroke risk in women age 55 to 79, but only if the risk of heart attack or stroke is higher than the risk of a stomach hemorrhage.

To determine this, your doctor will figure your risk of a stroke or heart attack within the next 10 years and compare it to your risk for stomach bleeding. Your doctor will only recommend baby aspirin if it is more likely to prevent a stroke or heart attack than to cause a hemorrhage in your brain or stomach.

Solve your barriers to heart-healthy exercise

Everyone tells you to exercise to protect your heart, but no one tells you how to solve the problems that keep you from exercising — until now. Use this how-to guide to change the "exercise rules" and take control of concerns and obstacles like these.

Obstacle #1: I am too old. You are never too old to benefit from the right kind of exercise. In fact, if you are a couch potato, getting very active can slash heart disease risk by an astounding 90 percent. An amazing German study suggests this even works if you are already over 40. All adults should aim for either 30 minutes of moderate exercise five days a week or 20 minutes of vigorous exercise three days a week.

But this does not mean you have to gasp, sweat, and strain your way to better heart health. The American Heart Association (AHA) defines moderate exercise as breathing harder than you normally do with a noticeably higher heart rate. But it will vary depending on your fitness level. For some people, moderate exercise means a brisk walk, while others get moderate exercise from a slow walk. If you cannot exercise this hard for 30 minutes straight, the AHA suggests you start small, perhaps by doing three separate 10-minute sessions of activity instead of one long one.

Obstacle #2: Exercise hurts. Before you do any physical activity — especially one that is painful or causes pain afterward — talk to your doctor. Pain is often a sign that you are exercising too long or too hard or doing the wrong kind of exercise. Start with gentler exercise, or cut back on the length and intensity of your exercise. If your pain is due to a health condition, stop exercising and talk to your doctor about what can be done.

Obstacle #3: I am too tired. Try exercising in the morning when you are fresher. If that's not possible, then make up your mind to get moving whenever you can. Believe it or not, exercise will boost your energy.

Obstacle #4: Exercise is too boring. Experiment with several fun activities like waltzing, line dancing, swimming, biking, or golf. Or take a tip from recovering heart patients in the Cardiac Friends program in Wisconsin. They volunteer to walk dogs at the local animal shelter three times a week.

Obstacle #5: Exercise does not work. Exercise may not work the same way as prescription medicine, but studies show it still gets the job done.

- Walking 30-45 minutes just three times a week slashed the risk of a heart attack by 50 percent in women past menopause, researchers found.

- A study of over 13,000 women discovered that those who were the most physically active during middle age were more likely to live to at least age 70 without physical disabilities, poor mental health, dementia, or chronic diseases like cancer, diabetes, heart disease, or stroke. This even worked for women whose sole exercise was walking.

- Many studies show physical activity reduces blood pressure, cuts "bad" LDL cholesterol, raises "good" HDL cholesterol, and improves other risk factors that contribute to heart disease.

Obstacle #6: Exercise takes too much time. Combine exercise with other activities. For example, instead of meeting a friend for coffee, take a walk together. As long as the exercise reaches moderate intensity and is an addition to your regular activities, it counts toward your 30 minutes for the day.

Hidden heart threat for thin people only

Being thin could mean you are at higher risk for a heart attack than you realize. In fact, up to 30 million slender Americans may face this danger, Mayo Clinic researchers say. Find out whether you are one of them — and what you can do about it.

Determine your risk. Extra body fat raises your risk of heart attacks and strokes. That is why experts recommend you maintain a body mass index (BMI) between 18.5 and 24.9. This "normal" BMI means your weight is appropriate for your height, and you are neither obese nor overweight.

But when Mayo Clinic scientists examined more than 6,000 people with normal BMI, they discovered that some of those people had a lot of body fat despite their slim appearance. And those with the highest percentage of fat had a much higher risk of heart trouble than people with the least amount. They also found that:

- higher body fat was associated with lower "good" HDL cholesterol and with higher "bad" LDL cholesterol, triglycerides, and C-reactive protein, a marker of inflammation.

- people with the highest body-fat percentage had four times as much risk of metabolic syndrome as people with the least body fat.

- men with the most body fat had an increased risk of high blood pressure, high LDL cholesterol, high triglycerides, and low HDL cholesterol.

- women with the most body fat had higher odds of dying from heart disease.

One thin person may have more danger of heart disease than another because two people with the same BMI can still have different amounts of body fat. BMI includes both weight from fat and weight from bone and muscle. So a daily jogger who lifts weights on rainy days may have less fat and more muscle than someone who is sedentary, even if both people have the same BMI.

Mayo Clinic researchers say you have a condition called "normal weight obesity" if you have a normal BMI and a body-fat percentage of at least 23 percent for men or 33 percent for women. That is important because fat cells spew out compounds that promote inflammation in your body, and inflammation raises your risk of heart trouble. That is one reason your body is safer with more muscle and less fat.

Take action if needed. Researchers and medical experts have yet to agree on what percentage of body fat is best, so tests for body fat are not required to figure your heart-disease risk. Future research may determine whether expensive body-fat tests should be part of your medical exams. But for now, your local health or fitness club is more likely to offer a body-fat test than your doctor's office.

Some experts recommend measuring your waistline to roughly estimate your body fat. According to the Mayo Clinic study, men with waistlines of 34 inches or more and women with waistlines of 32 inches or more were at higher risk for heart problems. People in this range may need to reduce their body fat, even when BMI is normal. Experts suggest two ways to do this.

- Aim for a healthy diet to help control your weight. But do not try to lose weight until you check with your doctor, and mention that you want to focus on losing fat. If you just restrict calories, you will lose muscle tissue as well as body fat, leaving you weighing less but with possibly the same percentage of body fat as before.

- Get more exercise, and include weight lifting to help increase your lean muscle mass. Ask your doctor first to make sure the extra activity and weights are safe for you and to find out how often and how much weight you should lift. For easy exercises you can do while seated, see *Get fit while sitting* in the *Belly fat* chapter.

QUICK*fix*

You can improve your heart health in six ways just by making one change to your day — take the stairs instead of the elevator. When inactive employees at the University Hospital of Geneva tried this, they lowered their blood pressure and LDL cholesterol, slimmed their waist measurements, lost weight and body fat, and got more aerobically fit in just 12 weeks. The employees averaged 20 flights of stairs a day. If you don't have that many stairs to climb, fill in the gap by parking farther away from the store when you shop, walking while talking on the phone, and taking a walk during your coffee break or after dinner.

Super vitamin watches over your heart

Come up short on vitamin D, and you may be 80 percent more likely to have a heart attack, stroke, or heart failure, even if you do not have heart disease. But that is not all this super vitamin can protect you from.

Heart disease. Compared with older adults who got the most vitamin D, those on the low end of the scale were more likely to die from heart disease as well as other causes, a University of Colorado study found.

Metabolic syndrome/diabetes. Those with the highest blood levels of vitamin D have 43 percent less risk of heart disease, metabolic syndrome, or diabetes.

Stroke. Higher blood levels of vitamin D are also linked with less narrowing of the neck arteries, which may lower your risk of stroke.

Heart failure. People who are deficient in vitamin D can reduce their risk of heart failure and coronary artery disease by raising their vitamin D to normal levels, suggests a University of Utah study.

High blood pressure. Harvard research shows that men who do not get enough vitamin D may be five times more likely to develop high blood pressure. Other studies suggest that vitamin D can help lower blood pressure.

Peripheral artery disease. People with the lowest blood levels of vitamin D have more risk of peripheral artery disease.

Most adults do not get enough vitamin D, especially as they age. The recommended vitamin D amounts are 400 International Units (IU) or 10 micrograms (mcg) for people age 51 to 70 and 600 IU or 15 mcg for anyone age 71 or older. But many experts say these numbers are too low and will change soon.

To make sure you're not low on vitamin D, ask whether your insurance company covers a vitamin D blood test called the 25-hydroxy-vitamin D test. If they do, tell your doctor to test you. If your insurance does not cover the test, ask your doctor to recommend an inexpensive way to get tested.

If you need more vitamin D, talk to your doctor about how you should get it. Some experts recommend a few minutes in the sunshine several times a week, but this option is controversial and may not work year-round if you live too far north. Fish and foods fortified with vitamin D, such as cereals, milk, and orange juice, can help add vitamin D. But if your levels are low enough, your doctor may also recommend dietary supplements. Check your multivitamin or calcium supplement to see how much vitamin D you're already getting before you buy extra supplements.

Lower blood pressure with sweet treats

Cereal with raisins and almonds, yogurt mixed with tropical trail mix, banana smoothie. These treats may not sound heart-smart, but they give you magnesium, calcium, and potassium — three minerals that help you control your blood pressure. Load up on these, and you'll also say "bye-bye" to your high risk of heart disease and stroke.

Calcium. Four out of five women turn their backs on the mineral that could be saving them from diabetes, high blood pressure, colon cancer, weak bones, and more. Scientists say so.

- Diabetes. A Chinese study found that the more calcium and magnesium women got in their diets, the less likely they were to develop diabetes within seven years.

- High blood pressure. Not getting enough calcium raises your risk of developing high blood pressure, but studies suggest that adding calcium to your diet helps. Calcium also helps lower high blood pressure if you already have it.

- Colon cancer. The more calcium you get, the lower your risk of colon cancer, reports a study from the National Cancer Institute. But aim for no more than 1,300 mg a day. Higher amounts don't seem to help.

- Weak bones. Your body needs a regular supply of calcium to keep bones strong. In fact, many studies show calcium supplements can put the brakes on bone loss in older women. So give this lifesaver a chance. All you have to do is eat tasty and easy-to-get foods like yogurt, low fat milk, low-fat cheeses, spinach, Total cereals, canned salmon, and canned baked beans.

Magnesium. Foods like bananas, raisins, and almonds can help you prevent metabolic syndrome, a group of conditions that lead to heart disease and diabetes. These foods are rich in magnesium, and studies show that more magnesium means less risk of this dangerous syndrome. You have metabolic syndrome if you have any three of the following:

- too much fat around the middle

- high blood pressure

- low HDL cholesterol

- high triglycerides

- high blood sugar

But the more magnesium you get, the lower your blood sugar and Body Mass Index (BMI) tend to be, research shows. Lower BMI may mean less fat around your middle. Studies also link getting plenty of magnesium to higher HDL, lower blood pressure, and lower triglycerides. So enjoy more magnesium-rich foods like tropical trail mix, pumpkin seeds, beans, brown rice, nuts, and baked potatoes.

Potassium. Although a high salt diet can raise your blood pressure, more potassium from foods can blunt salt's effects on blood pressure. That is why it is called the "un-salt," because of its amazing ability to keep blood pressure low. Try three tasty snack foods just loaded with it — dates, raisins, and tropical trail mix — to get started.

Although the Institute of Medicine recommends 4.7 grams of potassium a day, high amounts can be dangerous for some people, so talk to your doctor before adding more potassium to your diet. If your doctor agrees, eat more potassium-rich foods like papaya, yogurt, bananas, and dried plums.

Simple SOLUTION

People with intermittent claudication (IC) who tried walking with poles similar to ski poles found they had less leg pain, could walk farther before pain started, and increased their total walking distance.

"Nordic pole walking" is like cross-country skiing except that you walk instead of ski. The poles take some of the weight off your legs while still giving you a wonderful workout. That is important because walking difficulties from IC can make daily activities so difficult that people become housebound or dependent on others. But research suggests exercise can help prevent that.

To find Nordic pole walking lessons and poles, ask your doctor or physical therapist, check with local gyms and hospitals, or look for information online.

Eat smart for a healthy heart

Lowering your blood pressure and cholesterol are two smart ways to keep your heart in shape. Two eating plans that will help you meet these goals are the DASH (Dietary Approaches to Stop Hypertension) and TLC (Therapeutic Lifestyle Changes).

Both diets conform to powerful heart-protecting guidelines set up by the American Heart Association (AHA), but the DASH diet primarily helps lower your blood pressure while the TLC reduces cholesterol. These diets help you avoid heart attacks and strokes by managing fiber, fat, cholesterol, dairy, salt, and protein. Here's a glance at how they work.

Ingredient	DASH	TLC
Fiber	At least 30 grams of daily fiber from 6 to 8 servings of grains, 4 to 5 servings of fruits, 4 to 5 servings of vegetables. 4 to 5 servings of nuts, legumes, or seeds per week.	At least 6 servings of grains, cereals, and breads a day. 3 to 5 servings of vegetables, beans, or peas a day. 2 to 4 servings of fruit every day.
Fat	Limit total fat to 27 percent of daily calories. Limit saturated fats to 6 percent of daily calories. Choose monounsaturated oils, such as olive oil.	Get 25 to 35 percent of calories from fats. Get less than 7 percent of your daily calories from saturated fats.
Cholesterol	Limit to 150 mg a day.	Limit to 200 mg a day.
Dairy	Include 2 to 3 servings of nonfat or low-fat dairy products.	Limit dairy to 2 or 3 low-fat or nonfat servings a day and eggs to two yolks or less a week.
Protein	Choose modest amounts of fish and skinless poultry. Limit to no more than 6 ounces a day.	Limit meat, poultry, and fish to 5 ounces or less a day.
Salt	Limit to 2,300 mg or 1 teaspoon a day.	Limit to 2,300 mg or 1 teaspoon a day.

In recent years, the AHA has issued additional diet recommendations that can make the DASH and TLC diets even more effective. For best results, give these a try.

- Limit trans fats to less than 1 percent of calories.

- Make half your grain servings whole grains.

- Limit foods and drinks with added sugar.

- Eat fish at least twice a week.

2 famous heart diets you should know about

You might be surprised to learn that a diet can be good for your heart even if it does not meet the American Heart Association's (AHA) diet recommendations. Neither the Mediterranean diet nor the Ornish diet meet the AHA's fat guidelines, yet both are famous for their heart-protecting powers. But these diets are not necessarily right for everyone.

Meet the Mediterranean diet. This diet reflects the way people traditionally eat near the Mediterranean Sea in Greece, Crete, and southern Italy. Studies suggest the Mediterranean diet can not only protect you from heart disease, it can also help those who have previously suffered from heart attacks or angina. But to get this protection, you must follow guidelines like these.

- Eat mostly plant foods like fruits, vegetables, grains, nuts, and seeds.

- Get 25 to 40 percent of calories from fats — mostly unsaturated fats like olive oil.

- Limit dairy to daily low-to-moderate consumption of cheese and yogurt.

- Eat fish or poultry twice a week.

- Limit sweets to a few times a week.

- Limit red meat to a few times a month.

- Season foods with garlic, onions, and herbs.

But plan carefully because the Mediterranean diet has a few pitfalls. For example, this diet's higher fat content may cause weight gain. You could also come up short on iron and calcium.

Understand the Ornish plan. The Ornish diet is an extremely low-fat diet that only allows 10 percent of calories to come from fat while increasing carbohydrates to 75 percent. Because it is a demanding program, most people find it hard to follow for very long.

According to AHA experts, some people with high LDL cholesterol or heart disease who are highly motivated may benefit from very low-fat diets, but they must be carefully supervised by their healthcare provider. Do not consider any very low-fat diet if you have high triglycerides or insulin-dependent diabetes. And, of course, always talk with your doctor before changing your diet plan.

4 'bad' vegetables you should be eating

Some naturally healthy vegetables are like Rodney Dangerfield — they "get no respect." But white potatoes, celery, iceberg lettuce, and sweet corn should move from your "avoid" list to your "must eat" list — especially if you want to lose weight, save your vision, and lower your blood pressure.

White potatoes. Drop high blood pressure like a hot potato — with a hot potato. Potatoes are healthier than anyone guessed and can even keep you slim.

Potatoes seem like a nutritional villain because they are often eaten as greasy French fries, high-fat potato chips, or as a baked potato drowning in butter, sour cream, cheese, bacon, and chili. But without fatty toppings, the baked potato is a good source of potassium, resistant starch, fiber and more.

The potassium in potatoes makes them a super addition to the DASH diet for lowering blood pressure. Too little potassium in your diet can raise your blood pressure, but a potassium-rich diet may help bring it down. In addition, researchers recently discovered that potatoes contain kukoamines, compounds that have also been linked to lower blood pressure.

Potatoes may also help you lose weight, thanks to their resistant starch. Resistant starch is a fiber-like compound that leaves you feeling more full and satisfied after a meal. That may help you eat fewer calories so you keep trim — or even lose weight. Try a baked potato with spicy salsa, and enjoy other good sources of resistant starch like beans. You may be pleasantly surprised at the results.

Celery. Like potatoes, celery is a good source of pressure-lowering potassium. But celery also contains compounds called pthalides. Pthalides relax your arteries so they can dilate and ease your blood pressure. Pthalides also help reduce hormones that constrict blood vessels and raise your blood pressure. Animal studies suggest that pthalides may help lower blood pressure by up to 14 percent, but you will need to eat four celery sticks a day for results like that. To sneak more celery into your diet, add chopped celery to tuna fish salad, soups, casseroles, chicken salad, and stir-fries.

Sweet corn. A small ear of corn can give you up to 6 percent of the daily value for potassium. That is important because high blood pressure can threaten your vision as well as your heart. If you have uncontrolled high blood pressure for too long, it can damage the blood vessels that deliver blood and oxygen to your retina — a serious problem called hypertensive retinopathy.

This gradually narrows these blood vessels until blockages form and blood and fluid leak out. In the worst cases, the optic nerve swells, resulting in vision loss. Fortunately, this condition can take years to affect your eyesight, but don't wait. Add more potassium to your diet with corn, potatoes, celery, and other DASH diet foods, and take extra steps to lower your blood pressure, so you never face this threat to your vision.

Iceberg lettuce. Early research suggests people with low vitamin K intakes may be more likely to develop hardening of the arteries. That is why eating a good source of vitamin K like iceberg lettuce or other leafy greens may mean extra protection against heart attacks and strokes. But that's not all. People who ate three cups of low-calorie salad before a meal ate fewer total calories, one study found. So try a lettuce-loaded salad before your meals, and you may start shedding pounds.

3 secrets to make you want breakfast again

You might think skipping breakfast is a great way to sneak in more sleep, lose weight, or get more done, but new research suggests eating breakfast may help you look better, feel better, and spend less time in the doctor's office.

Helps drop the pounds. You can have your extra time and eat breakfast too if you eat whole-grain cereal. This speedy breakfast may help you keep your weight down — or even shed excess pounds if you are overweight. A recent study found that breakfast skippers are four and a half times as likely to be obese as people who eat breakfast regularly.

Breakfast may also be a secret of the National Weight Control Registry, a group of more than 4,000 people who have lost at least 30 pounds and kept it off for at least a year. Scientists report that three out of four people in the Registry eat breakfast every day, and cereal and fruit are their favorites. It's no wonder. High-fiber foods like whole-grain cereals leave you feeling more satisfied for longer, so this hearty breakfast may help you avoid extra between-meal snacks or overeating during meals.

Revs up your metabolism. Many people hit a slump in the last half of the morning. They get sleepy, can no longer concentrate, and just generally feel bad until lunch. Skipping breakfast is often a prime reason. Your body has simply run out of gas. Top off your personal gas tank by eating breakfast, and you'll jump-start your metabolism and feel a whole lot better when 10 a.m. rolls around.

Keeps the doctor away. The more your odds of heart disease go up, the more likely you will be spending extra time with your doctors. Oddly enough, eating breakfast can help. Unlike taking drugs or seeing a doctor, eating breakfast is the one easy thing you can do every day to lower your cholesterol. A small British study discovered that women who skipped breakfast every day for two weeks developed significantly higher total cholesterol and LDL cholesterol than when they ate a whole-grain cold cereal for breakfast every morning. Other studies found similar results.

Eating hot whole-grain cereals may be even better. An analysis of several studies found that eating oatmeal might help lower LDL cholesterol as much as 4.9 percent. If your cholesterol is 200, that is nearly a 10-point drop without taking cholesterol-lowering drugs. But to get these benefits, you must find time to prepare and eat breakfast. Fortunately, that may not be as hard as it looks. Try these tricks to make getting your daily whole-grain breakfast easier.

* Make oatmeal in your slow cooker overnight so it will be waiting for you when you wake.

- Make your cereal portable, and eat when you get where you are going. Drop whole-grain cereal and dried fruit into a resealable bag, and take a regular or Styrofoam bowl with you. For cold cereal, either pack a small carton of milk, or plan to eat your cereal trail mix style. For hot cereal, pour hot water into a small thermos.

Liven up breakfast with heart-smart treats

Breakfast pastries may not be heart smart, but that doesn't mean you can't have a sweet treat for breakfast.

Whether you like blueberry muffins, berries in your oatmeal, or berry breakfast smoothies, berries are the breakfast fruit you should be eating. In fact, berries significantly lowered total cholesterol, triglycerides, insulin, and blood sugar levels in a recent study.

Get the scoop on berries. Researchers tested three groups of animals prone to obesity. Two groups ate a diet that was 2-percent powder of freeze-dried blueberries while the third group ate a normal diet. After three months, the blueberry eaters had lower cholesterol, lower triglycerides, better insulin sensitivity, and lower blood sugar — four key risk factors for heart disease and metabolic syndrome. The blueberry eaters also trimmed their "apple shape" — that extra abdominal fat that promotes inflammation and pushes heart attack risk even higher.

But that's not all. At the start of the study, the researchers assigned the blueberry eaters to either a high-fat or low-fat diet. By the study's end, the low-fat diet group weighed less and had lower body fat than the high-fat group. Of course, animals do not always respond to diet the same way people do, so more research is needed. But other studies also suggest berries can make a difference in preventing heart disease.

"Berry" your heart attack risk. Researchers in Finland asked middle-aged study participants to eat moderate amounts of berries and berry juice every day. Two months later, the participants had raised their HDL cholesterol by 5 percent and lowered their blood pressure. These changes were equivalent to about a 10-percent reduction in the risk of heart disease, experts suggest. The researchers suspect berry polyphenols deserve the credit for this because study participants developed higher blood levels of polyphenols like quercetin, p-coumaric acid, and vanillic acid.

Participants had no trouble eating the required 3 ounces of berries every day since they were provided a delicious variety, such as whole bilberries (a cousin to the blueberry), black currant or strawberry purée, and small amounts of juices like lingonberry nectar (similar to cranberries) and raspberry-chokeberry juice. But you do not need exotic ingredients to add more berries to your breakfast. Try these ideas to help you start.

- Blend a breakfast smoothie by mixing blueberries, blackberries, strawberries, or raspberries with milk, yogurt, or juice.

- Add fresh berries to whole-grain pancakes or dried berries to low-fat muffins.

- Enjoy whole-grain toast slathered with strawberry, blackberry, or blueberry preserves.

- Add fresh, frozen, or dried berries to cold breakfast cereal or hot oatmeal.

- Eat fresh berries out of hand.

When you cannot have berries at breakfast, mix berries into cottage cheese or yogurt, add fresh berries to salads, or add dried berries to trail mixes or baking mixes.

SimpleSOLUTION

Enjoy these five delicious, inexpensive foods that keep your arteries clear.

- Apples. Try an apple a day. Studies suggest the pectin in apples helps keep cholesterol from being absorbed.
- Brown rice. This whole grain can help squelch cholesterol by giving you 14 percent of the daily value for fiber.
- Chickpeas. Canned chickpeas (garbanzo beans) helped lower cholesterol 3.9 percent in an Australian study.
- Kidney beans. Recent research suggests red kidney beans, black beans, and lentils can help keep your LDL cholesterol from turning into oxidized LDL, the kind of cholesterol most likely to coat your artery walls and narrow your arteries.
- Oats. The soluble fiber in oats has made oatmeal famous for its power to reduce LDL cholesterol.

4 ways whole grains safeguard your heart

The Philadelphia Phillies baseball team began using whole grains and other nutritional strategies to improve their performance in 2007. In 2008, they won the World Series Championship. Whole grains are not the only reason the Phillies did well, but players think these high-fiber foods are important for good performance. What's more, whole grains are not just a short-term fix. Eating these delicious foods can help protect you every day for the rest of your life.

Reduce blood pressure. Choose your sandwich bread carefully. Instead of limp white bread, pick a yummy whole-grain bread that lowers blood pressure. A small study suggests adding more whole grains to your diet helps bring blood pressure and weight down. This may happen because whole grains retain more of their fiber and nutrients, while refined grains do not. Both soluble and insoluble fiber have been associated with lower blood pressure.

Help you lose weight. Women who eat whole grains have significantly lower body mass indexes (BMI) and smaller waists than women who avoid whole grains, research shows. But eating refined grains like white bread can make things worse. In a recent study, people who ate the most white bread expanded their waist size three times faster than people who ate a healthy whole-grain-rich diet similar to the DASH diet for high blood pressure.

Fortunately, higher intakes of fiber from cereal — especially whole-grain cereal — have been linked with lower body fat in older adults. Even better, a Pennsylvania study found that overweight people who ate whole grains lost more fat from their midsections than those who ate refined grains.

Slash heart danger from diabetes. People who have diabetes are twice as likely to develop heart disease, but the bran from whole grains may help. Women with diabetes who got the most bran had the least chance of dying from heart disease, researchers found.

Prevent heart failure. Congestive heart failure is a condition where your heart cannot pump enough blood to meet your body's needs. A study of more than 14,000 people found that people who ate more whole grains were less likely to develop this crippling condition.

It helps to be "in the know" when looking for whole-grain products. Some contain a mix of whole-grain and refined-grain flour. To avoid getting only a fraction of the whole grains you expect, use these tips.

- Look for products labeled "100 percent whole grain."

- Products that contain 51 percent or more whole-grain ingredients by weight can include this language on their labels: "Diets rich in whole-grain foods and other plant foods, and low in total fat, saturated fat, and cholesterol, may reduce the risk of heart disease and certain cancers."

- Whole-grain bread should have at least 2 grams of fiber in each serving.

- Words like "multigrain," "7-grain," "enriched flour," "bran," and "wheat flour" do not mean a bread is truly whole grain. Instead, look for whole wheat, whole rye, oatmeal, barley, wheat berries, or brown rice as the first ingredient listed.

QUICK*fix*

How you cook your food can make a difference in your heart attack risk. Some kinds of cooking encourage advanced glycation end products (AGEs) to form. That is bad news because AGEs have been linked to hardening and narrowing of the arteries. Even worse, the older you get, the harder it is for your body to get rid of AGEs.

Some cooking methods form more AGEs than others, so limit browning, grilling, broiling, and frying — especially for meats. Instead, try roasting, boiling, steaming, or using your slow cooker. If you are not sure whether a cooking technique will promote AGEs, keep in mind that high heat and a lack of water usually add AGEs.

Play B-vitamin bingo to cut stroke risk

Stop strokes before they strike — by making your food even more delicious. Top Product 19 or Total Raisin Bran cereal with banana slices or strawberries. Or spread a turkey sandwich with blackberry jam, and eat it with a side of three-bean salad with garbanzo beans. Meals like these can help you avoid three vitamin-B deficiencies that may be the most overlooked risk for strokes and heart attacks.

Fight back with folate. Also called vitamin B9, folate is the heart-saving, brain-boosting, stroke-stopping, mood-enhancing B vitamin that you absolutely should not miss out on. Here is why.

* Helps you escape a deadly stroke. In 1998, the United States and Canada began fortifying all grain products with folic acid, the supplemental form of folate, so fewer people would be deficient. Before that time, American deaths from strokes dropped by only 0.3 percent each year, but after 1998, stroke deaths plummeted by 2.9 percent annually. Canadians saw an even larger drop — from 1 percent a year before 1998 to 5.4 percent afterward.

* Protects your arteries. Recent studies suggest that lowering homocysteine with folic acid supplements may not prevent heart attacks, but your arteries still benefit. According to research, even a mild B9 deficiency may boost your odds of atherosclerosis, the hardening and narrowing of your arteries caused by plaque buildup.

But adding folic acid may help fend off hardened arteries because your blood levels of this vitamin influence how well your arteries perform. Less folate may mean the lining of your arteries fails to dilate when it should, raising your blood pressure and risk of heart disease. That high blood pressure may damage your artery walls, making them even more susceptible to plaque buildup. Fortunately, supplementing with folic acid may reverse the artery lining's failure to dilate in people with heart disease — and that may be enough to reduce blood pressure and help prevent plaque buildup.

Maybe that is why a recent Japanese study found that women who got the most dietary folate and vitamin B6 were less likely to die from heart disease or strokes. What's more, men who got more of these vitamins had less risk of death from heart failure. So enjoy delicious folate-rich fruits like bananas, raspberries, and papayas, and you may help save your heart.

- Fends off dementia. Older adults with folate deficiency are three and half times more likely to develop dementia, a Korean study suggests. Earlier studies also found a link between mental impairment and folate deficiency.

- May help your mood. Deficiency in folate has even been linked to depression.

Help your heart with B6 and B12. The American Heart Association does not recommend B vitamin supplements to prevent heart disease and stroke because they are not proven to help. But research shows you should still be sure to get enough B6 and B12 from the foods you eat.

- According to a German study, people with the lowest blood levels of vitamin B12 had more risk of blocked or restricted blood flow in the brain — a key cause of strokes. The danger was even higher for people who also had low folate levels.

- Experts say high blood levels of C-reactive protein (CRP) mean you are at higher risk for strokes and heart attacks. A Tufts University study suggests low blood levels of vitamin B6 mean higher CRP while higher blood levels of B6 mean less CRP.

You can see why all three B vitamins are important. To make sure you get enough of each one, plan a meal by picking one food from each column in the chart below — just like you would if you were playing Bingo. But in this game, you not only reap a delicious meal, you may also win better protection against heart attacks and strokes.

B6	B9 (Folate)	B12
Brussels sprouts	black-eyed peas	rainbow trout
lima beans	collard greens	ham
baked potatoes	asparagus	canned clam chowder with milk
lentils	spinach	halibut
baked sweet potato	creamed corn	roast turkey
winter squash	navy beans	bottom round steak

Smart reasons to go meatless with beans

Imagine a delicious dinner of Cajun red beans and rice, and you can see that going meatless once in a while might not be so bad. Bean dishes are a thrifty way to cut back on meat because beans cost much less. Plus, they may help protect you from heart attacks, strokes, hospital stays, and more. Try going meatless with beans a few nights a week — or even more often — with disease-preventing dishes like these.

Lower your cholesterol with chili. Making meatless low-fat chili in your crockpot could be your first step towards good news at your doctor's office. Chili's kidney beans can help lower both total cholesterol and "bad" LDL cholesterol, a recent study found. Australian researchers saw similar results in people who ate lots of canned chickpeas.

But that is not the only way beans help keep your arteries clear. A laboratory study suggests the antioxidants in black beans, lentils, and red kidney beans may help prevent your LDL cholesterol from oxidizing. Oxidation of LDL cholesterol helps trigger artery-clogging plaque that can lead to heart attacks. So try bean dishes like black bean or kidney bean chili, lentil soup, or baked falafels with chickpeas. Pick up some Beano at the drugstore, and you'll get the cholesterol-dropping power of these dishes without the gas.

Defend against stroke with bean burritos. The more beans you eat, the better your odds of avoiding a stroke. Just replace the meat in your burritos, tacos, fajitas, or enchiladas with beans, and switch to low-fat cheese, and you have added another meatless meal to your week. That may help prevent two key risk factors for stroke — high cholesterol and high blood pressure.

Lowering your cholesterol helps because the same artery-clogging plaque that causes heart attacks also causes strokes. New research also suggests eating more meat-free bean dishes may help lower your blood pressure. The study found that people whose diets included the most protein from vegetables and the least protein from meats had lower blood pressure than people who got most of their protein from meat. So replace meat with beans regularly to help provide your first line of defense against stroke.

Lose weight with red beans and rice. People who eat beans are more likely to weigh less and have smaller waist measurements than people who avoid beans, research shows. Bean lovers are also less likely to be obese, even when they eat more calories than bean haters.

This may happen because beans are a rich source of fiber-like compounds called resistant starch. Recent studies suggest eating foods rich in resistant starch may help you feel full and burn more fat. Beans are also high in protein and fiber. These help you feel full sooner, eat fewer calories, and limit hunger between meals. So enjoying low-fat versions of red beans and rice or Spanish rice with black beans may help you lose weight.

Fend off cancer with baked beans. Whether you make them yourself or heat them from the can, even low-fat, vegetarian baked beans can be surprisingly filling. What's more, research suggests beans may help protect you from colon cancer and breast cancer. The fiber in beans may be one reason why, but beans are also rich in antioxidants called flavonols. People who get the most flavonols from beans, apples, and other foods may have less colon cancer risk, a study suggests.

A 4-season guide to heart-warming foods

You want to eat heart healthy, but raw fruits and veggies seem so bland and boring. Instead of making big changes, start small. Try to eat daily servings of foods rich in just one heart-healthy family of nutrients, and you can enjoy a menu of delicious foods that changes to match each season.

Cool off in the summer. Hot foods are the last thing you want during the sweltering August heat. Fortunately, you can turn to salads full of tomatoes, carrot slices, and lettuce or spinach. Top that off with a big slice of watermelon, and you'll have a heart-healthy meal that will cool you off and defend your heart. Carotenoids are the reason.

Carotenoids may sound like something from Star Wars, but they are actually nutritious food pigments that lend their color to some of your favorite fruits and veggies. For example, lycopene helps make tomatoes and watermelon red while beta carotene and alpha carotene help tint carrots orange. Other carotenoids, like lutein and zeaxanthin, lend color to spinach.

Just remember, most carotenoids are fat soluble. That means you must eat them with fat, so your body can absorb and use them. If your salad is fat free, drizzle a little low-fat dressing over it. The extra effort is worthwhile, because research suggests carotenoids can protect your heart.

Enjoy the riches of autumn. When leaves start falling, it is time for carotenoid-rich baked sweet potatoes, winter squash, and pumpkin recipes. These may help you avoid metabolic syndrome, a condition that raises your risk for heart disease and diabetes. You have metabolic syndrome if you have any three of the following — too much fat around the middle, high blood pressure, low HDL cholesterol, high triglycerides, or high blood sugar.

Dutch researchers recently found that the more lycopene or beta carotene people had in their diets, the lower their odds of metabolic syndrome. Lycopene lovers were also less likely to have high triglycerides. On top of that, eating more alpha carotene, beta carotene, lycopene, lutein, or total carotenoids was linked to smaller waistlines and less body fat. Experts suspect the antioxidant powers of these healthy nutrients may contribute to their heart-healthy effects.

Warm up in winter. After facing snow, biting wind, and chilled rain, a steaming bowl of tomato-vegetable soup or a plate of spaghetti with marinara sauce is perfect to warm you up and protect your heart. Both dishes contain lycopene with an added benefit — processed tomato products actually give you more lycopene than raw tomatoes.

Snack in the spring sunshine. Chilly spring mornings can quickly give way to warm — or even hot — afternoons. Fortunately, tomatoes and their lycopene are good for both. At mid-morning, a spicy salsa with baked tortilla chips can warm you, while a cool glass of delicious, low-calorie tomato juice may be ideal under the afternoon sun.

In a study of people with diabetes, people who drank two 8-ounce glasses of tomato juice every day made their LDL cholesterol more resistant to oxidation in just one month. Oxidized LDL is the kind most likely to lead to heart attacks and strokes, but the lycopene in tomatoes may prevent this dangerous artery-clogging cholesterol from forming. That is why foods rich in lycopene — like tomatoes and tomato-based foods — may help you dodge heart attacks and strokes.

Question & Answer

Can soy foods help lower my cholesterol?

Doctors once thought the isoflavones in soy helped lower cholesterol by up to 3 percent, but here is the real story. Most people eat soy-based foods in place of meats, dairy, and other foods high in saturated fat and cholesterol. It is the resulting drop in saturated fats and cholesterol that cuts your blood cholesterol — not soy. Besides, some studies suggest soy products may contribute to your risk of dementia, so only eat soy in moderation. If you need to cut back, substitute rice or almond milk for soy milk and soy-free veggie burgers for soy burgers.

3 not-so-nutty reasons to choose nuts

"Sometimes you feel like a nut, sometimes you don't ..."

You may remember that jingle advertising a popular candy bar during the 1970s. A candy coating may not be the healthiest way to eat nuts, but on their own, they are a powerhouse of nutrients. Just a handful of nuts a day can help lower your cholesterol, prevent Alzheimer's, and even keep your weight down. But make sure you pick the right kind — some popular nuts are potentially harmful to your heart.

Defend you against heart disease. Nuts have been recognized as potential heart defenders by no less than the U.S. Food and Drug Administration (FDA). After examining the research on nuts and heart disease, they approved a health claim for labels of six kinds of whole or chopped nuts.

 The claim, in a "nutshell," suggests that eating 1.5 ounces per day of most nuts as part of a diet low in saturated fat and cholesterol may lower the risk of heart disease. But the FDA only allows the claim for almonds, hazelnuts, peanuts, pecans, some pine nuts, pistachio nuts, and walnuts. Cashews, Brazil nuts, and macadamias have too much heart-threatening saturated fat to be heart protective, the FDA says.

How do nuts protect your heart? Study after study shows nuts can:

* lower your bad LDL cholesterol, possibly due to their high levels of fiber and unsaturated fats.

* control inflammation in your arteries, which may also contribute to heart disease.

* lower blood levels of compounds associated with inflammation.

* help raise blood levels of the anti-inflammatory compound called adiponectin.

* protect the lining of your arteries and prevent the blood clots that cause heart attacks.

Save your brain from Alzheimer's. Walnuts are the nut to choose if you want to improve your memory and help fend off Alzheimer's disease. In a recent laboratory study, researchers discovered walnut extract may help prevent beta amyloid protein in your brain from turning into brain-clogging Alzheimer's plaques. What's more, an animal study found that simply eating the equivalent of seven to nine walnuts a day for a couple of months was enough to improve working memory.

Control your weight. In spite of promising studies, some people still will not eat nuts because they are afraid nuts may pack on the pounds. But just because they are high in fat does not automatically mean they make you fat. A Spanish study found that people who ate nuts twice a week were less likely to gain weight over a two-year period than people who rarely or never ate nuts. Another study discovered that women who ate almonds every day for 10 weeks gained no weight. The trick is to use nuts to replace other high-calorie foods like unhealthy snacks, fatty desserts, or even fatty meats.

All nuts are not created equal. When choosing and eating nuts, keep these tips in mind.

- Nuts coated in salt, honey, sugar, or chocolate are less likely to benefit your heart. Eat nuts straight, or use them to replace a high-fat ingredient in your favorite salads, pasta, rice dishes, or cereals.

- Instead of eating nuts straight from the jar or can, repackage 1 1/2 ounces of nuts in a resealable bag or small dish, so you will not eat more than you planned. Remember, one handful is all you need.

Why '0 trans fat' may not mean healthy

Many restaurants have stopped using trans fats in their foods. Some cities have even gone so far as to ban their use, hoping to create a more healthful eating experience. That is good in theory since research shows these deadly fats not only cause heart attacks, but strokes as well. Unfortunately, banning these fats from restaurants and grocery stores won't necessarily protect you.

Trans fats form when food manufacturers add hydrogen to vegetable oil to turn the liquid into a solid. This process, called hydrogenation, makes the product and flavor last longer. But these newly created fats raise your "bad" LDL cholesterol and lower "good" HDL cholesterol, boosting your stroke and heart disease risk. A recent study found that women over age 50 who ate the most trans fats were 30 percent more likely to have a stroke compared with those who ate the least.

Fortunately, the FDA now requires trans fat content to be listed on the Nutrition Fact label — a change that made many food manufacturers drop trans fats from their products, or at least lower them.

The problem is that trans fats may still lurk in many foods — including French fries, donuts, fried chicken, vegetable shortening, some margarines, snack foods, pie shells, and any other foods made with or fried in partially hydrogenated oils. Even a product that promises "zero trans fats" may not be safe. A product's label can say it has 0 grams of trans fat if the per-serving content is less than 0.5 grams. That means a few servings of "zero trans fats" may actually deliver several grams of this unhealthy fat. You may also get small amounts of trans fats naturally through some meat and dairy products.

Some food makers replace trans fats with saturated fats such as palm oil or palm kernel oil. Since saturated fats help raise cholesterol, trans-fat-free foods may still boost your stroke and heart attack risk. Other food makers replace trans fats with the new interesterified fats, but these may not protect you either. A small study suggests interesterified fats may cut your HDL cholesterol and contribute to diabetes risk. More research is needed, of course, but take these steps if you want to play it safe.

- Limit packaged foods, especially baked goods.

- Make sure the Nutrition Facts label promises "0 g" of trans fat, but check the ingredient list, too. If you find no partially hydrogenated items, the product may be genuinely trans-fat free.

- Avoid fried foods, or limit them to once a week or less.

- Cook with liquid oils instead of stick margarine or shortening.

Surprising truth about red meat

Don't bring home the bacon. Eating bacon, sausage, or deli meat daily puts you at far higher risk for heart disease than a daily steak.

According to Harvard researchers, just 1.8 ounces of processed meat every day — such as 2 slices of bologna or deli ham — makes you 42 percent more likely to get heart disease than eating 3 1/2 ounces of steak or other unprocessed meats daily.

Processed meats may be more dangerous for two reasons. They have four times as much salt as unprocessed meats and roughly 50 percent more preservatives, such as nitrites, nitrates, and nitrosamine. The extra sodium may stiffen your blood vessels and raise your blood pressure, two problems that provoke heart attacks. Meanwhile, preservatives like nitrates may help clog your arteries and harm your blood vessels, adding to your risk of a heart attack or stroke.

To help prevent these problems, eat processed meats no more than once a week, and limit your serving to 1.8 ounces or 50 grams. This may not be as bad as it sounds. For example, 50 grams means six slices of pan-fried bacon or a couple of slices of pastrami, so you can still enjoy your favorite bacon or deli meat. Just keep to the weekly limit, and remember that processed meats include salami, weenies, sausage, pepperoni, processed luncheon and deli meats, smoked meats, and bacon.

The Harvard study also suggests unprocessed red meat like beef, hamburger, lamb and pork may not raise your risk of heart disease, but it doesn't lower it either. And it can still help put you at higher risk for cancer. So if you love steaks and burgers, you don't get a free pass to eat as much as you want. Follow the American Heart Association guidelines, and make sure saturated fats account for no more than 7 percent of your daily calories, regardless of where they come from.

SimpleSOLUTION

You do not have to give up eating out to have a heart-healthy diet. In fact, you can often find menu options that are low in saturated fat, trans fat, and cholesterol. Unfortunately, most menus will not tell you how much salt or fat is in a dish. But you can easily solve the problem if you have a computer.

Before you leave for the restaurant, go online to the restaurant's Web site. Many chain restaurants supply both their menu and nutrition information. If you have trouble finding the nutrition information, visit the menu page. You may find links to nutrition information there. And remember, check the data for both the entrée and the sides.

Hook these secrets to a well-protected heart

Sit down to a fish meal full of omega-3 fatty acids, and you will start improving your arteries today. Omega-3 helps your blood vessels become more flexible, and the effects start right away.

Stiff arteries contribute to high blood pressure and may promote the blood clots that trigger heart attacks. But EPA, an omega-3 fatty acid in fish oil, may help. Eating a meal loaded with EPA eased artery stiffness within hours, a recent British study found. What's more, Spanish researchers discovered people who frequently ate fish rich in omega-3 for three months also improved the flexibility of their arteries.

Omega-3 fatty acids may also protect your heart by:

- helping to prevent arrhythmias — problems with your heart rhythm that can cause heart attacks and sudden death.

- lowering your triglycerides.

- reducing blood pressure.

- preventing your platelets from clumping together to form blood clots.

- fighting inflammation that helps harden your arteries.

Don't cancel out the advantages of fish by making the wrong choices. Here are some secrets to getting all the omega-3 and fish benefits you have coming.

Watch the portions. The American Heart Association recommends eating at least two servings of fatty fish per week. A serving is 3 to

3 1/2 ounces of whole fish or 3/4 cup of flaked fish. Beware of restaurant servings, which may be 6 ounces or more. You may end up getting two or three 3-ounce servings from one meal.

Beware of contaminants. Avoid swordfish, shark, king mackerel, and tilefish, which are high in mercury, and eat a wide variety of fish. That cuts your risk of eating too many fish high in contaminants. As an added precaution, remove belly and back fat and skin from fish to strip away PCBs.

Resist the tuna temptation. Two out of the three brands of tuna tested in a recent study had higher mercury levels than the U.S. Food and Drug Administration permits. While this does not mean you should avoid canned tuna, the researchers say people in the most danger from mercury — such as children — should be limited to 3 ounces of chunk white tuna about once every two and a half weeks. The study also suggests canned light tuna is a better option as it contains far less mercury and meets government safety standards.

Limit the all-you-can-eat crab legs. You may love shellfish like shrimp, clams, lobster, scallops, or crayfish, but they won't give you the same heart protection as finfish. A South Carolina study found that people who ate shellfish at least once a week were just as likely to have heart problems as those who ate little or none. But shellfish are still a good alternative to red meat as long as you don't deep fry them or slather them in butter.

Prepare it the right way. Bake or boil your fish to lower your risk of dying from heart disease, a University of Hawaii study suggests. People who eat their fish fried, dried, or salted may have a higher risk.

If you are not sure which fish are safe to eat, visit the Environmental Defense Fund Web site at *www.edf.org,* and type Seafood Selector or Health Alert in the search box. Recommended choices include sardines, canned pink or sockeye salmon, shrimp, and black sea bass.

Question & Answer

Is it better to eat fish or take fish oil capsules?

The American Heart Association recommends eating a variety of fish twice a week for their heart-healthy omega-3 fatty acids. But fish oil capsules may be an option if you have heart disease and cannot get enough omega-3 from food, if you have high triglycerides, or if you are concerned about mercury and other contaminants in fish.

Fish oil capsules contain virtually no contaminants, but check with your doctor before taking them. Fish oil may interact badly with some medications, and high amounts may cause heavy bleeding. They may also be unsafe for some people with heart failure, an implanted cardioverter defibrillator (ICD), or angina.

4 super spices for tip-top health

Try these four must-have items for your spice rack if you want to use spices to help replace salt and sugar. Together they protect you against almost all the major diseases of aging — and they make your food taste better.

Substitute cinnamon for sweetness. Cook and season foods with this pungent spice, and you may find dishes need less sugar to taste great. What's more, animal research suggests the added cinnamon may help bring your blood pressure down, giving you more protection against heart attacks and strokes.

According to researchers at Georgetown University Medical Center, a high-sugar diet raised blood pressure in animals, but adding cinnamon to the diet helped reduce blood pressure in both those on a high-sugar diet and those on a regular diet. In one experiment, cinnamon even helped prevent the rise in blood pressure that sugar causes.

To eat more cinnamon, add it to baked sweet potatoes, cooked carrots, baked goods, and winter squash. Or sprinkle it on oatmeal, raw apples, baked apples, cereal, yogurt, and toast.

Enjoy ginger for a healthy heart. People with high cholesterol who took 1 gram of ginger three times a day lowered their LDL cholesterol and triglycerides more than people who did not take ginger, a recent study found. Ginger-takers also raised their "good" HDL cholesterol more.

Getting ginger from foods may be easier than you expect because 1 2/3 teaspoons of powdered ginger is around 3 grams, the daily total used in the study. But ginger is not safe for everyone, especially people who take blood thinners, so check with your doctor before you try it. You can add fresh or powdered ginger to sweet potatoes, stir fries, rice dishes, and baked apples.

Turn to turmeric for antioxidant power. Doctors use a test called the Mini-Mental State Exam to help check for memory and cognition problems and the possibility of Alzheimer's disease. Low scores on this test may be a bad sign. But a Singapore study found that people who occasionally or often ate curry scored higher on this test than people who ate curry less than once every six months.

The turmeric in curry may be why. Turmeric contains curcumin and other compounds with anti-inflammatory and antioxidant powers. An earlier animal study suggests these powers may help prevent plaques — a hallmark of Alzheimer's — from forming in your brain.

If you would like to try turmeric, curry is not your only option. Add turmeric to fish, cauliflower, lean meats, or sauces. Add a dash of black pepper as well to boost turmeric's protective power. Piperine, a natural compound in pepper, boosts your body's absorption of curcumin. But consider skipping this spice if you:

- have gallstones or gallbladder disease.

- have diabetes, low blood sugar, or take drugs to help lower blood sugar.

- regularly take blood thinners, anti-platelet drugs, aspirin, or nonsteroidal anti-inflammatory drugs like ibuprofen.

- have liver disease.

Cancel colon cancer with garlic. Colon cancer is the second deadliest cancer in the United States and the third most common, but garlic may help you avoid it. A review of both animal and human studies found that more garlic meant less risk of this dangerous cancer. Early evidence suggests garlic may also help prevent cancer of the esophagus, prostate, mouth, ovaries, and kidneys.

Enjoy garlic in Italian dishes, lean meats, fish, mashed potatoes, veggies, and more. Just remember to limit your garlic intake if you take warfarin or other blood thinners.

Sweet way to lower blood pressure

Overweight? Try eating chocolate. It sounds crazy, but chocolate could help open your arteries and lower your blood pressure.

That's what Yale researchers found when they served 45 overweight adults a different chocolate treat once a week for several weeks. Whether they ate a small dark chocolate bar, sugar-sweetened hot cocoa, or sugar-free hot cocoa, the participants' blood pressure dropped and their blood vessel function improved after each treat.

Problems with blood vessels can be an early sign of hardening of the arteries and a rising risk of heart attack. Studies suggest cocoa is high in healthy compounds called flavanols, which may help boost nitric oxide and protect your arteries. Nitric oxide relaxes the lining of your artery walls and helps prevent problems that lead to cholesterol buildup and blood clots — key contributors to a heart attack. But to get these benefits, you need to know which chocolate to eat and how to eat it.

Cocoa powder. Flavanols belong to a family of heart-healthy compounds called polyphenols. Unsweetened cocoa powder usually gives you more polyphenols than any other chocolate, but "Dutch" processed cocoa powder loses most of its polyphenols in processing. Check labels, and look for cocoa powder labeled either "cocoa" or "nonalkalized cocoa" in the baking aisle.

You can bake with cocoa powder or mix it in hot water or milk to make hot chocolate. You may like it better with sugar, but use as little as possible. The Yale researchers report that sugar-sweetened hot cocoa did not help blood vessels as much as sugar-free hot cocoa.

White chocolate. Cocoa content is the key to getting polyphenols. Since white chocolate has no cocoa, it does not provide you with heart-healthy polyphenols, either.

Milk chocolate. Think twice before you choose store-bought milk chocolate. American milk chocolate contains as little as 10 percent cocoa, so it cannot give you as many polyphenols. European milk chocolate is a better pick, with 25-percent polyphenols.

Dark chocolate. Choose dark chocolate if you prefer solid chocolate to hot cocoa. It has more cocoa and more polyphenols than milk chocolate.

Polyphenols do not stay in your body long, so you must eat chocolate or cocoa regularly to keep getting their heart-healthy benefits. But do not eat a lot. By one estimate, 3 1/2 ounces of dark chocolate every day — 1 1/2 to 2 bars —could make you gain up to 50 pounds in a year. Extra weight is hard on your heart and could erase your chocolate benefits — or even make things worse.

So how much chocolate should you eat? Participants in the Yale Prevention Center study only ate about 2 1/2 ounces of chocolate. But other studies have found heart-related improvements with even less chocolate — the equivalent of one or two Hershey's kisses a day or less than a quarter cup of semisweet chocolate chips.

So limit your chocolate to small amounts like these, and cut calories elsewhere if you eat solid chocolate or chocolate chips. But remember, unsweetened cocoa powder is low in fat and sugar. Use that to make hot cocoa instead of eating solid chocolate, and you can cut fewer calories from other parts of your diet.

Choices for a heart-healthy snack attack

Forget dry, crumbly bran cookies. You can enjoy delicious snacks full of ingredients that help lower cholesterol, blood pressure, and blood sugar; reduce your stroke risk; and can even help you stay slim.

Lower blood pressure with figs. The fig is one of the sweetest fruits you can eat, so it is a great treat when a sugar craving hits. But do not let all that delicious goodness fool you. Figs are also a good source of fiber, calcium, potassium, and magnesium.

Many studies suggest high-fiber diets help lower blood pressure. And still more studies have found that more magnesium, potassium, and calcium from fruits and veggies can also help lower your blood pressure. So eat fresh figs in season or dried figs when you are on the go. And if you crave a sweet, soft cookie with a fruity filling, you can even enjoy the occasional whole-grain Fig Newton.

Cut cholesterol with blackberries. Studies show high-fiber diets not only lower blood pressure but your "bad" LDL cholesterol, too. Because blackberries are rich in fiber, especially soluble fiber, this simple snack food could help lower your blood pressure and cholesterol.

Both soluble and insoluble fiber can help. Soluble fiber turns soft and sticky in your body and slows the progress of food through the intestine. This gives your body a chance to mop up excess cholesterol before it can get back into your bloodstream. The American Heart Association recommends eating insoluble fiber, as well as soluble fiber, to help prevent heart disease. That is why a handful of blackberries — or figs — can be a great snack for your heart.

But these fruits are not good for your heart alone. Uncontrolled high blood pressure can more than quadruple your risk of a stroke because it can thicken your artery walls. High cholesterol also contributes to stroke risk because cholesterol buildup helps narrow your arteries. Thicker artery walls and narrower arteries can help a blood clot block the blood flow to your brain, triggering a stroke.

Fortunately, lowering cholesterol and high blood pressure helps cut stroke risk. So aim for a diet high in the fiber, magnesium, calcium, and potassium that help fight high blood pressure and cholesterol. You will slash your stroke risk, too.

Battle blood sugar with oatmeal. Oatmeal is already famous for its cholesterol-fighting powers, but its soluble fiber may help control your blood sugar, too. The soluble fiber in oatmeal makes your body absorb sugars more slowly. As a result, insulin can convert that sugar to energy, so it never gets into your bloodstream. That may be why diets high in soluble fiber help lower blood sugar. For extra fiber, top your oatmeal with blackberries or chopped, dried figs.

Stay slim with cereal. High-fiber foods like whole grains and figs can make you feel full on fewer calories. In fact, one study discovered that the more cereal fiber and whole grains you get, the lower your body mass index (BMI) and cholesterol are likely to be. So grab a handful of hearty whole-grain cereal and eat it as a snack, or add dried fruit to make trail mix. You may find staying slim just got easier.

Simple SOLUTION

Good news for people with congestive heart failure — you can literally waltz your way to better fitness and increased ability to perform daily activities. A study of people with heart failure found that those who spent 21 minutes alternating between slow and fast waltzes three times a week became just as aerobically fit as people who followed a treadmill and cycling program. Waltz dancers also slept better and improved their ability to do housework and hobbies.

If you have heart failure, exercise can help lower your risk of hospital stays and death. Just remember, before you try waltzing or any other exercise, talk to your doctor first.

Blues-busting secrets that pep up your life

4 ways to stay on the sunny side of life

When God closes a door, He opens a window. Remember that promise, and you won't be brought low by the losses that often accompany aging.

As you get older and have changes in your life, you may feel rather lost and adrift. With the passing of friends and no job to provide social contact, even the healthiest golden years can get lonely. You may prefer to continue living in your own home rather than lose your independence by moving in with your kids. But being alone too much isn't good for you. In fact, the average person spends 80 percent of her waking time with other people, and that's when we tend to feel happiest.

Stay social to stay healthy. Research shows loneliness may be related to physical ills, including cancer, dementia, heart-related problems like high blood pressure, lower immunity, and even death in older people. Perhaps part of the reason is your close friends will encourage you to take better care of yourself by avoiding bad habits and getting medical help when you're ill.

Journalist Jeffrey Zaslow researched and wrote a book about 11 women from Ames, Iowa, who grew up together and remained friends into middle age. *The Girls from Ames: A Story of Women and a 40-Year Friendship* relates how these longtime friendships have improved their lives and helped them through times of trouble. When it comes to a strong social support system, your good friends may be even more important than your family members.

Staying social also may help keep you young, avoid a crippling fall, and keep your reflexes sharp, a new study has found. Researchers say seniors who have fewer opportunities for social activity are years older — on the inside — than those who remain socially active. That support network may also help you cope better with chronic pain.

Pick cheerful companions. Not all friends are created equal. Loneliness can spread, kind of like the flu, among people in the same social group. Research using information from the famous Framingham Heart Study shows you're 52 percent more likely to be lonely if someone in your social network is also lonely. The effect also works in the opposite direction — being around happy people can raise your own level of happiness.

Get out and get active. Staying physically active can help ward off the blues. Even better, find an exercise class you enjoy, and you get the added benefit of being with other people who share your interest. Consider yoga, tai chi, water aerobics, line dancing — whatever floats your boat. Check with your local senior center to see what classes are available.

Find your new purpose in life. Everyone needs a reason to get out of bed in the morning. Once your working life is behind you, find something else that is meaningful. Your new purpose could be volunteer work, taking part in church activities, or spending lots of quality time with your grandchildren — anything that gets you out of the house regularly. You'll feel better, and you may even live longer.

Simple guide to serious symptoms

Everyone feels a little down sometimes. That doesn't mean you have clinical depression. A minor bout of the blues may just need a little tender loving care at home, but major depression is a disease and calls for help from an expert. Here's how you can figure out where you stand.

You may have the blues if you:	You may be depressed if you:
have trouble concentrating when you read	have no interest in picking up a book
need convincing to go out with friends	refuse to go out at all
feel tired during the day	too exhausted
have trouble sleeping some nights	can't seem to sleep at all
get cheered by your grandchildren	have no interest in seeing visitors
continue to play in weekly bridge game	quit most of your usual activities
feel perked up when you hear good news	take no interest in even the best news
take longer to make decisions	can't make decisions at all
are disappointed in some aspects of life	feel like a complete failure
feel a bit restless	feel agitated and have trouble sitting still
notice some appetite changes	have lost or gained weight for no reason
want to change certain things about life	feel trapped in your life
make some plans for the future	have thoughts of suicide

These mood characteristics are not all-inclusive and are based on the depression screening test available at the mental health Web site *http://psychcentral.com*. If you have access to a computer, check out the many other resources available on this Web site. If you're not sure how severe your mood problems are, seek professional help.

Question & Answer

People keep telling me my depression is all in my head, since nothing is really wrong in my life. So why can't I just snap out of it?

Depression can result from genetic and biological factors as well as influences from your environment. You may feel depressed because your brain chemistry is out of balance. You can't snap yourself out of that any more than you can talk yourself out of having the flu. That's why professional help is often your best option.

Quick counseling is just a click away

Think you're too shy to lie on a couch and spill your problems to a therapist? If you have a computer, you have another alternative.

Researchers in Australia offered counseling to people with mild depression that used e-mail along with online lessons. The participants also did weekly homework assignments and participated in discussions with other depressed people — all using their computers. After eight weeks, they showed about as much improvement in their depression as would be expected from traditional therapy. Other researchers in Kentucky had good results with a similar eight-week program for depressed people.

One great benefit of online therapy is you don't need to live close to a counselor to get help. Instant messaging (IM) or live chatting with a therapist through short typed messages can let you carry on a conversation with someone far away. You can locate a therapist who is available online through two Web sites.

- **Help Horizons,** at *www.helphorizons.com*, can link you with psychologists, psychiatrists, marriage counselors, and other therapists. You can make an appointment to chat with a specific therapist or meet with the counselor on call. Fees run $40 to $100 per hour.

- **My Therapy Net,** at *www.mytherapynet.com*, is a similar online link to therapists. You pick your counselor, then chat using IM or a live video feed. Sessions cost about $1.60 per minute, depending on whether you chat for 15, 25, or 50 minutes at a time.

If you're not looking for live therapy, perhaps a video will do. The program *Good Days Ahead: The Interactive Program for Depression and Anxiety* helps you work through your sadness without a therapist. You watch videos to learn steps to help you overcome your problems and feel better. The program, created by psychiatrists, is available on DVD at *www.mindstreet.com* and costs about $99.

Simple**SOLUTION**

Get yourself a four-legged companion. Adopt a pet, and you'll gain good company and a brighter mood.

A dog or cat in your house gives you someone to talk to, take care of, and share affection with. That's why having a pet can ward off loneliness. When you take your pet out for a walk, you have an automatic conversation starter. Comments on your cute Yorkie can be a bridge to socializing.

Look for your next pet at a local animal shelter. You'll feel good knowing you're giving a home to a creature in need.

Beware quacks with no credentials

Pretty much anyone can hang out a shingle offering counseling or "life coaching." Even a person who calls herself a "psychotherapist" doesn't necessarily have special training or expertise. But other titles do signify certain qualifications.

- Psychiatrists are medical doctors who can practice therapy, prescribe medicine, or hospitalize patients. Your family physician can also prescribe medicine for psychological problems.

- Psychologists have Ph.D. degrees in either clinical or counseling psychology. They can practice various types of therapy.

- Social workers typically have a master's degree in social work and may help individuals, families, or groups work through their problems.

- Psychiatric nurses have special training in helping people with mental and emotional problems.

Don't be afraid to ask questions and check credentials before you settle on a therapist. Ask if they're licensed and how many years they've been practicing. Find out if they have experience treating your type of problem and what kind of treatment they prefer. Also be sure you feel comfortable on a personal level with the therapist, since that can make a difference in the success of treatment.

To find a qualified therapist near you, check your local phone book under Counseling Services or Psychologists. If you have a computer, you can also search online. Try these Web sites.

- *www.apa.org*. At the Web site of the American Psychological Society, click on the "Find a psychologist" link, then type in information about your location to find licensed psychologists near you.

- *www.academyofct.org*. Visit the Academy of Cognitive Therapy (ACT) to find a certified cognitive therapist near you. Click the box "Find a certified cognitive therapist," and input information about where you live.

Natural help for haywire hormones

Hormones are like hard-working ants, marching to every corner of your body to keep all systems going strong. Several types of hormones can affect your mood, including those related to digestion, growth, and sleep. Here is how to keep the peace, hormonally speaking.

- Thyroid hormones. If your body doesn't produce enough of these, you may feel depressed, tired, or foggy. Your doctor can order a test of your level of thyroid stimulating hormone (TSH) to see if thyroid problems are at work.

- Ghrelin, the "hunger hormone," tells your body to eat and wards off depression and anxiety.

- Cortisol, the "stress hormone," can cause depression if you produce too much, as happens in Cushing's disease.

- Melatonin, which controls your body's sleep cycle, may affect mood.

Most important when it comes to mood are the sex hormones. Estrogen and progesterone, female reproductive hormones, play a role in mood, especially around the time of puberty, pregnancy, and menopause. That is good news, since you can look forward to an end to some of this hormone-related turmoil after you've passed through the change in life. Before that happens, you can fight the power of hormonal surges with these natural remedies.

Omega-3 fatty acids. You can get these from fish oil supplements and flaxseed, and they may help with typical middle-age blues. Research shows women found relief from 500 milligrams (mg) of omega-3 three times a day.

Exercise. Regular physical activity helped middle-aged women feel happier and fight night sweats and hot flashes. Just three hours a week of walking or yoga did the trick.

Soy. Some women swear by the phytoestrogens — plant-based estrogens — in soy as an alternative to hormone therapy. Evidence remains sketchy, but if you decide to try soy, stick with whole foods like tofu and soy milk rather than supplements.

Question & Answer

Isn't depression just a normal part of getting old?

Depression and aging don't have to go together. It may seem normal to feel sad when you realize you're losing your edge, whether it's physical strength or mental sharpness. In addition, as you get older, so do your friends and relatives. You could be losing them to illness, death, or relocation. Other losses may include your professional identity and even your purpose in life.

Battle the blues by accepting the changes in your body and your life. Some experts say as you get older, you gain the ability to block out negative events and focus on the positive. That can actually help you be more content than younger people.

Why drowning your sorrows is a mistake

A glass of wine when you're unhappy and stressed may seem like the perfect solution. But alcohol can't fix your foul mood. In fact, it may make it worse.

The Bible warns of the link between alcohol and depression. "Who has woe? Who has sorrow? ... They that tarry long at the wine." (Proverbs 23:29–30)

Research shows some 30 to 50 percent of people who are alcoholics are also depressed. If you have a family history of either problem, you're also at a higher risk for the other condition.

Don't buy into the good-time myth. Alcohol depresses your central nervous system by acting as a sedative, or calming agent. Drink a little, and you may feel more relaxed and carefree. Problems may seem to slip away. But as drinking becomes a habit, you need more and more to feel good. Eventually, the good feelings disappear.

Drink enough, and alcohol impairs your speech and muscle coordination and may bring on sleep. Drinking too much can actually depress the vital centers of your brain to bring on a life-threatening coma.

Having more than three drinks a day for women or four drinks for men raises your risk of heart disease, liver disease, sleep problems, cancer, bleeding gums, and more. Even if you've been a moderate, safe drinker for years, you can develop problems as you age. Alcohol can start to affect you more strongly as you get older, or you may need to take drugs that don't mix well with drinking.

Steer yourself away from the bar. If you decide you want to cut back or stop drinking, give these tricks a try.

- Measure and keep track of how much you drink, and stick to your limits.

- Space out your drinks by alternating with nonalcoholic drinks or waiting a certain time between drinks.

- Drink alcohol only with meals, so the alcohol is absorbed more slowly.

- Find alternate activities and places that don't involve alcohol.

- Plan how you'll handle urges. What will your strategy be when a friend pressures you to share a beer? Decide first, and you won't be blindsided by temptation.

If these don't work for you, or your problem is more serious, see your doctor for help. He can prescribe medication and counseling if needed.

Common drugs linked to depression

The drugs you take to treat various ailments may affect your mood. (*See the table below.*) Talk to your doctor if you think your drugs are making you depressed.

Health condition	Drug class	Drug name
pain	nonsteroidal anti-inflammatory drugs (NSAIDs)	ibuprofen (Advil) Ultracet (combination of acetaminophen and tramadol)
high blood pressure	antihypertensives	clonidine (Catapres)
heart problems	beta blockers	propranolol (Inderal)
asthma	bronchodilators	pirbuterol (Maxair)
asthma, allergic reactions	corticosteroids	prednisone
infection	antibiotics	ciprofloxacin (Cipro) gemifloxacin (Factive)
heartburn	histamine blockers	ranitidine (Zantac) cimetidine (Tagamet)

Happy outlook builds a better body

A sad outlook on life is bad not only for your mind, but your body, too. Develop a happy nature, and you can protect your physical health.

Don't let bones take a beating. People who are depressed also tend to have lower bone mineral density, meaning they're at risk for the bone-thinning disease osteoporosis. Part of the reason may be that chronic moodiness changes your levels of an important brain chemical that also affects your bones. In addition, certain drugs that treat depression, including selective serotonin reuptake inhibitors (SSRIs), increase your chances of breaking a bone. They also put you at risk for suffering a serious fall.

Prevent bad-mood belly fat. You may feel unhappy when you're carrying a few extra pounds around the middle, but it's not all about dissatisfaction with your body. Belly fat also changes your body chemistry to make depression more likely. Some research shows that people with type 2 diabetes, often related to being overweight, are more likely to show signs of depression. And the problem can go both ways, since some antidepressant drugs can make you gain weight.

Adopt a heart-saving attitude. The same belly fat that makes depression more likely also puts you at risk for heart disease. In fact, suffering from depression raises your chances of a heart attack by 50 percent or more. Experts used to think the link was excess chronic inflammation, which can damage your blood vessels and start the heart disease ball rolling. But new research suggests the problem may be partly due to behavior. When you've got the blues, you may be too moody to bother with exercise or other good-health measures. That can bring on heart problems.

But your body is not doomed to break down just because of the blues. If you can motivate yourself to engage in even simple physical activity, you may find some relief.

Clean house clears mental cobwebs

When you're feeling down, you're like a caterpillar in its cocoon. All you want to do is hide away and be still. Break out of your cocoon and get active, and you may magically find yourself feeling better.

Researchers in England wanted to find out if getting off the couch could help with mental distress. They surveyed nearly 20,000 people, asking questions about physical activity and happiness. The survey found that people who were physically active for as little as 20 minutes a week had less depression. More activity made for an even better mood. Even activities like vigorous housecleaning — enough to make you breathe hard — lowered the risk of depression by 24 percent. So mop the floor, vacuum the carpets, and put a shine on those windows. Your cleaner house may also help clear out the cobwebs in your brain.

If the thought of cleaning makes you cringe, try another form of physical activity to pull yourself out of the dumps. Exercise is an important part of beating a low mood, whether or not you're taking other steps to feel better. When the experts reviewed a big batch of research, they concluded that aerobic activity like running or walking, performed at least three times a week for five weeks, helped lift mood better than a placebo and just as well as talk therapy.

Getting active can help for many reasons:

- Your body pumps out endorphins — natural hormones that make you feel good — when you exercise.

- Getting active lowers other signals of poor health, like inflammation, glucose intolerance, and heart risk factors.

- Slimming down if you need to lose weight can make you feel happier.

- If your activity results in a cleaner house or more beautiful garden, you'll get the added boost of a pleasant environment.

Activities that require deep breathing, such as yoga, have their own benefits because they encourage the flow of oxygen to all parts of your body. Even better, if you pick an activity that's fun, you also add play to your life. It's not just for kids, and it can help banish depression and stress. So plant some flowers, take a long bike ride, or go for a swim at the YMCA.

Some research has even suggested that the older you are, the more helpful physical activity may be in boosting your mood. One reason could be that, when you take part in social activities like dance or group tai chi classes, you get the added benefit of socializing with your friends. That in itself can boost a low mood.

Shared interest creates 'sunshine'

Janice was used to making new friends, having moved numerous times. But after her husband passed away and Janice moved to be near her daughter, she had trouble fitting in and finding companions.

Then Janice thought about what she'd always done after a move — join the local quilt guild. She checked the newspaper and found an ad for a group that met monthly at the local senior center. Janice felt at home among these ladies who shared her favorite pastime. After six months, Janice had new friends and was involved with a small group that made charity quilts for preemies at a local hospital. She enjoyed the meetings, along with lunch and shopping trips with the girls. Janice finally felt at home.

Secret to finding happiness

"If only I had (fill in the blank), then I'd be happy." Do you find yourself falling into the trap of wishing for that one thing you think will make you happy? Let it go. Research shows people are often wrong about the things they think will make them happy.

One classic study examined people who had won the lottery and others who had suffered spinal cord injuries. Although the winners reported being more happy than they were before and the injured reported less satisfaction with life, changes were not nearly as profound as you'd think. In other words, the winners were not super happy and the injured people were not deeply depressed, as might be expected in their situations.

Find joy in giving. So if winning $1 million won't make you happy in life, then what will? The good news is that researchers are trying to help you figure out what makes people happy. A recent PBS documentary, *This Emotional Life*, focused on this research, finding it's not so much what we have that makes us happy, but what we do. Specifically, showing compassion, offering forgiveness, and practicing altruism all tend to make people happy.

Anyone can develop the quality of altruism, or being concerned for others and sharing your riches. It's not just for the wealthy. In fact, after you have enough money to cover the necessities in life, more money won't make you any happier. But research shows how you use your money can affect your happiness, with more generous people finding greater happiness. As you give away your money, time, or talents, you're able to focus on other people and forget your own troubles.

Take the story of Cami Walker, a woman with multiple sclerosis who found relief, joy, and a new lease on life by starting a one-woman movement. She decided to give a gift daily for 29 days. Some of the gifts were material, but others were small kindnesses like listening to the story a neighbor wanted to tell or saying a kind word to the bank teller.

By the end of the 29 days, Walker felt happier, healthier, and more in tune with life. She found herself laughing more and felt closer to her family. Amazingly, she also felt physically stronger and was able to return to work. To share her experiences, Walker wrote a book and created a Web site, *www.29gifts.org*, encouraging others to try the 29-day experiment of giving.

Pick your passion. You already have all you need to start your own habit of altruism.

- Give money to a cause you believe in, like your church or your favorite charity.

- Volunteer your time where you see a need, whether it's building houses through Habitat for Humanity, taking care of tots in the church nursery, or running errands for a homebound friend. Research shows seniors who spend time doing volunteer work may benefit by keeping their brains sharper and perhaps even living longer.

- Use your skills to make items that help others if you can't commit to a certain volunteer schedule. Knitters can make caps for newborn babies, quilters can sew comfort quilts for wounded veterans, beaders can make rosaries to give away, and woodworkers can make toys for children in the hospital.

You know what you have. Give it away, and you'll gain happiness in return.

Energy **BOOSTER**

Zinc adds zing to your exercise routine. Your body needs this mineral to support all your hard work. Otherwise, you may feel more fatigued than fabulous.

When you exercise, your body pumps out carbon dioxide with the help of a special enzyme called carbonic anhydrase. That enzyme needs zinc to function, so when zinc is lacking, the enzyme can't do its job properly.

Eat more meat, poultry, beans, and fortified cereals, and you'll keep your body supplied with this essential mineral.

Simple ways to ease your grief

It's normal to feel sad when a relative or friend dies. That is the natural process of grief at work. Experts say you're better off dealing with the loss rather than trying to skip the pain of bereavement. You can come through it and enjoy life again.

Give it some time. In the past, a widow wore black mourning clothes for at least a year after her husband died. That was a sign she was grieving. Experts say you may mourn as long as two years, but everyone is different when it comes to grief. Don't put pressure on yourself to meet a schedule.

Grief is more than just sadness. You may also notice a lack of motivation, trouble concentrating, anxiety, and trouble making decisions. Some people experience confusion, memory loss, or a desire to be alone. The good news is that most people begin to pull out of the worst part of their grief by about six months after the loss.

Make an effort to carry on. If your problems are serious, your doctor may prescribe an anti-anxiety drug like alprazolam (Xanax). But these drugs can be addicting, so you may want to find other ways of working through your grief.

- Don't try to forget your loved one. Remembering him can keep him close in your heart. But accept that death is a part of life.

- Talk to people about your loss. Sharing your feelings may help. Look for a grief or support group if your family isn't helpful.

- Take care of your body. Eat right and go for walks for your physical and emotional health.

- Try to notice the good things around you, like the beauty of your garden or the happiness in a child's smile.

- Give to others to avoid thinking too much about your loss. Find opportunities to volunteer, or be creative and make something for someone else.

- Organize — your kitchen, closets, or photos — to give yourself a sense of control.

- Get creative through writing, painting, or another outlet. This can be a way of expressing your feelings and pulling yourself through the grief.

Straight talk about death and dying

Get advice about issues relating to death at *www.thecheckoutline.org*. It's a Web site featuring journalist Judy Bachrach, who offers advice to people who are terminally ill, have relatives who have recently died, or are otherwise impacted by death. Bachrach is a longtime writer and editor who has dealt with a close friend's death and has volunteered with hospice.

The Web site offers advice and blogs by other people with similar problems. Common topics include whether to choose cremation, discussing mourning with friends, and how best to support a grieving friend. The service is free.

Put worries to rest with special message

Help your family deal with your passing by leaving a personal message. In this electronic age, you can make it permanent and private.

You can leave messages to comfort your loved ones at the Eternal Message Web site, *www.eternalmessage.net*. Only the person you specify — and give your password to — can read your message. It's one way to ensure you're able to share those last thoughts privately. Not even the Web site owners can read what you've written.

The service is not expensive. For $10 you can post one message of up to 1,000 words. If you have more to say, you can post up to three messages for $20. Your loved one simply enters the password and reads your message for free. And you're doing one final generous act, since 10 percent of the proceeds are donated to charity.

Count your blessings for a sunnier outlook

"There is nothing either good or bad, but thinking makes it so."

Shakespeare's moody hero, Hamlet, had the right idea. A positive outlook on life can go a long way to brighten your mood, no matter the circumstances. Now research in psychology proves it's true.

Doctors sometimes tell their patients to try certain behavior changes to calm anxiety-producing thoughts. One trick is to keep a list of positive events or circumstances in your life, or say a daily prayer of gratitude. The idea that you can think yourself happy is part of the positive psychology movement.

Focus on keeping the glass half full. Physician and author Susan Vaughan discusses the benefits of positive thinking in her book *Half Empty, Half Full: Understanding the Psychological Roots of Optimism*. She suggests focusing on your abilities and skills rather than your weaknesses and telling yourself you have the power to get what you want.

"Train yourself to think like an optimist and you will gradually become one," she writes.

Vaughan also encourages "downward comparison," or thinking about the good aspects of your situation rather than envying what you don't have. Research shows you'll be more happy with yourself if you try to focus on people less well off than you. In addition, Vaughan suggests you change your surroundings — the music you listen to, the view from your window, the people in your life — to choices that make you calm and happy. Just as a baby in a nursery starts to cry when another one cries, so you're affected by the moods of other people.

Feel good by being grateful. This idea is expanded in the book *Thanks!: How the New Science of Gratitude Can Make You Happier* by psychologist Robert Emmons, Ph.D. He suggests keeping a daily or weekly gratitude journal in which you write down five things you're grateful for. Emmons explains how this activity helps you recall the positive things in your life.

"Gratitude is the way the heart remembers — remembers kindnesses, cherished interactions with others, compassionate actions of strangers, surprise gifts, and everyday blessings," he writes.

Research has shown this activity may help both healthy people and those suffering from neuromuscular diseases. Those who kept gratitude journals for 10 weeks felt more positive about life, didn't focus on hassles, felt better physically, and were able to do more exercise.

The act of writing down specific good things is just one method of cultivating gratitude. Emmons discusses several others:

- Learn prayers of gratitude and thanksgiving, perhaps specific to your religion.

- Use visual reminders, like a note on your desk or a quotation posted on the fridge, to keep you on track.

- Spend time with people who share your desire for gratitude, so their efforts will rub off.

- Pay attention to your choice of words, since language affects how you think and act. Pick positive words like "grateful," "fortunate," and "blessing" rather than negatives words like "lack," "loss," and "regret."

- Go through the motions — fake a smile for example — as you work to develop this new, positive attitude.

The real challenge is to be grateful for what you have even when things aren't going well. But this can be done, as the Biblical example of Job shows. And as you have success changing your thoughts about your life, you'll find your outlook and moods change as well. It takes effort — give it a try.

QUICK*fix*

Curl up with the right book, and you can read away your bad mood. It's called bibliotherapy, and research proves it works.

If you have mild-to-moderate mood problems — not full-blown depression — bibliotherapy can help you think about your problems in a new way. There are plenty of self-help books in the store that promise to cure your blues. Skip the losers, and pick one that's proven to have benefits. Experts suggest you try one of these titles.

- *Feeling Good: The New Mood Therapy* by David D. Burns, M.D.
- *Control your Depression* by Peter M. Lewinsohn, Ph.D., and others.

Look to a Higher Power for help

"Seek the Lord while he may be found; call on him while he is near." (Isaiah 55:6) This Old Testament advice may be your best ticket out of the blues. Many people feel better when they pray or attend a worship service. Science has finally caught up with what spiritual people have long known — a Higher Power can help with your unhappiness.

Pray your blues away. Research among more than 1,000 members of the Presbyterian Church in the United States found that people who pray more also enjoy better mental health. Those who prayed at least two times every day — some 42 percent of the group — had the best mental health. Praying even more than that seemed to bring on even greater feelings of well-being.

Practicing your spiritual beliefs, including prayer, worship, and meditation, benefit both body and mind. Science has found that the simple act of sitting quietly, relaxing and breathing deeply, and trying to calm and focus your mind can help shut out the clutter and problems of life, making you feel better. You'll enjoy these benefits while you pray:

- reduced stress, so less release of stress hormones like norepinephrine and cortisol

- increase in positive emotions, like hope, love, and forgiveness, along with decrease in negative emotions such as hostility

- slower rate of breathing

- lower blood pressure and heart rate

- stronger immune system

In addition, as you address a Higher Power in prayer, you strengthen the bonds you feel between the two of you. That may help you feel more connected and less alone. And if you pray in a group setting, like in a church service or Bible study, you get the added benefits of socialization and group support. That can help you avoid loneliness.

Find some spiritual healing. Other studies have found that people who have a higher degree of personal spirituality or "religiosity" — the importance of religious beliefs and activities in their lives — have a lower chance of suffering from depression. It seems that strong religious faith gives you something to cling to when bad things roll around.

You may even live longer if you're spiritually active, whether on your own or as part of an organized religion. Physicians are taking note, looking for ways to encourage spirituality in their patients to help improve their ability to cope with illness, quality of life, anxiety, and depression.

But even experts who report on the benefits of spirituality warn that anything can be taken too far. Don't use your religious beliefs as an excuse to avoid seeing a doctor or getting help for your physical or mental problems.

Don't let dieting get you down

Nobody expects to feel their mood soar when on a diet. After all, you're probably doing without some of your favorite snacks. But you also don't want to hit rock bottom. Pick the right plan, and you can shed those excess pounds without shedding your sunny outlook on life.

Watch the calorie count. Some research has found that women with a history of depression shouldn't cut back too far on calories. Doing so may put them at risk of another bout of the blues. This effect seems to be related to lack of tryptophan, an amino acid that can boost your mood.

Women in this study ate only 1,000 calories a day — rather Spartan fare, even for those trying to lose weight. The low-calorie diet lowered tryptophan levels equally in both groups. But the women with a history of depression could not adjust to the lower levels, as the other women did, and their mood dropped.

Pick low-fat over low-carb. Even if you've never battled serious depression, a low-carbohydrate diet plan may lead you down the path to moodiness. Researchers in Australia pitted low-carb diets against low-fat plans to see what effect each had on mood. The low-carb diets allowed only about 4 percent of calories from carbohydrates and 61 percent from fat, while the low-fat plans were about 46 percent carbs and 30 percent fat. The Atkins diet is an example of low-carb, while the Ornish diet is one well-known low-fat eating plan.

At first, both groups lost weight and felt happy — no surprise, since they could bask in their success. But by the end of the one-year study, the low-carb dieters saw their moods plummet, while dieters in the low-fat group continued to enjoy chipper moods.

The reason for the difference may be that making huge changes to your typical eating habits, as happens with low-carb dieting, is difficult and puts people in a funk. Or it could be the low-carb plan allowed for too few carbs in your body, bringing on lower levels of serotonin, a feel-good brain chemical.

Other research has confirmed the benefits of eating carbs for mood. Older men in Japan who ate moderate amounts of carbohydrates, vitamin C, and carotene, had less risk of moodiness than those who didn't get enough of these nutrients. So go low-fat when you diet, and be sure to get enough essential nutrients. You can lose weight and still feel great.

Spiritual fix for a hurting heart

Candace lived alone since losing her husband, but she didn't feel down in the dumps until her heart attack. After she came home from the hospital, she never got back her old sunny disposition.

Candace's sister noticed the change and encouraged her to get involved in her church again. So Candace made the effort to get to services every Sunday and felt uplifted by the folk choir's music. She also joined a senior ladies' Bible study that met weekly.

"Once I got back into reading God's word and trying to find His plan, I felt better about changes in my life," Candace says. "Now I have a fresh outlook, plus I look forward to seeing my friends every week."

Fabulous foods that will lift your mood

You're heard of comfort food — certain dishes that make you feel good just thinking about them. Maybe yours is macaroni and cheese, or perhaps chicken noodle soup. But for best mood enhancement, look to healthy protein. A high-quality protein snack — say some tuna salad made with light dressing — gives you three great ingredients to battle the blues.

Tryptophan. This amino acid is considered nature's antidepressant and is behind the legend that warm milk at bedtime will help you sleep. In fact, tryptophan does have a mild sedative effect, and it allows your body to produce melatonin, the brain hormone that controls your body's sleep clock. After it's digested, tryptophan is converted into the feel-good brain chemical serotonin to boost your mood. Experts think lack of tryptophan may be one cause of depression, bipolar disorder, and some other serious mental problems.

You'll find lots of tryptophan in high-protein foods like meat, fish, turkey, and peanuts. But you'll need carbohydrates to help boost this amino acid into your brain. Make that tuna salad into a sandwich, and you'll be on your way to a happier mood.

Omega-3 fatty acids. These "healthy" fats, abundant in fatty fish like salmon and sardines, are famous for how they help your heart. They're also important to ward off the blues.

One study looked at more than 3,000 people over a span of 20 years. It found that women who got more omega-3 fatty acids from fish and other foods had fewer symptoms of depression. Middle-aged women in another study who took 1 gram of fish oil every day for eight weeks enjoyed lower depression rates. The women also found relief from hot flashes. Finally, other research has noticed that people who stick with a Mediterranean diet, abundant in fish and olive oil, have lower rates of depression.

How does this fantastic fat help bring on a sunnier outlook? Your brain is full of fat, a lot of it essential fatty acids like omega-3. A lack of omega-3 in your system changes how the neurotransmitter serotonin works, altering your mood. In addition, the specific omega-3 fatty acids eicosapentaenoic acid (EPA) and docosahexaenoic acid (DHA) have anti-inflammatory effects in your brain, which may have an effect on mood.

Vitamin B12. Snapper, tuna, and salmon — high in omega-3 — also provide a megadose of this brain-boosting vitamin. If you don't get enough vitamin B12, you may be at risk of serious moodiness. One study found that women who were deficient in vitamin B12 had double the risk of being depressed. It also affects how your brain thinks and remembers, so getting enough can help keep your brain sharp.

As you work to get enough good-quality protein, pick whole foods over processed, and avoid sugar to help beat those middle-age blues. Researchers found that eating whole foods like fish, fruits, and vegetables benefits your mood because the nutrients work together to battle disease, including depression. Also, experts say a processed-food diet puts you at higher risk for inflammation, which also contributes to depression.

Energy **BOOSTER**

It's not your imagination. That bite of chocolate really does make you feel better.

Chocolate, especially the dark variety, boasts lots of polyphenols. These antioxidants work to raise the level of the feel-good brain chemical serotonin. Too little serotonin may fuel a foul mood.

People who suffered from chronic fatigue syndrome discovered that eating chocolate every day made them more peppy, one study found. Other research reported people who ate dark chocolate enjoyed lower levels of certain stress hormones, plus it helped their digestion. That's gotta feel good.

Just don't go overboard. The studies were based on about 1.5 ounces of dark chocolate a day, or nine Hershey kisses. That alone will set you back 180 calories.

Natural pick-me-ups fight the blues

Get a burst of energy — mental and physical — the natural way. You don't need to take drugs when you can feel better with old-fashioned herbs.

Boost your mood with St. John's wort. This funny-sounding herb, an extract from the yellow flowering plant *Hypericum perforatum*, is a traditional remedy for mild depression. It's the most commonly pre-scribed antidepressant in Germany, plus it gets an A rating from respected American experts.

Scientists think St. John's wort works by changing levels of serotonin and other feel-good brain chemicals, similar to how some antidepressant drugs work. It's no surprise that research shows St. John's wort works as well as some drugs to control mood.

A typical remedy is 900 milligrams (mg) a day of St. John's wort, divided into either two or three doses. You may have to wait two to four weeks to see results, so be patient.

Fight fatigue with Alpine herbal wonder. The herb known as *Rhodiola rosea*, or goldenroot, is a traditional Chinese remedy for stress. It's made from the roots of a plant with lovely yellow flowers that grows at high altitudes in Europe and Asia, and it's believed to make you feel better by fighting mental and physical fatigue.

Like ginseng, *Rhodiola rosea* is classified as an adaptogen, or a plant that works in a vague, nonspecific way to increase your resistance to stress — whether physical, chemical, or biological. *Rhodiola* works on your central nervous system by changing levels of serotonin and other natural brain chemicals.

Research shows depressed people who took *Rhodiola* supplements felt better within about six weeks. The herb also helped doctors working the night shift fight off fatigue and improve their mental performance. Successful studies used *Rhodiola* supplements twice daily. You'll get a boost with no caffeine or artificial additives.

Be aware of side effects. Although herbal remedies are natural, that doesn't mean they're free of side effects. St. John's wort can interact with a number of drugs, including some medicines used to treat depression. Rhodiola may produce restlessness, irritability, and insomnia if you take too much. But generally they are safer than prescription antidepressants, which can plague you with:

- weight gain.

- bone loss and fractures.

- falls. They are more likely among older depressed people who take common antidepressant drugs in the class of selective serotonin reuptake inhibitors (SSRIs), such as Fluoxetine (Prozac) and sertraline (Zoloft).

- stroke. New research shows that postmenopausal women who take antidepressants — both the tricyclic class of drugs and SSRIs — have a higher risk of suffering one.

Even the best drugs can take a long time — as long as 12 weeks — to work, and they may never work for some people. Before prescribing antidepressants, your doctor should do a physical exam and ask questions about your life and medical history. An antidepressant prescription should not be automatic for everyone suffering from moodiness. Ask whether a natural remedy might work just as well for your situation.

QUICK *fix*

Eat three square meals a day — even if you live alone and don't enjoy cooking. It will help your mood.

Your blood sugar can drop when you skip a meal. That means your brain is starved of the sugar it needs, so you'll feel the effects of hypoglycemia, including the blues. Find a way to eat right at every meal.

- Fix large batches, then freeze leftovers to eat later.
- Take turns hosting dinner with friends.
- See if your church has volunteers to help with cooking.
- Look into local Meals on Wheels programs, which may deliver at least one balanced meal a day.

Surefire ways to beat the winter doldrums

It's mid-December, and life is looking a bit bleak, just when you should be looking forward to the holidays. Two common complaints can make you feel down at this time of year.

Fight off holiday gloom. It's time for celebrations, family gatherings, and a well-deserved vacation from work. But not everyone feels their best when the holidays roll around. Instead, you may feel extra pressure to buy just the right gift or cook the best turkey dinner ever. Holidays can also bring back memories good and bad, and they can remind you that time is passing and you're getting older.

Don't let the holidays hit your mood like a ton of bricks when you can take steps to avoid the blues.

- Notice if you tend to have this problem, and don't put extra pressure on yourself to be happy all season.

- Spend more — or maybe less — time with your immediate and extended family. Figure out which works best for you.

- Cook your favorite meals, and make time for an activity you really enjoy. Don't follow tradition if it doesn't suit you.

- Talk through your problems with a trusted friend, or seek professional help.

Get smart about SAD. For some people, the winter blues are related to shorter days and longer nights, a condition known as seasonal affective disorder (SAD).

People are like potted plants — they need the right amount of sunlight to thrive. Regular exposure to bright light in the morning and darkness at night helps keep your body's internal clock, or circadian rhythm, in sync. Anything that upsets that balance, including the shorter days of winter, can alter your body's levels of melatonin. This natural hormone can affect your mood. Lower levels of vitamin D also may contribute to the blues. You can get this vitamin from sunlight, but only if you're out and about during daylight hours.

SAD affects about 5 percent of the U.S. population. If you think you're in that group, follow these steps to help yourself feel better.

- Keep a regular schedule, going outside into the sunlight at the same time every morning.

- Minimize your exposure to bright lights in the evening, including computer screens.

- Ask your doctor about a special light box that emits a wide spectrum of visible light, similar to sunlight. Some people with SAD get relief from sitting in front of such a light box — maybe reading or eating breakfast — for just 30 minutes each day. A good light box gives off 10,000 lux, a measurement of light, while typical indoor lighting is about 100 lux. Boxes have ultraviolet light filters, so you won't get sunburned.

Simple**SOLUTION**

Feeling lonely? Let your computer help you reconnect. Research has found that the Internet can actually help you feel less isolated and alone.

You can use e-mail to communicate for free with grandchildren thousands of miles away or keep up with friends via a social-networking site like Facebook or MySpace. You can also forge bonds with others through a support group or game playing, or meet people who share your odd interests. Just type your topic — say, stamp collecting or mead brewing — into a search engine, like *www.google.com*, to get started. Free e-mail is available at sites like *www.yahoo.com* and *www.gmail.com*.

Find treatment when money is tight

Don't assume you can't afford treatment for your lingering blues. A new law may be your ticket into the therapist's office. Even if the law doesn't work for you, help is available for people with limited funds.

Get a hand from Uncle Sam. The new Mental Health Parity Law ensures that you may be able to get a full course of treatment for your mood problems.

According to the law, employee health insurance policies that include coverage for both mental health and physical health must be fair. They can't make the mental health coverage more limited than that for physical health. For example, the plan can't place a limit on the number of office visits with a therapist that will be covered during a year, or limit coverage for depression drugs differently from heart drugs. That may mean you'll get more complete coverage for depression if you need to see a therapist.

But this new law won't help everyone. It applies only to companies that employ more than 50 people. And if your company's health insurance doesn't already cover mental health, the law doesn't require that it be added. If the change is too expensive, your company could choose to eliminate coverage for mental health problems altogether. Check your policy so you'll know exactly how much coverage you can expect if you need it.

Look to other sources for help. Even if this law doesn't help you, there are other ways to find affordable mental health care.

- See if your employer offers an employee assistance program. You may get a few sessions with a therapist for free.

- Look for a local community mental health center, which may let you pay on a sliding scale based on income. You may be charged just $10 or $20 per session if you have little or no income.

- Seek advice from your pastor, who probably has training in counseling.

- Find a support group for the specific problem that is bothering you. For example, you might attend Al-Anon meetings if you have a relative with an alcohol problem, or meet with a similar group for people coping with a job loss.

- Look for help on campus if you live near a university. Advanced graduate students often staff university mental health centers, providing free or cheap counseling to people from the local community. The graduate students work under close supervision from professionals, so you're in good hands.

Sounder sleep puts new life into your days

Simple way to add years to your life

Don't speed up aging any more than you have to. You can slow it down simply by getting enough sleep. Experts say you don't automatically get insomnia just because you're older. You may take longer to fall asleep or wake once or twice during the night, but unless health problems interfere, these changes should be minor. If your sleep problem is more serious, research suggests plenty of reasons why you should not just learn to live with it.

Heart disease. According to a report from the Sleep Health Centers of Boston, getting less than six hours of sleep increased the risk of dying from heart-related diseases over an eight-year period.

High blood pressure. Middle-age adults who slept less were more likely to develop high blood pressure over a five-year period, University of Chicago researchers found.

Diabetes. According to one study, people who slept less than six hours a night during the work week were nearly five times more likely to develop "impaired fasting glucose," a blood sugar problem that can lead to diabetes. Another study found that people prevented from getting their normal dose of "slow wave" or deep sleep for just three nights developed problems with glucose tolerance and insulin sensitivity. These are two more signs of an increased risk of diabetes. So how well you sleep can be just as important as how long you sleep.

Metabolic syndrome. Another study found that people who sleep less than seven hours a night are more likely to get metabolic syndrome — a condition marked by belly fat and high sugar levels — than people who get between seven and eight hours of sleep.

This doesn't mean you're doomed if you have insomnia. In fact, you have a number of drug-free options to help you sleep, and you'll find plenty of helpful tips within this chapter. Take steps to avoid these life-shortening conditions — like sleeping more — and you'll possibly add years to your life. Avoiding these conditions also means escaping their symptoms, which can make you feel far older than your real age. So while getting a good night's sleep may not be the fountain of youth, it might be the next best thing.

Question & Answer

Does eating Thanksgiving turkey make you sleepy?

Turkey may stand accused of putting you to sleep after your holiday feast, but this poor meat has been framed. It's true that turkey contains the sleep-promoting compound tryptophan. But tryptophan works best if you take it on an empty stomach without any other protein. Since turkey naturally has protein, it remains an innocent victim.

The real culprits behind Thanksgiving drowsiness are the carbohydrates like mashed potatoes and stuffing. These trigger a chain reaction that helps concentrate the tryptophan at higher levels in your bloodstream and send it into your brain — and that's what makes you sleepy. Of course, overeating doesn't help, either.

Secret to stopping middle-age spread

Belly fat can creep up on you before you know it even if you're active and eat right. Surprisingly, your sleep habits could be the problem.

Scientists from Case Western Reserve University reviewed 23 earlier studies and found that 20 linked higher weight to less sleep. A study on nurses at Walter Reed Army Medical Center found that those who got less than six hours of sleep a night had a higher body mass index than those who slept longer, even though they were more active. The researchers suggest that lack of sleep could trigger hormones that encourage overeating. And according to a recent Korean study, shorter sleep not only may lead to an increase in weight but specifically a larger belly.

If you have trouble controlling your weight, check out the chapter *Belly fat: easy ways to slenderize and energize*. If you're having sleep problems, try these drug-free suggestions to help you fall asleep faster. The three S's of sweet sleep will help you catch a few more zzz's, which in turn will help banish belly fat.

Set a schedule. Decide what time you'll go to bed and what time you'll wake every day, and stick to this schedule. This trains your brain to expect to fall asleep and wake up at the times you choose. This simple trick may sound too easy and too good to be true, but it comes from Harvard University sleep experts. So this is one case where a tip may be simple but also powerful.

Say goodbye to nighttime liquids. Experts say the most common reason older adults lose sleep is overnight bathroom visits. In fact, more than half of all adults over 55 may be affected. As you age, your body loses its ability to hold liquids for long periods of time, so you go to the bathroom more often even if you don't drink more. To work around this problem, try these tips.

- Drink less during the last few hours before bed. You can make up the difference by drinking more fluids during daylight hours. Try a similar strategy with high-liquid foods such as soups, grapes, and watermelon.

- Cut back on coffee and tea, which irritate your bladder.

- Keep a record of what you drink, how much you drink, and when you drink to see if you can spot patterns or triggers that cause your nightly bathroom trips.

Frequent bathroom runs can also be a sign of sleep apnea, incontinence, benign prostatic hyperplasia, and other conditions. So if making the changes listed above doesn't help, see your doctor.

Start a sleep diary. A sleep diary may help you pinpoint what is causing your insomnia. Include each of the following:

- the time you go to bed, the time you wake, and how many times you wake and fall back to sleep during the night.

- how well you slept and anything that interfered with your sleep.

- which foods, drinks, and medications you take, including the time you take them.

- when and how long you nap or exercise and how you spend your evenings.

- how sleepy you are during the day.

Examine the diary for possible links between your worst nights and either the things you do or the conditions you sleep in. If you can't find any connections, talk to your doctor about your insomnia, and share the sleep diary with her.

Quick fix for CPAP woes

Cynthia hated the noisy, uncomfortable air leaks from her CPAP mask — not to mention the red mark it made on the bridge of her nose. Then someone recommended RemZzzs, a thin liner from *www.remzzzs.com* that fits over the rim of the CPAP mask.

"I didn't think it would do anything, but it has been a wonderful help to my problems," Cynthia says. Her mask doesn't leak anymore because the liner cushions the space between the mask and her face. RemZzzs also absorbs oil and sweat and prevents the red mark on her nose. If you can't find a CPAP mask that fits well, a product like this may help.

Disarm 2 common sleep robbers

You sleep all night long, yet you always feel exhausted when you roll out of bed in the morning. Or maybe you wake easily enough, but you've struggled for weeks to stay awake during the day. You may be the victim of two sneaky sleep robbers that steal the rest from your nighttime slumber.

Uncover sleep apnea. If your bed partner complains that you snore, choke, and gasp during the night, you may have sleep apnea. That means you frequently stop breathing for 10 to 60 seconds and wake briefly to start breathing again. Most people with sleep apnea don't remember waking at all.

The scary thing is, this condition can impair you almost as much as drinking alcohol. The National Sleep Foundation reports that people with untreated, mild-to-moderate sleep apnea perform about as well as someone with a blood alcohol level of 0.06 — just 0.02 away from being legally drunk. Untreated sleep apnea has also been linked to reflux disease, depression, stroke, heart attack, high blood pressure, congestive heart failure, and diabetes. So if you think you might have sleep apnea, see your doctor. She may send you for a one-night sleep study, a test where technicians monitor your sleep and breathing. If you have this condition, your doctor has several ways she can help you feel — and sleep — better.

- CPAP. Your doctor may prescribe a continuous positive airway pressure (CPAP) device, a small machine that sends a stream of air into an attached nose mask that you wear. Using the machine keeps your airways open so you stop losing sleep.

- Pillow. People with mild sleep apnea may improve their snoring as well as their sleep with a special pillow that stretches the neck.

- Mouth guard. Dental appliances or mouth guards may help reposition your jaw and tongue to help keep your airway open. You'll need a dentist or orthodontist to fit you with the right one, but keep in mind that these probably won't work for side sleepers.

- Exercises. Research suggests that specially developed exercises for the tongue, soft palate, and throat may help mild-to-moderate sleep apnea. Ask your sleep doctor if she can recommend a speech therapist who can teach you these exercises.

- Surgery, or a small implant that can be put in at your doctor's office.

Whatever treatment you choose, be sure to lose weight if you're overweight, and avoid sleeping on your back. Experts say these simple strategies can be surprisingly effective.

Say good night to RLS. Creepy crawly things belong in the dark, but not in your bed, and certainly not on your body. If you feel crawling, prickly, or tingling sensations in your legs, and moving makes them feel better, you may have Restless Legs Syndrome (RLS). When these symptoms are severe enough, they can cause sleep loss and daytime exhaustion.

Eight out of 10 RLS sufferers also have periodic limb movement disorder (PLMD), which makes your legs jerk repeatedly while you sleep. The jerking doesn't wake you, but it may disturb your sleep enough to make you tired the next day. If you suspect RLS or PLMD is causing your insomnia, see your doctor for help as soon as possible. Meanwhile, try these tactics to ease your symptoms.

- Avoid caffeine, alcohol, and smoking.

- Get at least light exercise each day, and stretch or massage your legs before bed.

- Allow extra time for sleep whenever possible to help you get the rest you need.

Even if you have neither of these problems, you should still see your doctor about your insomnia if it lasts more than a few weeks. Insomnia may be caused by other conditions, such as acid reflux, depression, thyroid problems, high blood pressure, asthma, or allergies. By treating these problems, you may cure your sleeplessness as well.

Recipe for a perfect night's sleep

The foods you choose really can affect how you snooze. Humorist Lewis Grizzard wrote "Chili Dawgs Only Seem to Bark at Night" after severe indigestion from a chili dog kept him from sleeping. On the other hand, many people swear a glass of milk sends them straight to dreamland. Here are five super-simple ideas on what to do, eat, and drink before bed to give you a perfect night's sleep.

Eat rice for more rest. You can fall asleep faster even without drugs, Australian research suggests. This study found that Jasmine rice helped men fall asleep more quickly than regular long-grain rice. Starchy carbohydrates like jasmine rice have a higher glycemic index than heartier fare. Although that means they raise your blood sugar more quickly, it also means they increase the tryptophan in your bloodstream. That is good news because tryptophan is a natural compound that can help you sleep.

To make tryptophan work for you, eat a starchy carbohydrate such as jasmine rice, pretzels, soda crackers, or French bread about four hours before bedtime. The study used 600 grams of steamed rice — a little over two-and-a-half cups — but you may want to adjust the portions to see what works for you. If you have diabetes, make sure your doctor approves before you give this plan a whirl.

Count calories instead of sheep. Experts have long warned against eating a big meal within four hours of bedtime. They claim your body has to work so hard to digest all that food that the resulting discomfort can keep you awake.

But now new research says that is only part of the story. A Brazilian study suggests the more fat and calories you eat during the day, the less time you spend in deep sleep, and the poorer your sleep will be. This is particularly true if you eat more of your calories or fat after dark. Another study even discovered that people who ate the most fat also spent less time sleeping. So try cutting back on fat and calories in the evening — or even all day — and see if it improves your sack time.

Rely on an old home remedy. The tryptophan in milk is supposedly what makes you sleepy, but now scientists say the protein in milk blocks tryptophan from working. But that doesn't mean this old favorite can't help you rest. The familiar and comforting ritual of drinking a glass of milk before bed may be enough to convince your brain it's time to catch some zzz's.

Try a snooze-worthy fruit. Cherries may not sound like a sleep remedy, but don't be fooled. These little fruits are a good source of the hormone melatonin. Your body makes this hormone to help you fall asleep and stay asleep. Studies have shown that getting extra melatonin may help you sleep through the night. Instead of a supplement, why not try a handful of fresh cherries? For even more power, try dried cherries or check your health food store or grocery store for cherry concentrate. You can enjoy delicious cherry juice just by mixing a spoonful of cherry concentrate with water.

Escape nighttime heartburn. Gastroesophageal reflux disease (GERD) is a common cause of sleep problems. In fact, this fiery heartburn pain may keep you awake at night. But take the following items off your menu and you may sleep better: peppermint, spearmint, chocolate, cinnamon, garlic, onions, salt, coffee, tea, sodas, fatty or spicy foods, acidic foods such as tomato-based products and citrus fruits, and alcohol.

Hidden danger of sleeping pills

At first, it seemed like good news. People who took zolpidem (Ambien) slept right through their acid reflux attacks instead of waking up with severe heartburn pain during the night.

But Philadelphia researchers discovered reflux episodes lasted far longer in people who took zolpidem than in people who took a placebo — regardless of whether they had gastroesophageal reflux disease or not. Longer-lasting reflux may put you at higher risk for dangerous Barrett's esophagus and deadly esophageal cancer. If you take sleeping pills, talk to your doctor about trying drug-free treatments for insomnia and, if you suffer from acid reflux, ask how you can be treated for that, too.

Fend off modern-day sleep stealers

Many people slept 9 1/2 hours every night back in the 19th century. Today we sleep far less. If you can't sleep well at night, perhaps these modern-day conveniences are the reason why.

Shut off your cell phone. A preliminary Swedish study found a link between sleep loss and cell phones. The researchers were not sure whether the sleep problems came from late-night phone use or cell phone radiation, so more research is needed. But meanwhile, if you have insomnia, consider limiting your cell phone use, especially after dark.

Resist the TV and computer. According to a recent American Time Use Survey, many Americans don't get enough sleep. In fact, most people go to bed later than they should whether they work more than eight hours a day or don't work at all. The survey also found that watching TV is usually the reason people don't get to bed early enough.

Meanwhile, a study from Japan has found that using the computer or watching TV before bed may make you feel less rested the next day — even if you didn't get less sleep. The scientists suggest that computers and television may affect either how well you sleep or the amount of sleep your body needs. Maybe that is why experts suggest you skip watching stimulating television shows as you get closer to bedtime. They also recommend avoiding exciting or stressful computer pastimes such as video games, finances, or work-related tasks. These activities just aren't the stuff that dreams are made of.

Take a look at your medicines. Many modern medications weren't available to sleepers in the 19th century. Examples of today's possible sleep stealers include moxifloxacin and ofloxacin (antibiotics,) propanolol (beta blocker), furosemide (for blood pressure,) lovastatin (cholesterol drug,) levothyroxine (thyroid drug,) and levodopa (for Parkinson's and Restless Legs Syndrome).

You should ask your doctor and pharmacist if any of your prescription or nonprescription drugs list insomnia as a side effect. Also, check to see if they contain hidden caffeine or other stimulants. Some common pain relievers contain caffeine while cold medications with pseudoephedrine or phenylpropanolamine may keep some people awake.

Simple**SOLUTION**

Hidden ingredients in your supper or evening snack could be keeping you up at night. Tyrosine and tyramine are natural compounds that can rev up stimulating hormones like adrenaline and norepinephrine in your body — making you wide awake. That's why eating foods rich in these compounds may cause insomnia in some people. If you're battling sleeplessness, avoid foods with tyrosine or tyramine after 4 p.m.

Foods with tyrosine include chicken, turkey, milk, cheese, yogurt, cottage cheese, soy foods, peanuts, almonds, lima beans, green beans, bananas, wheat, and pumpkin seeds. Tyramine-rich foods include beef, cheese, wine, beer, soybeans, fava beans, eggplant, sausage, bacon, ham, processed meats, sugar, tomatoes, lentils, sauerkraut, potatoes, and spinach.

Unexpected way to win the insomnia war

You could see dramatic improvement in your slumber just by temporarily restricting your sack time. It's not as crazy as it sounds. Scientists have found that temporary sleep restriction can help you fall asleep faster, sleep longer, and sleep more deeply.

Why less is more. The problem with insomnia isn't just that you spend too much time awake. You also spend too much in-bed time struggling to sleep as well as getting light, unrestorative sleep. This can literally lead you to dread your bed. Sleep restriction therapy helps ease your in-bed anxieties by limiting the time spent in bed to the average time you spend sleeping.

For example, if you set your alarm clock for 6 a.m. but usually only sleep five hours, your temporary bedtime will be 1 a.m. no matter how sleepy you get before that. Instead of struggling to sleep, you may now struggle to stay awake. But that's good for several reasons.

- The resulting sleep deprivation should increase your body's ability and drive to get to sleep and stay asleep.

- Your body should replace time spent in light sleep with deeper, more restorative sleep.

- Because you spend less time in bed, you'll soon spend more of that sack time sleeping. This helps your mind associate your bed with sleep instead of with wakefulness and worrying about insomnia. As a result, you may find it easier to fall asleep in the first place.

These changes can lead to dramatic improvement in your sleep in just a few nights or weeks. And as your sleep improves, you'll gradually increase the amount of time spent in bed until you're finally sleeping normally.

Secrets of success. Before you begin sleep restriction therapy, you must spend a week or two recording how much time you spend sleeping per night. Then average the results. If that average is higher than five hours, that number is your new sleep quota. If it is less than five hours, your new sleep quota is five hours.

Next, take the time that your alarm normally goes off, and subtract your new sleep quota from that time. This is your new bedtime. Do not go to bed or take naps before this time.

During sleep restriction therapy, keep tracking how much time you spend sleeping. Divide your total hours of sleep by time spent in bed, and multiply by 100 to get a percentage. When you've spent 85 percent or more of your sack time sleeping well for several weeks, set a new bedtime that's 15 to 30 minutes earlier. Keep adjusting your bedtime this way until you're getting a good night's sleep.

What to know before you start. Sleep restriction may not be right for everyone, particularly people with epilepsy, bipolar disorder, or sleepwalking. And it may be dangerous for some people who already have excessive daytime sleepiness or for those who need to drive or operate a heavy vehicle. It's best to try sleep restriction with your doctor's or sleep specialist's supervision. And if you can't sleep more than five hours after several weeks of sleep restriction therapy, tell your doctor right away.

Energy **BOOSTER**

You just can't understand why you're so tired at 10 a.m. Here's a hint. If you skipped breakfast, you've had little or no food for 15 hours. You're basically sitting on empty. Preparing breakfast doesn't have to take long. Research shows that just one cup of high-fiber cereal can be enough to jumpstart your day.

Experts also say that combining protein and carbohydrates may help give you long-lasting energy. For a more portable breakfast, try a slice or two of peanut butter toast with a piece of fruit.

Action plan for a good night's sleep

You can improve your thinking and your sleep in just two weeks, and you may have a lot of fun doing it. Find out how putting more play in your day may mean more rest and relaxation at night.

Put sleep problems to rest. It sounds too good to be true, but a small Northwestern University study says this really works. Older adults who spent 90 minutes a day socializing and exercising said they started sleeping better after just two weeks. They also scored higher on tests of memory and thinking.

But the study participants didn't spend 90 straight minutes exercising to get these results. They started with a 30-minute session of walking, stretching, or doing exercises in place. Then they spent 30 minutes chatting while playing card or board games. And they finished up by doing 20 minutes of dancing, rapid walking, or calisthenics followed by 10 minutes of cool down exercises.

When it's as easy as walking, playing games, and dancing, why not try this drug-free remedy today? Start by pulling out your calendar and planning a half hour or so of socializing every day. You can plan lunches with family, evening card games with friends, or whatever suits your fancy. But don't forget to exercise. One study found that physical activity can be just as good at helping you fall asleep as prescription sleeping pills.

Exercise your right to a restful night. Physical activity doesn't just help you fall asleep. Many studies show it also helps you wake less during the night and spend more time in deep sleep. And if you choose the right exercise, you may only need nine minutes a day to improve your sleep, energy, mood, and memory.

That amazing exercise is tai chi. Don't let the strange name put you off. It's a remarkably easy workout of slow, gentle movements that takes you through various poses and stances. It's so simple that almost anyone can do it — even people in poor health. And you'll love the results. One study found that older adults with moderate sleep problems started sleeping better after just nine weeks of tai chi. And once you start sleeping better, you may find you have more energy, too.

On top of that, a study of people with dementia showed that five months of tai chi and cognitive behavioral therapy improved their mental abilities. Tai chi may also help ease depression, tension, and anger.

If you'd like to try tai chi or any other exercise, remember two things. First, clear it with your doctor. Then, set aside a time to exercise in the morning or before dinner each day. If you wait until after dinner, the stimulating effects of exercise may keep you awake.

Question & Answer

A relaxing weekend should lead to easier sleep on Sunday night, so why do I end up with insomnia?

If you use weekends to stay up late and sleep in, you may train your body to expect a new and later bedtime by Sunday night. Keep the same bedtime and waking time throughout the week — including weekends. Also, if you're worrying about the coming week's responsibilities, you may not be able to relax enough to sleep. Write a quick to-do list so you know you haven't forgotten anything, then focus on calm, relaxing activities after dinner.

9 ways to survive after a sleepless night

You're planning to see your doctor about your insomnia, but you still have to get through today. Try these fatigue-fighting tips to help keep you awake after a bad night.

Take a quick walk. Research has shown that just 10 minutes of moderate exercise, such as rapid walking, may ease fatigue and improve your energy and mood. So the next time you need to recharge, take a brisk 10- to 15-minute walk. If you're at work, walk during your lunch hour or break. Use the stairs or walk up and down hills for best results.

Let the sunshine in. Try walking outdoors, or sit outside where you can enjoy the sunlight for a few minutes. Bright light tells your brain to stop releasing melatonin, a hormone that helps make you sleepy. Spending some time in bright light may make you more alert.

Practice energy management. If possible, try not to do too much. Set priorities, keep expectations reasonable, and pace yourself. Plan to get things done when you feel most energized, and schedule breaks when your energy is low. Be sure to conserve energy when you can. For instance, don't waste energy standing when you can sit.

Use quick pick-me-ups sparingly. Caffeine and sugar raise cortisone levels, making you more alert, but you'll soon feel tired and drained when those levels plummet.

Plan a smarter lunch. Cut back on sugary and refined starchy carbohydrates like white rice, white bread, soda, and fruit juice in your lunch. They give you an initial rush of energy, but it will quickly fade, leaving you sluggish and sleepy. For better results, mix complex carbohydrates with lean proteins like fish, fiber-rich foods, and healthy fats like olive oil. This slows the energy rush from carbohydrates, spreads it out over several hours, and keeps your energy levels more stable. And here's a bonus tip — a large lunch may make you sleepy so stick with a smaller meal. Take the calories you remove from lunch, and spread them out across the day by eating small energy-boosting snacks like almonds, hummus, and fruit.

Try cinnamon and peppermint. Research shows that the smell of cinnamon or peppermint can help you stay more alert and focused. Peppermint may also reduce fatigue. Put peppermints or cinnamon sticks in a resealable plastic bag and take a whiff to wake up, or keep a potpourri or sachet in one of these scents. NASA suggests chewing gum as one way to help pilots stay awake, so chewing cinnamon or mint-flavored gum may be an even better bet.

Play your slump away. Give yourself an energy tune-up. Do a crossword puzzle, jigsaw puzzle, or computer game like Solitaire to get your mind going.

Sweep out the cobwebs. If you're at work, clean out your In Box or straighten up your workspace. If you're at home, do some light straightening in one room.

Thrill to the chill. Splash cold water on your face, or brush your teeth and gargle with minty mouthwash. Or to avoid getting too warm and cozy, turn on a fan, or rub a cool cloth or cold canned drink over your face and neck.

Little sleep tips that pack a big punch

Some sleep advice just seems hard to take seriously, even when it comes from your doctor. Surely keeping my bedroom dark isn't really powerful enough to help me sleep, you may think. But scientists say some "simple" tips can actually tweak the brain chemistry that helps you fall asleep and stay asleep.

Keep your room dark. As the world outside grows dim, the lack of light triggers your body to release melatonin, a hormone that helps you fall asleep and stay there. But if you're exposed to light, especially bright light, the pineal gland in your brain stops releasing melatonin, and your sleep may suffer. So keep your bedroom as dark as you can. And if you wake during the night, use just enough light to clearly see where you're going or what you need to do. Try not to turn on bright lights if you can safely do so.

Avoid having a nightcap. While it's true that alcohol can help you fall asleep, it also plays several tricks while you snooze. First, it interferes with your body chemistry, so you spend far less time in deep sleep and more time sleeping lightly. As a result, you wake up less rested and more tired. As if that's not enough, alcohol also relaxes your throat, making snoring more likely. If you have Restless Legs Syndrome, alcohol may also help trigger or aggravate your symptoms.

Relax with the right background noise. Thunderstorms, barking dogs, street noise, and snoring are like fire alarms for your brain. These noises force your brain to sit up and take notice even when you're trying to fall asleep. Animal research suggests loud sounds can also stimulate your brain out of deep sleep, making your sleep fragmented and less restful. "White noise" such as a fan or radio static masks these stimulating noises so your brain doesn't respond to them. This leaves your body free to fall asleep and stay sound asleep.

Visit the no-smoking zone. The nicotine you get from smoking may relax you at first, but then it turns into a stimulant. In fact, it revs up your brain wave activity, raises your heart rate and blood pressure, and makes your body pump out the same adrenaline you get when you face a scary situation. Try to have your last cigarette at least four hours before bedtime. If you would like to quit, be aware that a nicotine patch delivers small amounts of the drug round the clock, which could greatly disturb your sleep. Talk to your doctor about how you can quit smoking without making your insomnia worse.

Time your last coffee break. Caffeine blocks the effects of adenosine, one of the sleep-promoting compounds produced by your brain. As a result, caffeine makes you take longer to fall asleep and cuts into the amount of deep, restoring sleep you get. It may also increase the number of times you wake during the night. Caffeine's effects can kick in as quickly as 15 minutes and take three to five hours to go away, so you may want to avoid it in the evening. Some experts suggest having your last round of caffeine no later than six hours before bed.

QUICK*fix*

Create a relaxing routine during the last half hour before bed, and stick with it every night. This lets your body know it should be getting ready for sleep. You can include light, pleasant reading; gentle relaxation exercises; or other soothing activities. Over time, you'll program your brain to expect this routine to lead to sleep — helping you drift off more easily.

4 late-night fairy tales laid to rest

Experts say some of the things you've always heard about sleep aren't true. What's more, insomnia may play tricks on your mind, making you believe things that aren't accurate. Set the record straight on these four common fairy tales you probably tell yourself every night.

I must get eight hours of sleep. While it's true that eight hours of sleep is good for you, getting a little less may not be so bad. In fact, one study found that people who slept seven hours nightly had less risk of dying than those who slept eight hours or more. So aim for eight hours, but don't panic if you come up an hour short.

I'll never be able to fall asleep tonight. Once you've had trouble sleeping for awhile, you may dread getting ready for bed, going to bed, and trying to fall asleep. After all, you've been struggling to sleep for so long, you now worry that it can't be done. That anxiety can make your body produce norepinephrine, a natural compound that promotes wakefulness. This turns your fear of going to bed into a self-fulfilling prophecy. So instead of thinking, "I'll never get to sleep," repeat more relaxing thoughts such as "I always fall asleep after awhile" in your head. If you're still distressed after 20 minutes in bed, get up and do something soothing to ease the stress. Come back to bed when you're sleepy.

Horrible things will happen if I don't sleep soon. Insomnia naturally makes you worry that you won't perform at your best. In fact, many people expect insomnia to lead to disaster the next day. For example, you may worry that poor performance at work could make you miss out on a raise — or worse. But sleep experts point out that bad things can happen even after a good night's sleep. They say you shouldn't assume that lost sleep is the cause of a problem or that it guarantees a bad day. After all, you've probably managed to get through the day after a sleepless night once or twice before. So instead, remind yourself repeatedly, "I may not thrive tomorrow, but I'll probably do OK." This may help you relax enough to sleep.

Only sleeping pills can help. A recent study discovered that sleeping pills aren't as good or as long lasting as a newer, drug-free treatment for insomnia. That's good news because sleeping pills can be harmful in several ways.

- They may cause short-term memory loss, dizziness, high blood pressure, rebound insomnia, nausea, or grogginess.

- They may interact with other medications and cause uncomfortable or even deadly side effects.

- Some pills may be habit forming or make you do strange things like eat or drive during your sleep.

What works better than sleeping pills is something called cognitive behavioral therapy (CBT). Whereas sleeping pills treat the symptoms of insomnia, CBT treats the causes. In formal CBT, a professional works with you to debunk sleep fairy tales like the ones listed above.

He can also help you change unhealthy beliefs about sleep and fix behaviors that prevent sleep.

If you'd like to try CBT, get your doctor's permission. If she says yes, contact your insurance company to find out if they cover it. They may recommend a CBT professional, and some even offer computer-assisted CBT for free. Studies show that CBT programs on the Internet really can improve your sleep.

If your insurer or employer does not offer one, you can try a CBT program for around $25 at *www.cbtforinsomnia.com*. If you would rather work with a cognitive behavioral therapist, get a recommendation from your sleep doctor, or visit *www.academyofct.org*. If your insurer does not cover CBT sessions, expect to pay up to $150 per session for the five or so sessions needed to ease your insomnia.

Energy **BOOSTER**

Your body is smart — it gives you hints when it needs a break. Here are three quick ways to tell if your body craves some additional shut-eye.

- You're irritable and depressed.
- You've recently become forgetful.
- You drink more afternoon coffee.

You may think you're getting enough sleep, but these could be signs you need more. Getting a 20-minute nap helped people get through their afternoon slump better than a cup of coffee, a small British study found. By taking a short nap, you'll recharge your energy, improve your thinking, and feel much better.

Pros and cons of a midday siesta

Some people love to take naps, while others consider them a waste of time. Even experts are divided on the benefits of naps, especially for those who suffer from chronic insomnia. Learn what scientists on both sides of the argument say about when naps are good for you and when they mean trouble.

Protects your heart. A large Greek study found that midday siestas reduced men's odds of dying from heart disease. Frequent nappers had 37 percent less risk than non-nappers while occasional nappers had 12 percent less risk. Men who worked saw the most benefit while retirees saw almost none. The researchers suspect the possible stress-releasing powers of naps may be the reason they help working men more.

Makes you smarter. Studies suggest a good night's sleep improves both learning and memory. But daytime naps can help boost memory, too. In fact, one study found that a nap of only six minutes helped learning and memory a little bit while longer naps helped even more.

Question & Answer

Will I really feel better if I "sleep on it"?

Facing a thorny problem might be easier after a good night's sleep, but "sleeping on it" may not be wise if you're angry. Studies of people with and without heart disease have found that, in both cases, those who expressed their anger before going to bed slept better, but people who held that anger in slept more poorly. If someone or something has made you mad, go ahead and talk about it tonight. Then you really might feel better in the morning.

Studies like these may be one reason why a Harvard expert recommends naps for people who don't have insomnia. He says naps can be beneficial as long as they don't cause problems with your sleep at night.

Signals a problem. Napping has been associated with depression and diabetes, and daytime sleepiness can be a sign of sleep apnea or Parkinson's disease. When your health problems deprive you of sleep, naps can help you recover your lost energy. But if you don't know why you're so sleepy, or if you regularly sleep more than nine hours a day, see your doctor. He can help find and treat the cause of your problems, so you can start sleeping — and feeling — better.

Contributes to insomnia. Authorities have long said that people with insomnia should not take naps because it may interfere with nighttime sleep, particularly if you have chronic insomnia. Yet one study has recently suggested naps may not sabotage the nightly sleep of older adults, even for poor sleepers. So perhaps your best bet is to follow this expert advice. If you must nap during the day, limit your snooze to 30 minutes or less. And don't nap after 3 p.m. or within six hours of bedtime.

6 fun sleep-triggering tricks

Being awake in the middle of the night doesn't have to be miserable. In fact, doing something fun and relaxing while you're awake may help you get back to sleep faster. So if you haven't slipped back to slumber after 15 minutes, give these a try.

Turn yourself into a rag doll. Progressive muscle relaxation is a good tension-reducing technique that doesn't require much effort. Just sit or lie in a quiet, comfy place. Pick one group of muscles, like your right foot muscles, and tense them. Keep them tight for 15 seconds and then relax them. Do the same with the muscles in your other foot. Gradually move up your body tensing and relaxing each muscle group. Your body and mind should feel much better when you're done.

Take a dream vacation. Try to remember your last vacation spot, or imagine a luxurious vacation you'd like to take. Picture the trip in vivid detail including the sights, sounds, smells, and tastes. Don't leave anything out.

Create your own sound spa. Listen to soothing music or nature sounds.

Read 'em and sleep. Reading a favorite book is a time-honored way to get to sleep. Just make sure it's relaxing or uplifting rather than exciting. And definitely avoid any book or other reading that you "can't put down."

Follow the write route to rest. Keep paper and a pen by your bed, and try writing down your dreams or starting a poem or story. If the problem is tomorrow's to-do list, then go ahead and write it down along with an action plan for each item. Once you're done planning, you may be able to unwind and go to sleep.

Tame the midnight munchies. If you often wake up hungry, try keeping a small, sleep-encouraging snack like dried cherries on your night stand. Cherries are a good source of the natural slumber-promoting compound melatonin.

Whatever you choose to do when you wake during the night, keep these points in mind.

- Don't watch the clock. That just makes you more distressed about the sleep you're losing, and distress just keeps you up longer.

- Try to avoid bright lights or anything that might make you more awake than you already are.

- Avoid activities that are intriguing, exciting, or stimulating, especially those that might tempt you to stay awake. Instead, stick with enjoyable activities that relax your mind and body and will help you get back to dreamland sooner.

Nature's picks for sounder sleep

Take over-the-counter (OTC) sleeping pills long enough, and you could end up with thinking and perception problems or even dementia, new research suggests. The problem may be the drug diphenhy-dramine, more commonly known as benadryl. A review of studies found that sleeping pills containing benadryl, like Tylenol and Excedrin PM, may raise your risk of dementia and possibly Alzheimer's disease. But OTC sleeping pills also have side effects like dizziness, urinary problems, and constipation, even when the pills don't include benadryl.

Prescription sleeping pills are even worse. They may cause side effects like short-term memory loss, dizziness, incontinence, high blood pressure, nausea, and grogginess. And the older you are, the more likely these side effects will become a problem. Some pills may even be habit-forming or make you do strange things like eat during your sleep. Before using any type of sleeping pill, consider trying something more natural first.

Relax with chamomile. Remember the story of Peter Rabbit? After his narrow escape from Mr. McGregor's garden, Peter's mother gave him chamomile tea to help him sleep. Mrs. Rabbit had the right idea. Chamomile contains a compound called apigenin, which may have a gentle sedative effect. To make your own chamomile tea, steep one heaping teaspoon of flowers in hot water for 10 minutes. You can also buy store-brand tea, but it won't be as strong. Drink up to three cups a day. But don't use chamomile if you're allergic to ragweed, asters, daisies, or chrysanthemums because it's in the same family.

Wake up alert with valerian. Studies suggest valerian capsules can help you fall asleep faster and sleep better, but without morning grogginess or risk of addiction. One study even found that valerian worked as well as the prescription sleep aid oxazepam but with fewer side effects. Take 300 to 600 milligrams (mg) of valerian before bed every night. You should see results within a few weeks.

Sleep soundly with melatonin. Melatonin is a natural compound your brain produces to promote sleep. Although melatonin may not work for everyone, studies suggest that people who take melatonin supplements fall asleep faster and stay asleep longer. Melatonin may be particularly likely to help people whose natural melatonin levels have dropped — a problem more common in older adults. Research suggests taking a 300-microgram (mcg) capsule before bed. You can find higher doses, but they may keep you awake.

To get the best results from natural sleep aids, use these tips.

- Tell your doctor and pharmacist before you try an herb or supplement because even natural products may interact with medications, and some may not be safe for people with certain health conditions.

- Dietary supplements are not regulated, so some contain less active ingredient than promised and some may be contaminated. Ask your doctor or pharmacist to recommend a brand, or visit *www.consumerlab.com* to learn which products are uncontaminated and deliver what they promise.

- Do not take chamomile, valerian, or melatonin with any sedative or sleep aid or with alcohol.

- Taking valerian, chamomile, or melatonin may mask insomnia caused by a hidden medical condition, so see your doctor if your insomnia lasts more than a few weeks.

Best bets for banishing night sweats

Menopause may bring night sweats and hot flashes, but you don't have to live with them. Some products are made specifically to cool you down at night. Margaret favors the bed fan, which she found online at www.bedfan.com. It is a specially shaped fan you put at the foot of your bed, which blows cool air between the sheets. "I can now control night sweats," she declared after trying it out. "It really works."

Cooling pillows may also help. Some are filled with crystals that stay below room temperature, while others are filled with water you chill before bed. Alice uses one for her hot flashes. "I keep it next to my pillow and just roll over for instant relief," she says.

9 easy ways to kiss snoring good-bye

The snores of one British grandmother were recently clocked at 111 decibels — louder than a low-flying jet. No wonder her snores were waking her at night and causing her husband to flee to the guest room. But since the sound measurements were taken, the woman has found ways to improve her snoring without drugs or surgery. You can too.

If you're wondering what the big deal is about snoring, listen up. Snoring has been linked to a higher risk of diabetes, heart disease, high blood pressure, stroke, and traffic accidents. So steps you take to prevent snoring may help protect you against these dangers, too.

Plus, you may improve things on the marriage front. According to a National Sleep Foundation survey, 23 percent of those whose partner snores or has another sleep problem choose to sleep in another room. They are also more likely to report problems in their relationship and say that intimacy has been affected. Cutting out the snoring could not only make you a one-bedroom couple again but also strengthen your relationship.

Snoring occurs because something narrows your airway. The tighter space funnels air through your airway faster, which makes the walls of your throat vibrate and rattle, especially if they're slightly loose or relaxed. It's the vibration that makes that loud, obnoxious sound. So if you want to end snoring, you need to either keep your airway from narrowing or your throat walls from vibrating. Try these easy suggestions to help you do just that.

- Avoid sleeping on your back, which narrows your airway. Tuck pillows behind your back so you won't accidentally roll onto your back during sleep.

- Raise the head of your bed four inches. Try placing books or bricks under your headboard legs.

- Lose weight. Extra weight adds extra fat to your neck, constricting your airway.

- Get treated for allergies or sinusitis. A stuffy nose may make you breathe through your mouth while congestion may coat your throat and narrow your airway. See your doctor for medications that can help.

- Try nasal strips. These strips widen your nostrils and can help if allergies, colds, or sinusitis cause your problem.

- Avoid antihistamines. They tend to dry your throat, which promotes snoring.

- Stay away from sleeping pills. They relax your throat, which makes it vibrate more easily.

- Don't drink after dinner. Alcohol relaxes your throat muscles and narrows your airway for the first four hours after a drink.

- Quit smoking. Smoking irritates your throat and constricts your airway.

You can also try singing to strengthen your throat, dental appliances to help keep your airway open, or snore-fighting throat sprays.

Also, ask your doctor whether you have sleep apnea. If you snore loudly, gasp for breath during sleep, and experience daytime sleepiness, you may have this condition, where you temporarily quit breathing many times a night. Your doctor can order painless sleep tests to find out. Sleep apnea can be dangerous, so getting treatment may not only stop your snoring, it may also protect your health.

Fast fixes when you're too hot to snooze

Experts say you need to keep cool to sleep well. If your air conditioner is on the blink or you're suddenly having hot flashes, try one of these emergency "chill out" ideas to help you last through the night.

- Make a mini air conditioner. Fill a plastic milk or juice container with water until it's between half and three-fourths full. Put the lid on and stick it in the freezer. Or you can buy a pack of cold pops — those frozen plastic sleeves of flavored ice. Just before you go to bed, put either the pack of cold pops or the frozen container on a tray, and place in front of a fan. The frozen items will help chill the blowing air. To avoid disturbing your spouse, place the fan and its frozen partner close to you. Don't forget to refreeze your cold pops or jug for use the next night.

- Sleep with an ice pack. Dip a cloth in ice water, wring it out, and put it in the freezer for a couple of minutes. Then spread it across your chest, and turn the fan on in your direction. If you don't like the damp cloth, try wrapping a dry cloth around a frozen plastic bottle or an ice pack. You can also keep the ice pack by your pillow.

- Enjoy a cold glass of water before bed. Keep a thermos of ice water nearby so you can drink more if the heat wakes you during the night.

- Take a cool shower before bed.

- Wear a cotton gown or pajamas to bed, and use cotton sheets.

- Keep out daytime heat. If sunlight pours through your bedroom windows during the day, use light-blocking shades or dark curtains, and keep them closed. Keeping out the sunshine may make your bedroom cooler in the evenings.

- If all else fails, try sleeping downstairs. Heat rises so upstairs bedrooms may be hotter.

Secret weapon for pain-free rest

Your pillow isn't just a place to rest your head. When back pain and other health problems keep you awake at night, a pillow can become your secret weapon to help ease your symptoms and give you the shut-eye you deserve.

Relax back pain. Grab an extra pillow if back pain is keeping you up. Sleeping on your back puts heavy pressure on your spine. Placing a pillow under your knees can ease the pressure. For even better results, try to sleep on your side, and put a bed or sofa pillow between your knees. That takes even more pressure off your back.

Soothe allergies. Switch to a new pillow if allergies keep you up at night. An old pillow can harbor fungi and other allergens, especially if the pillow is made of synthetic materials.

Fend off leg cramps. Prop up your feet with a pillow if leg cramps often wake you during the night.

Cool heartburn pain. To fight nighttime problems with gastroesophageal reflux disease (GERD), pick up a wedge-shaped foam pillow. Sleeping with this wedge under your upper body raises your esophagus so acid stays in your stomach where it belongs instead of causing you pain. But if that's not a comfortable sleeping position, tuck the wedge behind your back to train you to sleep on your left side. This can help clear the acid out of your esophagus so you can fall asleep and stay asleep.

Tame neck pain. If your pillow tilts your neck and head upward or downward, it may be the cause of your neck pain. The right pillow places your neck in a neutral, untilted position that doesn't leave you feeling pained or strained in the morning. If you are seeing a doctor about neck pain, get his advice on what kind of neck pillow would be right for you.

QUICK*fix*

What you do during the day helps determines how well you sleep at night. Take these easy steps to help you sleep tight tonight.

- Morning: take a walk in the sunshine.
- Early afternoon: have your last caffeinated food or drink of the day.
- Late afternoon: exercise before dinner.
- Early evening: eat a light dinner and cut back on liquids.
- Evening: take a hot bath two hours before bed.

Pillow primer for perfect sleep

A bad pillow can keep you from getting a good night's sleep. Sometimes even expensive, new pillows can turn out to be slumber blunders. Before you buy your next pillow, consider these tips from a survey of pillow users on the Web site Sleeplikethedead.com. They may save you from buying pillows that steal your sleep away.

- Firm-pillow lovers should think twice before buying a down or down alternative pillow. User ratings suggest these are the softest pillows you can find. Instead, look for a pillow filled with buckwheat hulls or cotton. If you want something slightly less firm, memory foam pillows may also work well.

- If you want a pillow with good support, avoid buying feather pillows, down pillows, or down alternative pillows. Survey responders thought they got better support from pillows filled with cotton, microbeads, or buckwheat.

- If you're easily wakened by noises in the night, bypass buckwheat pillows, water pillows, and microbead pillows. When you shift position or move your head, the sounds made by buckwheat hulls, microbeads, or water may disturb your sleep.

- Don't choose down or feather pillows if you have allergies. According to user ratings, these may be the least hypoallergenic types of pillows. Stick with buckwheat, memory foam, latex, or microbead pillows instead.

For more details on pillow ratings and characteristics, visit *www.sleep-likethedead.com.*

Supercharged memory: amazing ways to age-proof your mind

Improve your memory in just two weeks

You can boost your brainpower in as little as 14 days. Scientists say that is exactly what occurred with people in a small study who followed a simple four-step program. And they didn't need special equipment, pills, or pricey "brain gyms." Here is what they did.

- ate five small meals each day instead of three large ones. They aimed for a diet loaded with omega-3 fats from fish and other foods, complex carbohydrates like beans and hearty whole grains, and antioxidants from brightly colored fruits and veggies.

- got heart-pumping aerobic exercise from brisk daily walks.

- did stretches and relaxation exercises to tame stress and help fine-tune their ability to concentrate.

- worked brain teasers, crossword puzzles, and memory exercises throughout each day to help focus attention and improve their memory skills.

After two weeks of these activities, the study participants not only scored better on verbal memory tests, but brain scans showed they had also begun using their brains more efficiently. Research suggests this program delivers a double reward for your efforts. It can help you improve your brainpower now and help reduce your risk of Alzheimer's disease in the future.

Of course, this is just the tip of the iceberg. For specific details on how to follow a plan like this one, keep reading. You'll discover ideas that go beyond this plan so you can do even more to stay sharp and help avoid dementia.

3 top dementia-defying tips

The lifestyle and nutrition choices you make every day may directly affect whether you eventually suffer from memory loss. Consider these examples.

- Stress management and what you drink and eat may affect the chemistry in your brain and help prevent plaques and shrinkage — sure signs of Alzheimer's disease.

- Good diet and sleep habits may help fend off inflammation in your brain. Chronic inflammation is also thought to contribute to Alzheimer's disease.

- Choosing antioxidant-rich foods will help you neutralize free radicals that promote damage in your brain. Good examples include deeply colored fruits and veggies like blueberries, spinach, and carrots.

Cut risk of memory failure in half

A funny-sounding fish from Down Under could be your ticket to better memory in your senior years. Barramundi, a native of northern Australia and parts of Asia, contains almost as much omega-3 fatty acids as wild salmon, making it a smart addition to your dinner plate. It is also easy to prepare and more contaminant-free than salmon. This fish may not be widely available so keep checking your local supermarket. Meanwhile, enjoy other omega-3 fish to start reaping fabulous brain benefits like these.

Prevent mental meltdown. A French study found that people over 65 who ate fish every week were 35 percent less likely to get Alzheimer's disease. After keeping tabs on hundreds of seniors for years, other scientists discovered older adults who ate three servings of fish a week had 47 percent less risk of any kind of dementia, including Alzheimer's disease. That is like cutting your risk in half. Omega-3 fatty acids like eicosapentaenoic acid (EPA) and docosahexaenoic acid (DHA) may be why. DHA is the most common fatty acid in your brain, and it is critical for normal brain function.

What's more, research suggests both DHA and EPA are inflammation fighters. They not only help prevent your body from making compounds that trigger inflammation but also help produce new ones to prevent inflammation. That is important because evidence is mounting that controlling inflammation is the key to preventing mental decline. Here is how it works.

One sign of inflammation is a substance called C-reactive protein (CRP). Doctors may order a certain type of CRP test to measure inflammation in arteries to determine heart disease risk. But a CRP test may also check inflammation in the rest of your body — including your brain. And in fact, research has found a link between high CRP levels and waning mental abilities. Studies even suggest inflammation may be the hidden factor behind Alzheimer's, diabetes, heart disease, and more. That is why the inflammation-fighting powers of fish may be crucial to your health.

Keep your brain plaque-free. Take in more DHA at the first sign of memory loss, and you may help prevent brain-clogging plaques from forming. Plaques are clumps of beta-amyloid protein that build up in your brain. They are also a possible cause of Alzheimer's disease. Fortunately, your body makes a protein called LR11 that may help stop plaques before they start. Like a natural Roto Rooter, LR11 helps scrub out proteins that form plaques.

The trouble is, some people have genes that prevent them from making enough LR11, a problem that may raise their risk of Alzheimer's disease. But a recent study found that DHA pushes brain cells to make more LR11. One study even found that DHA supplements may help fend off dementia in those who have the earliest signs of Alzheimer's. But why wait until memory loss sets in? Start eating fish rich in DHA before your memories start to slip away.

Top choices for brain-boosting fish

To get more omega-3 rich fish — especially those abundant in brain-healthy DHA — look for tasty choices like the ones listed below:

Fish	DHA grams per 3.5 oz.
Atlantic mackerel (not king mackerel)	1.6
Skipjack tuna	1.2
Lake trout	1.1
Lake whitefish	1.0
Atlantic herring	0.9
Anchovies	0.9
Sprat	0.8
Pacific herring	0.7
Sablefish	0.7
Sockeye salmon	0.7
Canned sardines	0.6

Get moving to expand your mind power

You can keep your mind sharp by growing a bigger brain. All it takes is a little aerobic fitness — even just walking the dog or square dancing — to help prevent mental decline.

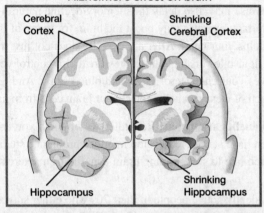

Alzheimer's effect on brain

Cerebral Cortex

Shrinking Cerebral Cortex

Hippocampus

Shrinking Hippocampus

One of the early signs of Alzheimer's is the shrinking of the hippocampus, a part of the brain that is critical for memory and learning. As the disease progresses, the cerebral cortex, which controls reasoning and judgment, also shrinks.

How do you "grow" your brain? By moving the rest of your body — quickly. According to brain scans by University of Pittsburgh scientists, older adults who were more aerobically fit had a bigger hippocampus than sedentary people. That is important because the hippocampus is the region of your brain associated with memory and learning. And Alzheimer's disease makes it shrink. *(See graphic above.)* In fact, the researchers found that fit individuals with a bigger hippocampus also performed better on memory tests.

Generate new brain cells. Brain scans show aerobic exercise improves your brain activity and helps add new brain cells to your hippocampus. Experts even say exercise may generate more new brain cells than anything else you can do.

This sounds like something you would expect from a revolutionary new drug, not from exercise. But one expert suspects you need an increased blood flow to the brain to create new brain cells and connections. And aerobic exercise is particularly good at rushing blood to your brain.

Preserve your memory. As if triggering new brain cells isn't enough, aerobic exercise may also delay the memory decline naturally caused by aging. In fact, exercise may boost the brain for many of the same reasons it helps your heart. After all, exercise does not just improve blood flow. It also lowers high blood pressure, helps control your weight, and improves your cholesterol levels and blood sugar. And research suggests each of these can help protect your brain cells from harm.

Reap the benefits at any age. Regardless of how old you are or whether you have started to develop memory problems, studies show it is never too late to start reaping brain benefits from exercise.

- Physically active people in their 70s who either stayed active or became more active significantly slowed their rate of mental decline, a study found. What's more, inactive older adults who started new exercise programs also improved their brainpower, especially their ability to process complex information quickly. All active study participants got their aerobic exercise from regular walks.

- Another study examined people who showed signs of mildly impaired memory. After six months, those who took three 50-minute walks a week — or did other aerobic exercise — scored better on memory and mental skills tests than people who did not exercise. Follow-up testing found this improved brainpower lasted at least 18 months.

Getting active does not have to be hard. A brisk walk in your neighborhood can make you more aerobically fit. You also get moderate physical exercise when you sweep out the screen porch, mow the lawn, shovel light snow, or hang clothes on a clothesline. Cycling, dancing, swimming, and jogging are more intense aerobic pursuits, but any activity qualifies that raises your heart rate and makes you breathe harder.

Slow path to better memory

Jogging, swimming and high-intensity aerobics probably are not right for you if you have trouble walking or rising from chairs. But you can still take steps to stay fit and maintain your brainpower. Discover three kinds of "slow" exercises that may help preserve your memory even when you are not in top shape.

Build mental and physical muscle. You do not have to spend hours lifting Olympic-sized barbells to keep your mind fit. A study of women age 65 and older found that lifting small weights for one hour twice a week can help you focus in spite of distractions, make better decisions, and solve conflicts.

The women in the study used free weights and weight machines for a year to get their results, but you do not have to join a gym. Stay at home and use substitute weights. You can lift cans of food, water bottles, soft drink bottles, or even a bag of sugar. Just remember to start slow, with perhaps two sets of 6-8 repetitions for each exercise, then increase the weight or the repetitions when the lifting becomes easy.

Stimulate memory with yoga. Yoga generally involves breathing exercises and a series of postures or poses — not exactly a recipe you'd expect to improve memory. Yet according to Indian researchers, men who spent 22 minutes alternating between yoga poses and relaxation exercises scored better on attention and working memory tests than men who simply lay still for 22 minutes. And these results occurred after just one session of yoga.

Boost your brain with tai chi. Like yoga, tai chi often involves a series of poses, but it also emphasizes gentle, circular movements between poses to loosen muscles and increase flexibility. Even though this is an exercise almost anyone can do, it may still benefit your brain. In fact, a small, preliminary study of older adults found that 10 weeks of tai chi helped improve "executive function" — the vital mental ability involved in planning, organizing, paying attention to details, forming concepts, and thinking abstractly. Future research will find out for sure whether tai chi improves memory as well.

If you would like to try strength training, yoga, or tai chi, ask your doctor's permission first. If she says you are ready for these exercises, get her advice on where to find classes, videos, or Web sites that can help you learn these slow but steady brain builders.

Simple**SOLUTION**

Good lighting and good shoes may help you prevent dementia and keep your quick wits. Here's why. Studies show head injuries raise your risk of both dementia and mental impairment. And according to the Brain Injury Association of America, falls are the most common cause of brain injury. Unfortunately, one out of every three older adults takes a tumble every year. Make sure you're not one of them.

- If you have balance problems, ask your doctor if your medications could be causing them.
- Be sure your home has good lighting, and keep your floors free of clutter.
- Get regular exercise to help improve balance. When walking, wear shoes with good support, and stick to well-lit areas.

Dementia prevention that really works

In 1988, researchers made an astonishing discovery. Mental tests had shown that a group of older adults were sharp as tacks and clearly had no signs of dementia, yet postmortem exams revealed their brains were riddled with signs of Alzheimer's, such as beta amyloid plaques. So how is it possible to have Alzheimer's and be symptom free?

After two decades of research, scientists think they may have the answer. The difference between healthy adults in the study and those with Alzheimer's was that the healthy adults had bigger brains and more neurons, a sort of "cognitive reserve" or mental savings account against the ravages of dementia. Later studies have suggested that at least 25 percent of older adults may already avoid Alzheimer's, thanks to this cognitive reserve. What's more, researchers suspect anyone can get these results just by frequently stimulating the brain with learning and other mentally engaging activities. This may work for several reasons.

- Neurons naturally shrink as you age, and your brain may shrink with them. This may even cause mild memory loss. But studies show mental exercise helps create new brain cells, adds new connections between them, and strengthens existing connections. That is like opening more roads in your brain so your brain impulses have more ways to get from point A to point B. Even if some of your brain's roads fail, your brain impulses have plenty of other routes they can use.

- Learning activities make your brain produce a compound called brain-derived neurotrophic factor (BDNF), a recent study discovered. BDNF is a kind of powerful mental fertilizer that helps brain cells operate at peak performance levels. BDNF is also an important ingredient for creating your memories.

- Mental exercise reduces the deposits that lead to beta amyloid plaques and clumps.

But you do not have to go back to school to get results like these. Experts say all kinds of mentally stimulating activities may help build your cognitive reserve, including leisure pursuits, learning, computer games and activities, and more. Perhaps the easiest mental exercise to try first is something called neurobics, a term created by the late neurobiologist Lawrence Katz in his book *Keep Your Brain Alive*. Neurobics means you stimulate your brain with novel experiences or by using your five senses in new ways. To get started, try neurobic activities like these.

- Use the opposite hand than you're used to for daily activities like brushing your teeth or fastening your seat belt.

- Take a different route to work. Or if you always take the same route through the grocery store aisles, start from the end of your route and work your way to the beginning.

- Listen to a radio station that has different music or content than what you're used to.

- Take your morning shower with your eyes closed, and use your other senses to do the things that help get you clean.

Just remember that once the challenge or novelty of the experience wears off, it is probably time to try something else new to your brain.

Question & Answer

Do you really use only 10 percent of your brain?

One expert calls this the "10-percent myth." Studies of brain scans show that most of your brain is active at any given time — even when you sleep. And by the end of a 24-hour day, experts say, you've probably used 100 percent of your brain.

Fun ways to fight memory loss

Neurobics is not the only way to build up a mighty defense against memory loss. Doing craft activities like pottery or quilting, playing games, reading books, or participating in computer activities may help slash your chances of memory loss by up to 50 percent, a Mayo Clinic study found. And that is only the beginning.

Find an activity that is fun, and chances are it will stimulate your brain as well. Take dancing, for example. You not only have to learn and remember your dance steps but also keep in step with your partner and make sure you don't step on his toes. Dancing may be fun, but it may also be serious preventive medicine.

A study in the *New England Journal of Medicine* found that dancing, reading, playing musical instruments and playing board games were linked to a lower risk of dementia. What's more, people who did these activities the most during an average week had 63 percent less risk of dementia compared with people who did them the least.

The reason this works is because your brain has something in common with your muscles. Bodybuilders regularly go to the gym to work out because using muscles more makes them stronger. Likewise, the more you "buff up" your brain, the stronger it becomes and the better it can resist memory loss. So when you sit down to a game of chess or put on your dancing shoes, you're not just playing. You're giving your brain a workout.

To develop the most mental muscle, research suggests you cross-train by doing more than one kind of mentally stimulating activity every week. According to researchers and experts, these activities are among the best ones to choose from:

- learning a second language
- writing
- playing card games

- doing crossword puzzles

- participating in group discussions

- knitting

- gardening

- traveling

- playing musical instruments

- dancing

- playing board games

- pottery

- quilting

- reading books

Search the Web for a mightier brain

Sitting down at your home computer may help you maximize your memory and limber up your thinking. So keep clicking your mouse, and you could be a snappy thinker for years to come.

Make the Internet your friend. You may already be doing things that help your brain. A Mayo Clinic study found that simply participating in computer activities may contribute to a lower risk of memory loss.

Two small, preliminary studies from UCLA suggest searching for information on the Internet not only stimulates your brain more than reading, but may also pump up the activity in the parts of your brain that support working memory, decision-making, and complex reasoning.

More research is needed to determine whether this really works, but meanwhile it can't hurt to make regular Internet searches a part of your routine.

Play "mind games" for more thinking power. Computer games are not just shoot-em-up time wasters anymore. While those types of games are available, you can also find more interesting games that may help you keep memory loss at bay.

For example, one research team taught older adults how to play a computer game that awards points for choices that turn a group of imaginary settlements into a prosperous and stable nation. Everyone trained on the game saw improvements in memory and reasoning. But those who became the most skilled also showed the most improvement in working memory and ability to juggle multiple tasks.

Since these are skills you use in day-to-day activities, experts suspect playing games like this may also improve your ability to accomplish the daily activities of independent living. In fact, the National Science Foundation takes this possibility so seriously that it recently awarded a million-dollar grant for research on whether computer games can help boost memory and thinking in older adults.

But your options do not end with store-bought computer games. Private companies offer "brain gym" Web sites or software full of games and activities that promise to help you pump up your brain for a fee. You can also find free Web sites full of puzzles or games online. Before you spend money for brain-training games, why not try some of the free options online such as *games.aarp.org*? You may be pleasantly surprised by the results.

12 easy ways to supercharge your memory

The newly crowned bronze medalist at the USA National Memory Championship admitted her memory probably wasn't all that good. But practicing with mental images and other tricks had helped her remember the order of all the playing cards in an entire deck. While you may not need to remember playing cards, you can boost your memory with similar techniques like these.

Picture it. Any time you learn new information — including names — create a mental image to go with it. For example, if your new friend's name is Katherine Queen, perhaps you'll picture Katherine Hepburn in *The African Queen*.

Try spaced rehearsal. Focus on learning new material for a while, and then put it aside. Revisit and relearn it every few hours, once a day, or every few days. This helps the information stick even better and longer.

Link it. Consider how new information relates to what you already know. This connection helps interweave the new memory with your existing knowledge.

Chunk it. To help remember a long string of items, break it into chunks. For example, you probably split your social security number into three groups of numbers when you say it, or perhaps you remember your pin number, 5647, as "fifty-six forty-seven."

Recall lists. To remember a group of items, try the tricks called mnemonics. For example, an acronym can help you remember the name of an organization (NASA for National Aeronautics and Space Administration) or the colors of the rainbow (ROY G BIV for red, orange, yellow, green, blue, indigo, violet). You can also use rhymes or stories to connect groups of items in your mind.

Focus on names. When you first meet someone, repeat the person's name to be sure you've understood it. You can even ask them to spell it for you. Use the name often in conversation to cement it in your mind.

Reinforce it. When you want to either remember something or remember that you've finished a task, say it out loud. For example, you might say, "It's 10 a.m. on February 2, and I just took my antibiotic."

Use all your senses. If you need to pick up peaches on the way home, picture them in your mind. Then imagine how they'll taste and smell, think of the feel of them in your hand, and say the word peaches aloud to yourself.

Organize. Make a place for every item, and always tuck that item back in its place. For example, always put your keys or cell phone in the same spot when you get home.

Put routines to work for you. Take your medicine at the same time every day.

Use productivity tools. When information overload hits, young professionals use a variety of tools to help. You can, too. Use to-do lists, schedule books or day planners, calendars, post-it notes, notepads, wristwatch or cell phone alarms, voice recorders, maps, file folders, or even hand-held electronic organizers. The time spent making notes and lists can help you remember things better.

Jog your memory. When a word or name is on the tip of your tongue, but just won't come to you, relax and stop trying so hard. Research suggests the answer may be more likely to come to you if you step back and let your brain work on it unsupervised. If you can't do that, recite the alphabet in your head. When you reach the letter that your word begins with, it may suddenly bring the word to your mind.

Question & Answer

Am I doomed to more memory loss if I don't have a college degree?

No. Just because people with less education may have a higher risk of dementia and mental decline does not mean you can't do anything about it. People with less education who regularly spent time reading, doing word games or puzzles, writing, and attending lectures scored just as well on memory tests as people with more education, a Brandeis University study found. So stop worrying about how much learning you may have missed in the past, and start hunting for fun, new ways to jump-start your brain.

QUICK *fix*

Keep your mental edge with these tips. According to the latest research, they really work.

Brush and floss. Studies suggest people with either inflammation from gum disease or tooth loss have a higher risk of dementia. Practice good dental care, and see your dentist regularly.

Limit TV. Watching less than seven hours of television a day may halve your risk of mild cognitive impairment, a less severe form of memory loss that may lead to dementia.

Know your ideal weight. Being underweight can raise your risk of dementia, researchers recently discovered. Ask your doctor how much you should weigh. If you are underweight, get his advice on any problems that affect your weight.

Socialize to stay sharp

Having a large social network may cut your risk of dementia. But what do you do if you recently retired to a new town and don't know anyone yet?

Starting your social life over from scratch may seem intimidating, but don't let that stop you. A Harvard study found memory declined twice as rapidly in people who were the least socially involved compared to those who were the most socially active. And that simply meant participating in volunteer activities, being married, or having contact with parents, neighbors, and children.

The researchers say many aspects of socializing may help maintain your memory. For example, the thinking and memory skills required by a social gathering may help keep your brain busy and active. On the other hand, spending time with people you care about may give you a sense of purpose that may have positive effects on your brain.

Socializing may even help prevent high blood pressure and other health conditions that may lead to memory loss. Other studies have also found a bigger social network, extra emotional support, and higher levels of social involvement can help you keep more of your brainpower for longer, while also cutting your risk of dementia. In one study, women's dementia risk dropped 26 percent because of their active social life.

To help gain these advantages for yourself, start with these tips.

- If you live alone, start simple and get a pet. Not only do experts count time with pets as socializing, but you may meet all sorts of interesting people when you take the dog — or rabbit — out for a walk.

- Now that you have moved, reconnect with the people from back home or with other friends or relatives you have not communicated with for a while. They will probably be glad to hear from you.

- Volunteer at a charity, hospital, or any other organization that promotes a cause you believe in. Or find out whether the Experience Corps has a program in your new town. People who volunteer with this organization help school children improve their reading and library skills. One study found that Experience Corps volunteers improved basic planning, problem solving, and reasoning skills needed for normal daily living. The improvement in brain activity even showed up in brain scans. To find the nearest Experience Corps program, visit *www.experiencecorps.org*, or call 202-478-6190.

- Make some homemade bread or a favorite dessert, or pick some flowers from your garden. Take this to your new neighbors so you can get to know them better.

- Buy a newspaper, or seek out your new town's Web site to find out what free activities or classes are coming up soon.

- Take a class in something that interests you. If classes are not available, look for clubs that match your interests.

- Get involved in your favorite fitness activity. Join a walking club or gym, or take a tai chi or water exercise class.

- Find out what is available at the senior center or local offices for aging.

- Learn what kinds of activities and courses are available at your community center.

3 ways to give your brain a tune-up

Making just a few simple changes in your life can help you avoid forgetfulness, Alzheimer's, and even the common "brain fog" of advanced age. Even better, these changes can help you today and for many years to come.

Sleep your way to a better memory. Your fading memory and concentration may not be as bad as you think, especially if you battle insomnia, sleep poorly, or often skimp on sleep. According to the National Sleep Foundation, people with insomnia have trouble concentrating. What's more, you must have regular sleep for your memory to work well.

While you sleep, your brain processes recently learned information so you can remember it better. This is also when your brain turns short-term memories into lasting, long-term memories. In fact, studies show people get better at remembering information learned the previous day once they have had a good night's sleep.

Sleep helps protect your memories in several other ways. Research suggests sleep loss or poor sleep can raise your odds of diabetes, which increases your risk of Alzheimer's disease. A University of Chicago study found that people prevented from reaching the deeper stages of sleep for only three nights developed problems with glucose tolerance and insulin sensitivity, two signs of a higher risk of diabetes.

Another study discovered that people who sleep less than six hours a night are nearly five times more likely to develop impaired fasting glucose, a blood sugar problem that may also lead to diabetes. Additional research shows that people with type 2 diabetes have a higher risk of Alzheimer's disease and other types of dementia. Some experts suspect this may happen because an insulin deficiency or insulin resistance may damage brain cells and lead to inflammation in the brain.

If falling asleep, staying asleep, or sleeping well is hard for you, see the chapter *Sounder sleep puts new life into your days* for powerful, drug-free ways to get the sleep you need so you can think better, remember more, and send brain fog packing.

Manage stress for mental success. Stress may not seem all that harmful, but it spells trouble for your body — as well as your mind. According to experts, high stress can:

* interfere with your memory.
* inhibit recall.
* reduce your ability to pay attention.

- raise your risk of dementia.

- release hormones that may damage your brain cells.

Scientists think long-term stress can even shrink the part of the brain associated with memory and learning. Fortunately, fixing this problem can be easy. When stress prevents you from remembering something, slow down and relax, and it may pop into your mind.

For long-term stress, start down the road to tranquility by learning relaxation techniques, like deep breathing. And to really tame stress, visit *Stress busters that set you free* and discover invaluable tips that can help you defeat stress. Your brain will thank you.

Focus attention to remember more. Information overload and distractions are common today. In fact, researchers suggest some memory lapses occur because you can't give your full attention to the information you want to remember. So try an experiment. Use these tactics to see if they help you remember.

- Take extra time to block out all distractions. Think "this is important" to help you focus. If necessary, go someplace quiet and free of distractions.

- Avoid multitasking. Trying to learn or remember two things at once makes it harder to retain either one.

- Concentrate exclusively on what you want to remember for at least eight seconds.

Little-known memory stealers

Your allergy medicine, painkillers, or prescription drugs could put you at higher risk for dementia. Maybe you've even suddenly started having problems with concentration, attention, and problem solving. But don't panic. Finding out what you're up against may make a significant difference in your symptoms and your risk.

Meet the mind robbers. A recent review of research found a possible link between brain disorders, like dementia, and certain prescription and over-the-counter (OTC) drugs. These drugs were also linked to two other conditions:

- delirium — a sudden, severe mental confusion that may be accompanied by delusions

- cognitive impairment — mild memory loss or reduced thinking and intellectual abilities

The class of drugs that may raise your risk of these problems is called anticholinergics. Anticholinergics block acetylcholine, a compound your brain needs for memory and learning. Unfortunately, hundreds of prescription and OTC drugs contain anticholinergic ingredients. For example, one anticholinergic drug called diphenhydramine is an ingredient in some cold and allergy medicines like Benadryl, sleep aids like Unisom or Sominex, and in some painkillers with "PM" at the end of their names — like Tylenol PM. Other anticholinergics may turn up in some prescription medications for high blood pressure, asthma, insomnia, incontinence, depression, anxiety, Parkinson's disease, cholesterol, and heart failure.

Know your risk. So why doesn't everyone who takes diphenhydramine develop dementia? Taking anticholinergics alone isn't enough to guarantee problems with your brain. Other factors, including age, also matter. For example, experts say you are more likely to be affected as you grow older for several reasons.

- The average older adult takes five or more prescription drugs. The more drugs you take, the more likely you are to take anticholinergics. And the more anticholinergics you take, the more likely you may be to develop dementia or another brain disorder.

- Older adults are more sensitive to the anticholinergic effects of these types of drugs.

- As you age, your body takes longer to eliminate medications.

Protect your brain. If you're worried about your risk of Alzheimer's or if you're an older adult experiencing memory or thinking problems, make a list of every medication you take. Include both OTC and prescription drugs. Ask your doctor and your pharmacist if medications on the list have side effects or drug interactions that can cause memory or thinking problems. If your doctor or pharmacist says yes, ask to switch to another medication. One expert believes long-term use of anticholinergics may triple your risk of Alzheimer's, so eliminating these medications may help. What's more, if your memory and thinking symptoms come from a drug, they're likely to disappear after you switch to a new medication.

A word of caution — never stop taking a drug your doctor prescribed without his approval.

Surprising cure for memory loss

Harry and his wife first noticed that his 89-year-old mother had begun to have problems with memory loss when they saw her at Christmas. "By the time we visited again in July," he explains, "Mother's memory loss had gotten much worse, and she was easily confused by simple daily activities."

In desperation, Harry checked medical sites on the Web to learn more about dementia. That's when he stumbled across an article about the side effects of a bladder control medicine his mother was taking. Severe memory loss was one of them. Harry and his wife helped his mother switch to a new bladder control medicine. "Within three months, she was completely back to normal," Harry says.

What to drink to save your memory

What you drink with breakfast may help protect you against dementia and memory loss. While not all morning beverages can help, here are a few that can.

Discover the power of fruit juices. People who drink fruit or vegetable juice three times a week were 76 percent less likely to develop Alzheimer's than people who drink juice less than once a week, a Vanderbilt University study reported. Other studies suggest this even includes commercial juices made from concentrate, so the orange juice you had this morning may be more helpful than you thought.

Free radicals and inflammation in the brain may contribute heavily to Alzheimer's disease, experts suspect. That's partly why the Vanderbilt researchers think juices rich in polyphenols may work best to cut your risk. Polyphenols have antioxidant and anti-inflammatory powers. What's more, research has shown that polyphenols in apple, grape, and citrus juices have more power to protect your brain than antioxidant vitamins. And recent studies suggest the polyphenols in apple and citrus juices can make their way into your brain for on-the-spot protection.

But other juices may also help. A small study found that older adults with memory problems significantly improved their learning and memory test scores after 12 weeks of drinking 2 1/2 cups of blueberry juice a day.

Add brain cell "bodyguards" with coffee. Many people like to start their day with a cup of coffee, thanks to the extra energy boost they get from caffeine. But that boost may come with extra benefits. Older men who drank coffee showed less mental decline than those who didn't, researchers reported. One cause of mental decline is a compound called beta amyloid, which can damage your brain cells. But the caffeine in coffee may trigger a chain reaction that sends special compounds to defend your brain cells against beta amyloid damage.

If you drink coffee, just remember to avoid it late in the day. Otherwise, the caffeine may keep you awake at night.

QUICK *fix*

Tofu lovers beware. Too much of a good thing may lead to dementia. A recent study found that older Indonesian men and women who ate the most tofu were more likely to have memory loss. Researchers think the phytoestrogens in soy may have harmful effects on older brains. Eating tempeh, a fermented soy product, was not associated with memory loss. Tempeh may be safer because the fermentation process increases its folate content — and folate protects your brain.

Another study of Japanese men found that those who ate tofu twice a week or more were also more likely to develop memory problems as they aged. Limit your tofu to once a week and replace tofu with tempeh whenever possible.

8 snacks to keep you smart

Snacking can be good for you. Turn your next snack attack into an excuse to eat "brain foods" that can help defend your mind. Start with these delicious choices.

Blackberries. Studies suggest inflammation and free radical damage contribute to the mental decline that comes with aging or dementia. Fortunately, antioxidants can prevent free radical damage.

Laboratory studies show that blackberries have very potent antioxidant and anti-inflammatory powers. Maybe that is why a recent animal study found that blackberries can help improve memory. The secret behind this blackberry success may be polyphenols called anthocyanins. These anthocyanins not only give blackberries their familiar dark color, they also supply extra antioxidant and anti-inflammatory power to defend your brain. Other polyphenol-rich choices include blueberries, walnuts, strawberries, cranberries, spinach, and plums.

Bagel. Bagels are rich in folic acid, an important B vitamin, and they taste particularly good with blackberry jelly. One study found that risk of Alzheimer's disease was up to 50 percent lower in people who got the most folic acid. To make sure you get enough of this vital vitamin, enjoy foods like enriched white rice, lentils, black-eyed peas, pinto beans, black beans, and asparagus.

Cereal. Cereals like Product 19 and Special K are good sources of vitamin B12. That is important because a recent study found that older adults with the highest blood levels of B12 were six times less likely to experience brain shrinkage, a problem that can lead to memory loss or dementia. Older adults absorb less of this vitamin so feed your body as many foods rich in B12 as you can. Good choices include meat, fish, milk, and fortified cereals.

Many cereals are also excellent sources of vitamin D. That is good news because low levels of vitamin D in your blood have been linked to dementia. You need vitamin D to help protect your brain cells. Unfortunately, people over age 60 are more likely to be deficient in this vitamin. Talk to your doctor about whether you should be tested for vitamin D deficiency. Meanwhile, eat plenty of foods high in vitamin D like milk, fish, and cereal.

Apples. Apples are not only rich in antioxidants, they are a good source of the trace mineral boron. A research nutritionist with the U.S. Department of Agriculture suggests not getting enough boron in your diet may affect your memory and thinking processes. He also points out that most people may not be getting enough boron for brain health. To add more boron to your diet, eat apples, peanut butter, and raisins.

Walnuts. Adding a handful of walnuts to your diet may help improve short-term memory, an animal study suggests. But don't eat more than nine walnuts a day or your waistline may expand.

Brown rice. For busy days, make this snack ahead of time. Cook up some brown rice, mix in raisins, sprinkle with cinnamon, and mix in a little honey. Brown rice is rich in vitamin B3 (niacin). But when niacin gets in your body, it becomes another form of B3 called nicotinamide.

A recent animal study found that extra nicotinamide helped prevent thinking and memory problems in animals with dementia. Although more research is needed, you might want to start eating more foods rich in vitamin B3, like brown rice and chicken.

Cauliflower. Add cauliflower to chopped veggies and dip them in your favorite dressing or veggie dip. The cauliflower can give you something extra — a compound called citicoline. A recent animal study found that extra citicoline helped prevent a kind of brain damage that may lead to vascular dementia, the second most common type of dementia. It may also have positive effects on memory and learning ability. To give your body extra citicoline, enjoy more fish and peanuts.

Cocoa. Dark chocolate bars and dark chocolate hot cocoa can be good for you in small amounts. That is because they contain antioxidants called flavanols. In a small study, people did better on challenging math problems and experienced less mental fatigue on days when they drank hot cocoa high in flavanols. Researchers aren't sure why, but they suspect the flavanols increase blood flow to the brain. That's a good excuse to keep some dark chocolate hot cocoa on hand for days when your brain needs an extra boost.

How to take dementia off the menu

Every meal you eat could help trim your risk of memory loss or bring you one step closer. The key is to know which foods belong on your menu and which ones mean trouble.

Choose the right fats. People who ate the most saturated fats and trans fats were twice as likely to develop Alzheimer's disease as people who avoided these fats, one study suggested. Another study of healthy adults over age 65 found that those who ate the most saturated fats and trans fats showed the most mental decline during a six-year period.

Saturated fats are the kind you find in meat, whole milk, cheese, and butter. Trans fats are common in fast foods, fried foods, and packaged foods. Replace trans fats and saturated fats with unsaturated fats from foods like fish, olive oil, canola oil, avocados, natural peanut butter, and nuts.

Beware the low-carb diet. Weight may not be the only thing you lose on a low-carbohydrate diet, particularly if you kick off your diet by eliminating carbohydrates completely. A small Tufts University study found that women who completely stopped eating carbohydrates did more poorly on memory tests than women on a low-calorie diet with carbohydrates. When the no-carb women switched to a diet that allowed small amounts of carbohydrates, their memory test scores improved.

Anytime you eat carbohydrates, like grains, fruits, and vegetables, your body breaks them down into glucose. Your brain runs on glucose the way your car runs on gas. As a result, when you eliminate carbs, you cut off the fuel supply for your brain. The Tufts University researchers recommend keeping at least a few carbohydrates in your diet at all times.

Follow the Mediterranean way. Imagine yourself lounging on a sun-drenched Greek island in the Mediterranean sea and learning to eat like the locals. You would enjoy plenty of fresh fish, hearty whole grains and beans, vibrant fruits and vegetables, crunchy nuts, and healthy olive oil. This may not sound like medicine for your mind, but studies suggest that people willing to eat this Mediterranean diet may be at least 40 percent less likely to get Alzheimer's disease. That is a remarkable difference. Just remember these easy guidelines:

- Eat fatty fish, like salmon and herring, but very little red meat.

- Include only small amounts of chicken and turkey.

- Limit yourself to just a few eggs each week.

- Skip high-fat dairy products, like ice cream and whole milk. Choose skim milk and nonfat yogurt instead.

- Aim for seven to 10 servings of fruits and veggies every day. Stir-fry or steam any vegetables you cook.

- Enjoy whole-grain breads and cereals and try new choices, like brown rice, couscous, and bulgur.

- Add more walnuts, almonds, and other nuts to your diet, but skip salted or honey-roasted nuts.

- Find new ways to add beans to your diet.

- Eat more good fats, like avocados and olive oil.

Energy **BOOSTER**

Take a few enjoyable minutes in the morning to eat breakfast, and studies show you will improve your memory and stamina. It's true. Canadian research shows the fat, carbohydrates, and protein in breakfast can enhance your memory. Other studies agree. What's more, skipping breakfast means you probably go without food for at least 14 hours. No wonder breakfast improves your stamina.

Even more amazing, one study discovered that breakfast skippers are four and a half times more likely to become obese than people who eat breakfast. Another reason to enjoy a low-sugar, low-fat breakfast that is high in fiber, carbohydrates, and protein — like whole-grain toast with peanut butter and fruit.

Heart-smart tricks that keep your brain healthy

Heart-smart tactics could become your secret weapon against memory loss and dementia. A French study found that treating heart risk factors slowed the progress of dementia in people who already had it. That's a great reason to try these four simple ways to fend off heart attacks, strokes, and memory loss — all at the same time.

Take a weight off your mind. Dropping even a few pounds can help your heart, but it won't just be your heart that will thank you. According to one study, people who were obese at middle age were three times more likely to develop Alzheimer's than people at a healthy weight. This may happen because fat cells produce dangerous inflammatory compounds that travel into your brain. But a German study found that people who cut calories and lost 5 to 8 pounds scored better on memory tests after only three months.

Replace salt with spices. The problem with salt is it's almost half sodium. Too much sodium can raise your blood pressure. That's why eating less salt is a key way to fight high blood pressure, a problem that can lead to small, silent strokes or brain plaques that can affect your memory over time. Research shows that people who have high blood pressure during middle age were 60 percent more likely to develop dementia than people with normal blood pressure. Preliminary studies suggest taking steps to treat or avoid high blood pressure may help. So aim to keep your blood pressure below 120/80 mm/Hg.

Ditch fried and prepackaged foods. These often contain trans fats that can raise your bad LDL cholesterol and lower your good HDL cholesterol. A cholesterol level over 200 mg/dL may contribute to dementia-causing plaques in your brain or trigger problems that reduce critical blood flow to your brain. Maybe that's why high total cholesterol during middle age has been linked to higher risk of mental impairment and dementia. But that's not all.

A recent study suggests that people with HDL cholesterol under 40 mg/dL are 53 percent more likely to have memory loss than people with HDL above 60 mg/dL. Scientists suspect this happens because HDL may help prevent plaques in the brain. Good ways to raise your HDL include aerobic exercise, losing weight if you are overweight, avoiding trans fats, and quitting smoking. These tactics may also help lower your total cholesterol.

Eat more fiber. Eating fiber-rich foods, like whole grains, slows your body's ability to absorb the glucose that raises your blood sugar. Fiber may also reduce your risk of developing diabetes. That is good news because diabetes and high insulin levels can nearly double your risk of Alzheimer's disease. Here's how.

- Diabetes damages blood vessels in your brain.

- High blood sugar may damage your brain cells.

- High insulin levels may help prevent the natural breakdown of beta amyloid, a protein linked to plaques and Alzheimer's.

Fortunately, early studies suggest good blood sugar control may help prevent mental decline.

For details on these heart-smart tactics, see *Natural remedies that pump up your heart, Safe & steady blood sugar for nonstop energy,* and *Belly fat: easy ways to slenderize and energize.*

Straight talk about alcohol

Although heavy or binge drinking may raise your risk of memory loss, mild-to-moderate drinking may have the opposite effect. Drinking small amounts may help improve blood flow to your brain, some health professionals think. But if you don't drink, don't start. If you do drink, remember that a 12-ounce beer or 5-ounce glass of wine counts as one drink. Limit yourself to two drinks a day if you're a man and one if you're a woman.

Reverse 'false' dementia

Forgetfulness and confusion are not always a sign of Alzheimer's. Other medical conditions can cause similar symptoms that may diminish or even vanish once you get treatment. Before you worry that your symptoms are signs of Alzheimer's, follow this advice.

Talk to your doctor. One man who thought he had symptoms of Alzheimer's was amazed to learn he did not have dementia at all. Instead, he was diagnosed with normal pressure hydrocephalus, a condition where too much fluid presses on the brain. After medical treatment, his Alzheimer's symptoms virtually disappeared.

While not everyone will get such dramatic results, ask your doctor about this if you also have walking and incontinence problems. Other health issues may also cause memory problems, poor thinking, or confusion. Examples include diabetes, low thyroid function (hypothyroidism), and sleep apnea. Ask your doctor if you should be checked for these or any other conditions that can cause false dementia symptoms.

Check your B12. Vitamin B12 doesn't just affect your risk of getting dementia. A deficiency in B12 may fool a doctor into thinking you already have Alzheimer's disease — even if you don't.

Vitamin B12 helps keep your nerve cells healthy. Getting enough B12 becomes tougher as you age because your body does not absorb it from foods as efficiently as in the past. That makes your risk of deficiency go up. If you become deficient in B12, you may develop problems with memory loss and confusion that can be mistaken for Alzheimer's. If you develop these problems, ask your doctor if you should be treated for vitamin B12 deficiency. The earlier this deficiency is treated, the more likely you are to make a full recovery.

Track your liquids. As you grow older, your body's ability to make you thirsty diminishes. That may be one reason why dehydration causes nearly 7 percent of hospitalizations among older adults. Dehydration happens when your body gets too low on fluids. Research shows dehydration can cause poor mental performance, poor short-term memory, and slowed reaction times in decision making. Get your doctor's advice on how much water you need to drink every day, and keep track of whether you are meeting that goal. Drink extra water when conditions are hot or dry or any time you exercise or do physical work. And watch out for these signs of dehydration:

- dry lips and mouth
- dizziness or headaches
- forgetfulness, confusion
- rapid breathing
- increased heart rate
- dark urine, constipation
- weakness, lack of energy

Beware the alcohol trap. Alcohol may interact with some medications to cause memory loss. If you drink alcohol, ask your doctor or pharmacist for advice.

Think positive for better memory power

One reason your memory might get worse as you age is because you expect it to. Older adults who believed seniors perform more poorly on memory tests actually scored lower on those tests than other seniors, researchers found. Another study discovered that middle-age and older adults who expected to hang on to their memory and thinking skills outscored those who didn't.

Instead of worrying about memory loss, focus on what you are trying to remember or learn right now. This helps hone your memory skills. Keep replacing your memory worries with new memory challenges for your brain, and you may be surprised by how good your memory and thinking can be.

Stress busters that set you free

Eat your way to stress relief

Goodbye, stress balls and worry beads. Hello, whole foods and produce. The new way to battle your everyday stress involves your refrigerator — not your toy box. Get enough of the right essential nutrients, and you will de-stress, re-energize, and feel better starting today.

Replace mind-soothing minerals. Both magnesium and calcium can be excreted from your body quickly during stress, so you may not have the stores of these essential nutrients you need.

When you feel anxious, you have lower levels of glucose in your blood, which leads to a rise in catecholamines — fight-or-flight hormones like epinephrine that your body pumps out to handle the extra stress. This hormonal change, in turn, lowers the level of magnesium in your body. Research on college students found that during exam time students did indeed lose extra magnesium in their urine. But it gets worse. When you're under stress, you release cortisol, known as the stress hormone, which causes your body to excrete too much calcium. That's two important minerals down the drain.

Replace what you lose by getting more calcium and magnesium from food. Spinach, sunflower and pumpkin seeds, and navy or black beans are all great sources of magnesium. For calcium, look to low-fat dairy foods like milk, yogurt, and cheese, along with spinach and collard greens.

Keep cortisol in balance. Be sure you get enough of these other nutrients, which can affect your cortisol levels.

- Omega-3 fatty acids. Abundant in fish oil, this heart-healthy fat works as a buffer for excess stress hormones. Research among university workers at an Australian college found that taking omega-3 supplements for six weeks helped them feel less stress and hostility. They took 1-1/2 grams of a specific omega-3, docosahexaenoic acid (DHA), every day. The DHA seemed to lower blood levels of norepinephrine — one of those fight-or-flight hormones — and reduced levels of proteins that raise inflammation in your body. Try eating fatty fish like salmon and tuna to get this healthy fat from your plate rather than from a pill.

- Vitamin C. This important antioxidant vitamin supports adrenal gland function. Getting enough vitamin C will help stabilize your cortisol levels. You need some vitamin C every day, so look for good sources like strawberries, orange juice, sweet peppers, and broccoli.

- B vitamins. These water-soluble nutritional gems do a lot to help your body fight the damage of stress. Thiamin and pantethine keep your body from pumping out too much cortisol. In fact, pantethine, or vitamin B5, is sometimes called the anti-stress vitamin because it helps your body make adrenaline and boosts your stamina. Vitamin B6 helps you make certain brain chemicals that allow you to deal with stress. Get what you need from whole grains like oatmeal, brown rice, and whole wheat and rye flours.

SimpleSOLUTION

Biting your nails is a classic symptom of stress. Take control of your hands, and you will have lovely nails in no time.

- Rubber band therapy. Associate your bad habit — nail biting — with a bit of pain, and you can break the habit. Wear a rubber band around your wrist, and snap it every time you find yourself chewing on your nails.

- Quick cover-up. Apply artificial nails or Band-Aids on your finger tips. The physical barrier will keep you from biting and remind you to stop.

- Terrible-taste treatment. Creams or nail polishes that taste bad can help you remember to keep your fingers out of your mouth. Look for the products Mavala Stop or Control-It.

Tame tension with regular tea time

Sitting down to a nice cup of tea is a relaxing experience. New research shows it's not just the warm cup, tasty muffin on the side, or soothing company that gets the credit for putting you at ease. Ingredients in several types of tea actually lower your body's response to stress.

Kick back with black tea. A study of young men in London, a city of tea drinkers, found those who drank black tea four times a day for six weeks enjoyed a lower stress response. They were compared with men who drank a similar beverage that did not contain tea. Both groups were presented with a stressful event, like the possibility of losing their jobs or being accused of shoplifting. They then had to defend themselves in front of a camera. Researchers found the tea drinkers had lower levels of the stress hormone cortisol in their blood. They also had less evidence of certain heart risk factors and were more relaxed after the event was over.

Black tea has so many active ingredients, including flavonoids, polyphenols, and catechins, that experts don't know exactly what was at work. But they speculate it may have been theanine, an amino acid that can block the effects of excitement in your body.

Go green for a relaxing change. The traditional Chinese beverage of green tea can also be a relaxing choice, since it contains theanine just like its black-tea cousin. Both come from the *Camellia sinensis* plant. Research in Japan found theanine extract helped students relax — even right after they took a math test. Other studies found drinking green tea might lower your risk for depression and other forms of mental distress. Five cups or more per day had the greatest benefit. This powerful health booster may also help lower your blood pressure, slow hardening of the arteries, and keep your weight under control.

Calm down with chamomile. That old bedtime favorite, chamomile tea, is also no slouch when it comes to cutting anxiety. Researchers went to a group they were sure would be under stress — people having a heart catheterization procedure. Sure enough, more than 80 percent of people who drank two cups of chamomile tea were sound asleep within 10 minutes.

Chamomile tea is made from an herb, *Matricaria chamomilla*, not from the same plant as black and green tea. The active ingredient in chamomile that helps you relax is likely apigenin, a flavonoid. A study on mice found apigenin works like a tranquilizing drug to bring on relaxation.

Simple choices for stress control

Stress usually doesn't happen out of the blue. You can probably figure out the causes of your anxiety if you pay attention to what is happening in your life when you start to feel overwhelmed. Everyone is different, so pinpointing your personal stress triggers will help you avoid that stress and control your moods.

Create a mood map. Keep a log or "stress journal" for at least a week, tracking your moods at certain times of the day. Assign each page in a notebook to a new day. Divide each page into four or five sections, one per time of day:

- early morning

- late morning

- early afternoon

- late afternoon

- evening

Write down a short description of how you felt at each time of day, like "very anxious" or "medium" or "not at all anxious." Use a scale of one through five, with one indicating a very bad mood and five a very good mood. Also keep track of other important bits of information for each time segment. Key items might include what you think caused your stress, whether you felt physically sick, and how you behaved in response to the problem.

Look at your stress journal after at least a week, and try to identify patterns of stress, anxiety, or unhappiness. Was it often at the same time of day? Could it be related to drinking caffeine? Were you alone or with others? Did you feel hungry or rushed? Questions like these can help you identify your triggers or other sources of your stress or anxiety.

Take back control. You're not doomed to dealing with the same stresses day after day, week after week. You can fight back once you figure out what actions or events tend to cause problems. Try to handle your stressful situation in one of these four "A"+ ways.

- *Avoid* the stress so it's no longer a problem. This may mean you avoid certain people or situations.

- *Alter* the stress by changing it into something you can handle without anxiety.

- *Adapt* to the stress so you can handle it better. You may have to stop being a perfectionist or simply change how you think about a situation.

- *Accept* the stress if you can't change it. Some things in life are beyond your control.

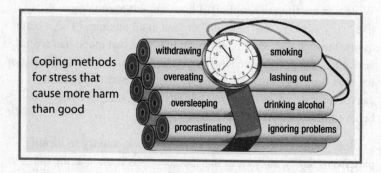

Coping methods for stress that cause more harm than good

withdrawing
overeating
oversleeping
procrastinating

smoking
lashing out
drinking alcohol
ignoring problems

Question  Answer

Is stress always a bad thing?

Excess stress that never seems to end can take a toll on your mental and physical health. But stress in small amounts is a normal part of life and gives some spice to your day. Without it, life would be tedious and dull. Learn how to manage the little stresses in life so they don't snowball into major problems.

Play now or pay later

When was the last time you did something just for fun? No goals, no plan for success, no timetable, simply wasting time having a good time. That's what it means to "play," and adults don't do it enough. Society teaches that play is for kids, and adults need to be productive and to avoid wasting time. But experts warn that failure to play may doom you to a life of gloom and unhappiness, with no release from the stresses of everyday life.

Play becomes even more important when times are tough, the economy is on the decline, or bad events happen. Research shows that chronic stress in animals shrinks the parts of the brain that take care of remembering and learning new tasks. In contrast, play lowers the levels of stress hormones in your blood, helping to keep your body healthy.

If your life lacks fun and frivolity, try these ideas to recapture the joy of playtime. Focus on relaxing and having fun rather than simply fitting more achievement into your day.

- Think back to the activities you enjoyed as a kid. Did you like to ride horses? Play basketball? Ride your bike? You can still do those things, and you may enjoy them just as much.

- Watch your attitude with grown-up games. If you're too serious about your golf swing or overly focused on improving your time when you run, then you're not having fun. That's stress — not play.

- Find a friend who knows how to play. Best bets include dogs and young grandchildren. They're interested in simply having fun, not in keeping a schedule or getting the highest score.

- Get out and plant. Cardiologist Meyer Friedman, who developed the notion of the high-stress type-A personality, suggested spending time with the three Ps: people, pets, and plants. All three can help nurture your creative side, and plants don't disagree or talk back. So get your hands dirty in the garden.

- Take another turn at the craft table. But don't try to paint the perfect picture or make a tooled leather belt fit for a king. Just have fun while you make something with your hands.

- Schedule a play date with your honey (wink, wink). That's right, if you and your spouse are healthy enough for intimate activity, get busy between the sheets. You'll feel relaxed while you block out the rest of the world, and you both will be rejuvenated afterward.

Energy **BOOSTER**

Stress can tire you out. Go from exhausted to exhilarated with these tips for beating fatigue.

- Eat breakfast to avoid the low blood sugar blues.
- Get the right amount of sleep.
- Learn to say no to lower your stress and save energy.
- Avoid large meals, which can leave you feeling sluggish.
- Banish negative people who sap your energy.
- Get a kick without caffeine to avoid rebound fatigue.
- Skip the midday cocktail. It will make you crave an afternoon nap.
- Don't smoke. Nicotine can hinder good sleep.
- Check side effects of your medications to see if they're bringing you down.
- Get a blood test to check for a liver or thyroid condition.

Relax your potbelly away

Stress is a part of life — even the good life. Unfortunately, it's often also a part of being fat. New research shows stress shifts fat to your waistline. It's all about hormones, but you can still do something about it — just get out and get active.

Here is how the stress-weight connection works. When you are under long-term stress, your body responds by pumping out lots of cortisol. This hormone product of the adrenal gland is sometimes called the "stress hormone." Too much cortisol in your system encourages your body to build up extra belly fat.

New research shows that animals put under stress started to gain more weight around their midsections — the equivalent of a person gaining belly fat. The same proved true with research on people. By learning how to relax and release stress, you'll help rid yourself of that potbelly for good.

Focus on being active. Stress has a helpful purpose — it prepares you to be in motion. That's the fight-or-flight response at work, and it's meant to allow you to escape from sudden danger. But when you're under stress for long periods of time and you don't get the chance to relieve that stress through movement, you end up stewing in your own stress juices, so to speak.

Taking part in exercise can teach your body how to handle stress without being damaged. In fact, evidence shows that getting into a long-term habit of exercise lowers your level of cortisol and raises levels of other hormones — the androgen DHEA and growth hormone — that protect you from the damage of chronic inflammation.

Physical activity also helps lower your feelings of anxiety and depression. Regular aerobic exercise, like swimming or cycling, works especially well for anxious people who take it up when they haven't been active before. In a review of research, only prescription drugs — not talk therapy or meditation — worked better than exercise to ease anxiety. Those are big results.

Do something you enjoy. You don't have to join a senior soccer team or train to run a marathon to get the mood-enhancing benefits of exercise. Pick your favorite of these helpful activities. You'll be in a better frame of mind, and you'll feel good all over.

- Walking. Research on middle-aged women in Philadelphia found those who started a walking program had less stress, anxiety, and depression. The women walked briskly for either 40 or 90 minutes five times a week. Those doing the most exercise saw the most benefit.

- Running, swimming, or riding a bike. Work up to one of these more strenuous pursuits if you can handle it. Experts say to aim for moderate physical activity for at least 20 to 30 minutes on most days of the week.

- Yoga. Women with rheumatoid arthritis who took yoga classes three times a week enjoyed better health after just 10 weeks. They reported improved balance, less pain and disability, and even better moods.

Be sure to consult your doctor before you begin a new exercise program.

Kick stress like the 'Grannies'

Head to a soccer field in South Africa's Limpopo Province, and you are likely to see some 80-year-old women practicing the sport. They're the "Grannies," a team of ladies who practice for an hour twice a week to play in an all-seniors league. They say the sport has helped them battle arthritis, diabetes, and other health problems of aging. It has even improved their outlook on life.

"Soccer for me relieves stress," says 61-year-old Chrestina Machabe. "I suffer from hypertension, but since I started playing soccer I have become healthier. I even sleep better at night." Chrestina has learned from experience how closely exercise is related to stress relief.

QUICK*fix*

Next time you feel overstressed and ready to burst, let out a big yawn.

That's right — this common sign of sleepiness may also help relieve stress. Yawning can help cool your body, and sometimes you do it on reflex. But you can use yawning to your advantage when you want to calm down quickly. Olympic speed skater Apolo Anton Ohno yawns on purpose before his big races, working to get more oxygen into his lungs to power his muscles. He also releases stress with these intentional yawns. Based on the eight Olympic medals Ohno has won, the trick seems to work.

A new route to relaxation

How can "cloud hands" or "grasp the bird's tail" help relieve your stress? When you practice these and other common movements of tai chi, you teach your body and mind to work together in harmony. That's why performing this ancient art can make you feel better, both physically and emotionally.

Get connected. The traditional Chinese martial art of tai chi, now mostly performed as a series of slow, deliberate postures and graceful movements, is believed to improve the mind-body connection. That's how it helps relieve stress. You have to pay attention to all the details of what your body is doing while you perform the movements of tai chi. That helps you stay focused and tune out all those other nagging problems that can make you feel overwhelmed.

Research on a small group of young adults found these tai chi beginners benefited both physically and mentally from participating. They felt better and reported less stress after taking tai chi classes for just 18 weeks. Psychological and physical tests proved they were not just imagining a lower stress level — the good results were real.

Help your body and brain. Here are some other great things tai chi can do for your health.

- Stave off memory loss. This form of relaxing exercise cuts back on stress, and it may also help you sleep better. Both stress and lack of sleep can bring about memory problems, so anything you can do to battle these two troubles may keep your memory at its best and make your brain stronger.

- Lower your blood pressure. Several studies of tai chi's physical effects found it may lower your systolic and diastolic blood pressure numbers — both the first and the second numbers in a reading. This finding has encouraged experts to recommend tai chi as a helpful non-drug treatment for people suffering from high blood pressure.

- Boost balance and flexibility. Tai chi can help you improve your fitness as much as running yourself breathless. Researchers found that older women who practiced tai chi for three months enjoyed better balance, flexibility, and leg strength. The tai chi program worked better than a brisk walking program did for another group of older women. Although you may think you're not working hard when you move through the poses, you're actually improving your aerobic capacity, or ability to use oxygen during exercise.

Start right with instruction. Many people learn tai chi in classes, led by an instructor who guides the class through a series of movements. You can also do the movements on your own once you get the hang of them. Some people find practicing their tai chi moves for 15 to 20 minutes is a great way to start the day every morning. Check with your local senior center, community education center, or YMCA to find a tai chi class that's a good fit for seniors.

Talk to your doctor before you try tai chi, especially if you have a joint or muscle problem like arthritis or tendinitis or any other medical issue that could get in the way of good balance. Also be careful if you take a medicine that makes you dizzy or lightheaded.

Novel pursuit brings fun and friendship

Gretchen spent 30 years as a preschool teacher. She never worried about finding time for exercise because she spent most days crawling on the floor or chasing children on the playground.

After Gretchen retired, she wasn't as active anymore. For a while she spent her days catching up on projects. Then her neighbor talked her into joining a tai chi class at the local senior center.

"I never considered doing anything that far out," Gretchen said. "But now I love my tai chi class. The movements are relaxing, and I have to concentrate hard to do the routine. Plus it's nice to see my new friends at class."

Breathe in some peace of mind

Take a deep breath, count to 10, and feel your worries fall away. Well, that's how it's supposed to work. In reality, you may have to practice more control over your breathing, and do it for longer than a count of 10. But the basic idea holds — you can change the way you breathe to get control of your stress level. Doing that may well boost your immune system, which in turn may add years to your life.

Give your immunity a leg up. Your immune system gets revved up for a short time whenever you encounter a sudden stressful event. That reaction is your body getting ready to fight off infection — or maybe a grizzly bear.

But if the stress remains for a long period, you wear down your immunity and your ability to fight off that infection. Too much pressure on the system over time simply causes more wear and tear. The cells of your immune system, made to fight off foreign invaders like harmful bacteria and viruses, do not function as well after you suffer long-term stress. Seniors and people suffering from another illness are at even greater risk. That's why living with constant stress raises your chances of getting sick.

Change the way you breathe. You take about 14 to 16 breaths each minute while you are at rest. But when you are in a stressful situation, you tend to breathe faster as your lungs work to take in more oxygen as part of the fight-or-flight response.

Here's how deep breathing helps. When you breathe deeply, you work your diaphragm, the powerful sheet of muscle that separates your lungs from your stomach. Taking a deep breath lowers your diaphragm, pulling your lungs down with it and pressing against organs in your abdomen to make room for your lungs to expand as they fill with air. Then as you breathe out, your diaphragm presses up against your lungs, pushing out carbon dioxide. This kind of deep breathing engages what is called the "relaxation response." That is the opposite of the stress response.

Research shows practicing deep-breathing exercises can lower your anxiety, stress, and depression while it increases your feelings of optimism. It's free and safe stress relief, and you can do it anywhere, at any time.

Follow the path to stress relief. Find time to do these deep-breathing exercises several times each day, even if you don't feel especially stressed. First, inhale through your nose slowly and deeply, counting to 10. Be sure your stomach and abdomen expand, but your chest does not. Then, exhale through your nose slowly, also while you count to 10. Concentrate on counting and breathing through each cycle to quiet your mind. Repeat the cycle five to 10 times.

Get your muscles in on the action. You can add progressive muscle relaxation, especially if your goals include cutting stress, relaxing, and getting some very important sleep. Small studies have shown it may even help lower blood pressure. Here's how.

- Lie down and get comfortable. Don't cross your arms or legs.

- Be sure you continue breathing slowly.

- Tense one muscle group tightly while you count to 10. Then release that muscle group and move on to the next one.

- Begin with muscles at the top of your head, then move downward through muscle groups like your upper arms, lower arms, hands, thighs, calves, feet, and so on.

- Concentrate on how relaxed and heavy your muscles feel when they're released.

Put anger to rest for better night's sleep

You're not alone if you've gotten angry today. An average person suffers through 15 anger-causing events every day. But anger is not always bad. Some experts say you can think more clearly while you're feeling angry. This powerful emotion seems to help your analytical thought processes. But too much anger, especially if you don't handle it right, can damage your health and keep you awake at night.

Research points to the downside of anger. One study of people with implantable defibrillators found that those who had strong reactions when they thought about something that made them angry suffered the effects later. They were more likely to have a heart rhythm problem within the next four years. Other research has shown that negative emotions of various types, including anger, are bad for your heart and raise your risk for heart disease. In contrast, laughter can help relax your blood vessels and benefit your heart.

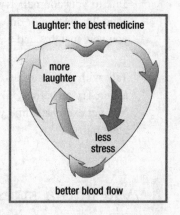

Laughter: the best medicine

more laughter

less stress

better blood flow

Don't sleep on it. Trying to keep your anger inside can interfere with sleep. When experts studied some 1,000 people with heart disease, they found people who tried to suppress their anger had trouble sleeping. It seems the habit of not venting your anger means you hold it inside, then stew on it all night. Other research suggests bottling up your anger can put you at risk for high blood pressure.

The problem may have a physical connection. When you are angry — even while asleep — it disrupts your limbic system. This system is the part of your brain that controls emotions, including anger. The disruption makes it hard for you to enter REM sleep, the deep sleep in which your brain is active and you tend to dream.

Uncork the bad feelings. Find safe ways to release your anger. Don't try to vent emotions in an unfocused way by crying, yelling, or laughing. Experts warn this "catharsis" method is not helpful but merely reinforces the anger. Try one of these tricks instead.

- Talk to the person who made you mad. Discuss your feelings, but don't place blame. Avoid taking out your feelings on a third party.

- Talk to your journal. Try to express and make sense of your anger by writing or drawing about it. This activity can bring you new insights and a different perspective on the issue.

- Talk with your muscles. Physical activity releases pent-up anger. Try an activity like boxing using a Wii game console. You get exercise while you "hit" something safely — plus you have fun.

Age into a stress-free life

The stereotypes of the high-strung youngster and the easygoing older person may be true, new research shows. A Gallup phone survey of more than 340,000 people in the United States found that people tend to have the most worry and stress when they're in their 20s. But people older than 50 showed less daily stress and more happiness. In fact, people in their 70s and 80s reported the lowest levels of negative emotions. Experts suspect many older folks learn to focus on their current happiness rather than worrying about the future.

Question & Answer

Is it true that a big shock or a stressful time in life can turn your hair gray?

New research shows stress is not what brings out the gray — it's heredity. A study of Danish twins found life stresses did not seem to have an effect on when the women showed signs of graying hair. Genetics, rather than a high-pressure job or unruly children, determines when your hair loses its color. Even better news, getting gray early does not mean you are destined to die young. You should celebrate your white locks as a sign of wisdom rather than of hard times.

Healing herbs give natural relief

Stress is as old as the ancient struggle for life, and as modern as our busy schedules. Check out these remedies that have been passed down through the years, and see if they can help put you on the road to relaxation.

Try valerian to chill out. This herb, from the *Valeriana officinalis* plant, is well known for its ability to cut anxiety and even help you get to sleep. Experts believe the combination of natural plant chemicals in the herb does the trick, behaving in your body similar to common anti-anxiety drugs. In fact, one study found valerian lowered anxiety about as well as diazepam (Valium).

Valerian may take several weeks to start working, so be patient. A typical dose is 400 to 600 milligrams (mg) of extract in a capsule.

Give ginseng a go. The traditional Chinese herbal remedy for stress also offers other possible benefits, like boosting your memory and strengthening your immune system. Active ingredients in ginseng are called ginsenosides, a type of natural plant chemical. Ginseng is known as an adaptogen, or a remedy that works in a nonspecific way to cut stress without doing your body any harm. Studies show ginseng seems to work on the adrenal and pituitary glands, which release hormones in response to stresses in your body.

You'll find several types of ginseng available, including American ginseng, Chinese or Korean ginseng, and Siberian ginseng. Experts suggest you look for a product labeled Panax ginseng that has been standardized to contain between 4 percent and 7 percent ginsenosides. Taking 200 to 400 mg daily for up to eight weeks is considered safe.

Ingredients in herbal supplements are not closely regulated by the U.S. Food and Drug Administration, so you need to be careful when shopping. Check the Web site *www.consumerlab.com* for trusted information on herbal supplements.

Popular herb warrants caution

One herbal stress buster may do the job, but its safety has a big question mark.

The herb kava is made from dried roots of the *Piper methysticum* plant. Research in Europe found it works as well as benzodiazepine drugs like Valium to treat anxiety and sleeplessness. Kava works fast, as quickly as just one or two doses.

But kava got a black mark when it was linked to liver damage several years ago. Contaminated batches of kava may have been partially to blame. But experts think kava may cause severe problems after long-term use or at higher-than-recommended doses. Don't try kava without talking to your doctor first.

A 'scent'sational way to relax

Many women find their favorite perfume can lift their mood with just a brief whiff of its familiar scent. It may be that it evokes a happier time or place, or perhaps they simply enjoy the scent of a particular flower or exotic spice. This is the power of aromatherapy, and you can use it in many ways to help you relax.

Certain fragrances, including lavender, rose, neroli, and frankincense are known for their ability to lower stress.

- Lavender has been used since ancient times for this purpose. In one study, linalool, a compound found in lavender and other scented plants like lemon and basil, lowered stress-related chemicals in rats after a stress test. In another study, intensive-care patients who were massaged with lavender essential oil had lower anxiety afterward. The flower also helped calm anxious dental patients who were exposed to the scent of burning lavender oil.

- You may know frankincense as one of the gifts from the three wise men. Frankincense is a tree resin that is made into an aromatic incense traditionally used in religious ceremonies in the Middle East and Europe. Research in mice shows a chemical released from frankincense when it burns works on certain brain pathways to lower anxiety.

If you want all-day aromatherapy benefits, look for perfumes or colognes that include these relaxing scents. Or simply select an aroma you particularly enjoy. A favorite scent can help banish stress by distracting you from your anxieties.

For a relaxing evening, use scented candles or bath products of your favorite soothing fragrance. You can also burn essential oils at home in a lamp ring or electric diffuser. Don't place essential oils directly on your skin or in a bath since they can irritate your skin.

QUICK*fix*

"Our life is frittered away by detail," wrote the famous writer and minimalist Henry David Thoreau. "Simplify, simplify." Try these 10 tricks to do just that and make your life easier to manage.

- Prepare for your day the night before.
- Get up 15 minutes earlier every morning.
- Write things down rather than relying on your memory.
- Make duplicate keys to everything possible.
- Say "no" more often to new responsibilities.
- Avoid negative people.
- Use your time wisely.
- Simplify your meals.
- Repair or toss things that don't work.
- Break large jobs into bite-sized tasks.

#1 feel-good way to soothe stress

Isn't it great to find a solution for your ills that is also enjoyable? That's the way it is with massage, a surefire helper when it comes to stress and anxiety. Massage makes you feel good, and even the experts agree it has benefits.

Pick best mode for your muscles. Several types of massage may help relieve your stress and bring on feelings of relaxation.

- Swedish massage, the most common type, uses long, smooth strokes and some kneading of muscles.

- Shiatsu is more vigorous, involving intense pressure applied to pressure points. You may feel some pain during treatment, but you'll be relaxed after the session is over.

- Reflexology focuses on pressure points in your hands and feet.

A massage therapist typically tries to create a calm and soothing atmosphere using dim lights, soothing music, and pleasant fragrances. All these factors make the massage experience pleasant and relaxing.

But the benefits go beyond simple relaxation. Getting a massage causes positive changes in your natural body chemicals, including lower levels of the stress hormone cortisol and higher levels of the mood-enhancers serotonin and dopamine. Experts also think massage helps by shifting your nervous system away from the fight-or-flight response and boosting your "rest-and-digest" response. That helps your heart rate and breathing slow, blood vessels relax, and digestive system become active.

Find an affordable venue. Spas and beauty salons are common places to get a massage, but they're on the pricey end. A one-hour massage typically costs $75 or more at a spa or salon. Look for lower-cost licensed massage therapists at sports fitness facilities, hospitals, nursing homes, or in a private office. See if your health insurance policy covers massage therapy as a healthy-lifestyle treatment along with weight-loss and stress-management programs.

Help yourself with at-home massage. You can do part of the job on your own with self massage. Try this trick to relieve anxiety fast. Locate the pressure point on the bottom of your foot and massage it with acupressure. Between your big toe and second toe, move your fingers up the webbing toward the center of your foot until you feel bones. Press firmly or rub in small circles on that tender spot for about 30 seconds to help tension melt away.

Or get your honey to help. Couples trained in "warm touch" techniques, including neck and shoulder massage, lowered their physical stress symptoms and stress hormones over a month's time, research found. Take this excuse to shower your favorite person with some extra affection.

Question & Answer

Can a stressful event or sudden surprise bring on a heart attack?

Yes. Sudden stress can stimulate your sympathetic nervous system to release stress hormones called catecholamines. They immediately raise your heart rate, blood pressure, and the force of your heart's contractions. That pressure can knock loose plaque in your arteries, which can then migrate and block blood flow. Possible result? Heart attack. Stress may also be related to heart rhythm problems, called arrhythmia, and may raise your risk for unhealthy high cholesterol. Keep your cool, and help your heart.

Wage war on clutter for a worry-free home

Wealthy New Yorker Langley Collyer died in 1947 after being trapped by fallen piles of belongings in his home. Firefighters worked for days to find his body, sorting through a three-story house that was chock full of old newspapers, books, scrap metal, tree limbs — even an old Model-T car.

Collyer suffered from compulsive hoarding, a condition that compels people to collect and save all kinds of stuff, whether it's useful or not. In the worst cases, a house can be filled to the rafters with useless belongings. But even milder cases of messiness can make you feel stressed and uncomfortable in your own home. Clean out the clutter in your house, and you may uncover a less-stressed you.

Get organized to clear your mind. Most experts agree a clutter problem usually is a personality problem, not a problem with the space in your home. Rather than try and fit things into boxes and bins, adopt the attitude that less is more, and get rid of items your don't need.

"There is a connection between mess and stress," says psychologist and organizing expert Kathleen Kendall-Tackett. "Life is substantially more stressful when chaos reigns. You end up taking longer to do the same amount of work. When your home is well ordered, people and things get to where they need to be, tasks get done, and family life is cherished. Organization allows you to have a life."

But lack of organization can interfere with your life. You can't take your medicine if you can't find it, and you won't go for a walk if you can't locate your tennis shoes. Too much clutter makes it hard to clean the house properly, so dirt and germs linger and may make you ill. You also run the risk of falling if you have to step around piles or boxes in your hallway.

Give clutter-busting secrets a try. Serious clutter may require a professional organizer to put your home to right. If you want to tackle the job yourself, use these tips to help keep it shipshape.

- Gather the proper tools. Keep a wastebasket in each room so you can throw out things immediately. Place cleaning supplies where they are needed, such as in the kitchen or bathroom. Store other items for easy access, like keeping an address book, stamps, envelopes, and checkbook all together for bill paying.

- Store thoughtfully, but not too much. Keep in-season clothes at the front of the closet, but put others in a separate place. As you move items back and forth at the start of a new season, you'll notice what you haven't worn and can toss it. In the kitchen, keep pots, pans, and stirring spoons near the stove, and knives and cutting boards in the food-preparation area.

- Get rid of nonessentials. Think about whether you really need something or whether it just gets in your way. If you need an item or bit of information later, can you find it somewhere else? Is that magazine or pair of shoes out of date? Sort through your possessions, and you may notice a pattern of gathering useless things. Stop the pattern.

- Think minimalist. Is that collection of vintage model cars worth the trouble of weekly dusting? Do you really enjoy watering and caring for 17 houseplants? You are not obligated to keep everything you own, so keep only the items that really make you happy. Find a thrift or consignment store to donate your extra goods, and let someone else enjoy them.

Get creative for a calmer mind

They say music can soothe a savage beast. It may also soothe your stress and anxious moods. Research shows being creative with either music or art can help you relax, even if you are dealing with a difficult medical problem. Pick up your paintbrush, dust off that oboe, and coax your mind back to easy street.

Chill out with music. Music therapy gained respect after it helped soldiers wounded in World War I and World War II get back to their old selves. It can improve your mood and relieve stress. Music therapy may include listening to music you enjoy or playing music. A music therapist may be there to help, and you may work alone or in a group of people. It may involve music that is live or recorded, vocal or instrumental.

Research shows music therapy works to battle stress and anxiety while it brightens your mood. People with heart disease enjoyed less stress, lower blood pressure and heart rate, and fewer medical complications when they listened to relaxing music. When you listen to music you particularly enjoy, you benefit from expanded arteries and better circulation, studies show. Best bets include tunes with a slow tempo, predictable harmonies, and no sudden changes. Stay away from music you dislike, which can actually make you feel more anxious.

You'll feel in harmony when you listen to enjoyable music. If you don't have a favorite soothing sound, check out the calming tunes played by harpist Sue Raimond, proven to soothe both people and pets. Her music CDs are available at *www.petpause2000.com*, or you can find other harp CDs in a music store near you.

But you may want to get into the act yourself. Sit down to your piano, get out your clarinet, and spend some time relearning an old hobby. Or consider joining a drum circle, where you can express emotions while you follow a leader playing rhythm patterns. Playing together — with each person on her own drum — fosters a sense of community and helps cut stress. Find a drum circle near you advertised in your local newspaper, or check out the listings at *www.drumcircles.net*.

Release your inner artist. Performing or listening to music is not for everyone, but you may enjoy drawing, painting, or working with clay to get stress relief. Art therapy allows you to share your thoughts and feelings without words. You benefit both by expressing yourself and by participating in a discussion of your life and how your art reflects it.

Experts have found that art therapy can help you deal with stress or trauma by reducing your anxiety and tension. You may also enjoy physical benefits to your immune system, nervous system, and heart. Besides all that, it's just downright fun.

As with music therapy, you can take part in art therapy sessions alone or in a group, with or without a therapist, in a single session or with repeated meetings. Many hospitals offer music or art therapy, or you can find a class at your local wellness center, community center, or with a therapist in private practice.

QUICK *fix*

Some people tend to worry — constantly, it seems — about all kinds of bad things that might happen. It's fine to plan ahead for potential problems, but constant worrying over unlikely catastrophes does not help anyone. But it can certainly hurt by taking a toll on your mental and physical health.

Try this trick to put a stop to that never-ending worry. Schedule a daily "worry break." Pick a block of about 15 or 20 minutes, and use that prescheduled time to give your worries all your attention. If they intrude at other times, try to put off those thoughts until your next "worry break." Then you can focus most of the day on living — not on worrying.

Easy ways to turn a frown upside down

You know the sound. That little voice inside telling you that traffic will be heavy, rain showers will come early, and you can't afford to fly to your daughter's house for the holidays. That's the sound of pessimism, and it can turn a half-full glass of refreshing milk into a half-empty glass of sour. When it comes to attitude, you're in control — but only if you can seize the power and shush that negative voice inside.

Identify your inner optimist. Don't think of an optimist as someone who can't see the reality of the situation, who doesn't appreciate how stressful life is, or who is simply lucky. You can look on the bright side without wearing blinders. Author Brian Luke Seaward, Ph.D., describes key traits of optimists:

- They see the positive, even in a bad situation.

- They count blessings instead of misfortunes.

- They're happy people who are nice to be around.

- They take things in stride and adapt to the situation.

- They have enough faith in themselves to work through a crisis.

Stop toxic thoughts. Experts point out that most of your background thinking consists of negative thoughts — blowing problems out of proportion, blaming others for your troubles, or expecting the worst to happen. All that negative thinking keeps you in a state of constant stress.

Don't let it happen. When you catch yourself thinking negatively, interrupt it, put an end to the toxic thought, and try to rephrase the situation in a positive light. This is a new habit, so you will need to practice the skill until you get it right. Psychologists call it "cognitive restructuring," or paying attention to your negative thoughts and consciously pushing them aside. Reframing your thoughts is a great tool to cope with stress.

Write yourself a new story. Replace those old negative ways of looking at the world with positive thoughts. You can improve your life and health by changing your "personal story," says Harvard physician Matthew Budd in his book *You Are What You Say*.

Budd describes how people tell themselves a story about life and their health, then tend to live up to that story. For example, if you tell yourself you are too busy to eat right or exercise, or that you are a victim of poor health, then that's exactly what will happen. It becomes a self-fulfilling prophecy. But if you decide not to live up to that negative story and instead decide on a different story, you can change your life and your health. The change may help you find relief from your chronic ills.

Budd even suggests you make use of the placebo effect by putting it to use in a positive way. The placebo effect is the tendency of people to believe that a remedy will work, and often to think it has worked — even a sugar pill, which has no real power to heal. But the placebo effect changes your expectations, and sometimes that changes your body. Put it to use by believing you will overcome your stresses.

Be happy, be healthy. You may even be able to heal — or at least better handle — certain stress-related physical problems just by changing your thoughts. Headaches, jaw pain, insomnia, stomach problems — all of these may be related to excess stress. That's the basis of the Ways to Wellness program developed at Harvard and used by health insurance organizations across the United States. But you don't need to join a program to heal yourself. Look inside and find the optimist within.

Save your teeth from the nightly grind

Jaw pain, worn-down teeth, morning headaches, and complaints from your spouse about the noise. These are all signs your stress is exploding in the form of nighttime teeth grinding.

Bruxism is the technical name for clenching your jaw or grinding your teeth. It typically happens while you sleep. Bruxism is often related to stress, so if you can stop the stress, you'll stop the grinding. In fact, some dentists notice more people having trouble with teeth grinding during tough economic times. In other cases, teeth grinding is related to your teeth not fitting together properly.

You may not even know you're grinding your teeth while you sleep, but your partner may let you know by complaining of the horrible noise. Your dentist may see the telltale signs of wear and tear on your teeth.

A clenched jaw is powerful, exerting up to 300 pounds of pressure and causing serious problems such as:

- wearing down tooth enamel, putting teeth at risk of decay. This can also speed up gum disease.

- breaking or fracturing healthy, undecayed teeth.

- pain and inflammation in your jaw joint, known as temporo-mandibular joint (TMJ) disorder.

You can save your teeth with a bite guard that protects your teeth at night. For about $300 to $1,800, your dentist will fit a guard to your teeth. The price can run up to $2,500 if it also corrects a misaligned bite. An over-the-counter bite guard may work for you as well, and you can find one starting at about $20.

Alternately, try to change your behavior, especially if the problem has progressed to TMJ pain.

- First, get in the habit of resting your tongue behind your upper teeth and closing your lips. This position keeps your jaw open and at ease.

- Second, place your computer screen up high and the keyboard down low. The posture needed to work in this position keeps your jaw from jutting out.

- Third, don't sleep on your stomach.

- Finally, try to reduce your stress.

Outsmart stress-related IBS

You have been looking forward to Sunday dinner with your family all week. Then, just as you're about to sit down to the roast chicken, an attack of diarrhea hits. You might not be so bothered if it happened only once in a while, but this goes on several times a week.

That's not unusual for someone who suffers from irritable bowel syndrome (IBS), a group of symptoms — not a disease — that can turn your life upside down. You may experience painful gas, bloating, and alternating constipation and diarrhea, which can lead to hemorrhoids, even though nothing is physically wrong with your gastrointestinal tract. Having these symptoms for at least three months may be a sign it's IBS, sometimes called spastic colon.

If it's not a physical problem, then what is going on? IBS may be related to how you handle stress. Strange as it sounds, your brain and digestive system are closely linked. Many of the same hormones and parts of the nervous system control both. Instead of the healthy, smooth contractions of the bowel wall called peristalsis, which move food along its digestive route, you experience painful spasms.

While you try other solutions to cut stress from your life, check out these changes to help with the physical symptoms of IBS. Everyone is different, so see what works for you.

Fill up on soluble fiber. People who eat white flour and processed grains often don't get enough of this nutritional wonder. That can make your digestion sluggish and bring on constipation and stomach pain. So adding fiber may be the first thing your doctor suggests to battle IBS. Both soluble fiber — from psyllium, oats, and fruits — and insoluble fiber from wheat bran may help speed up your digestion. But stick with soluble fiber to improve common symptoms of IBS, as research shows that works best.

Start with psyllium, made from the seed coat of plantain, in the form of an over-the-counter product like Metamucil. Or check out the Web site *www.helpforibs.com* for information on another type of soluble fiber, called acacia, which has produced good results in some people for both diarrhea and constipation. Of course, the best way to get your soluble fiber is from fresh foods like apples, citrus fruits, beans, barley, and oatmeal.

Pacify with peppermint oil. This natural remedy has been soothing upset stomachs for centuries. It works by relaxing the smooth muscles in your intestines, and it seems to improve many IBS symptoms, including pain. Try taking three to six enteric-coated capsules every day. Don't chew the capsules, or the peppermint oil may be released before it reaches your intestines.

Pack in the probiotics. Certain strains of helpful bacteria live in your gut and keep it working as it should. They crowd out disease-causing bacteria while they help digest fiber, and some types can stamp out IBS symptoms, including pain. You can add more good bacteria to the mix by eating probiotics in foods like active yogurt or kefir or in supplements. Look on the label for names of bacteria strains like *Lactobacillus* and *Bifidobacterium*, aiming for 10 to 100 billion bacteria a day. Your supermarket probably carries common brands of probiotic yogurt like Stonyfield Farm, Activia, and DanActive.

Energy **BOOSTER**

This ancient movement stimulates the nervous system to boost your energy in 20 seconds. You can do the simple yoga move called an arm swing anywhere, at any time. Here's how.

- Take three breaths while you sit up in your chair. Stretch your arms straight ahead, parallel to the floor, while you breathe in and out.

- Take a deep breath and push your chest out while you swing your arms to the sides. Then swing them backward as far as you can comfortably reach.

- Release your breath as you bring your arms to the front once again, slouching slightly forward. Relax.

- Repeat three to five times.

If you have shoulder pain, like arthritis or bursitis, take it easy.

Muscle power:
live long and strong

Muscle your way to a powerful future

Poverty of the flesh. That's what sarcopenia means in Greek. It's the gradual wasting away of muscles as you get older, and it can start creeping up as early as your 30s.

Sarcopenia often brings with it frailty, loss of independence, falls, and fractures. It's a common reason for entering a nursing home, where some 60 percent of residents suffer from the condition. But you don't have to accept increasing frailty when you can boost your muscle power with a little bit of effort.

Use it or lose it. When it comes to your muscles, this adage pretty much says it all. Continue working your muscles as you age, and you can maintain muscle mass.

Every year from age 30 to 60, you typically lose one-half pound of muscle — while you gain a pound of fat. The gradual change may not be obvious, since your weight may stay about the same. Experts say this wasting away of muscle is due to a combination of factors, including inflammation, hormone shifts, and oxidative stress.

Happily, resistance training — lifting weights — helps people of all ages slow this aging and wasting of muscles. It's an activity not just for bulking up body builders. Lifting weights two or three times a week increases your strength by building muscle mass and bone density.

One study found that older people who lifted weights twice a week for six months boosted their muscle strength by 50 percent. They performed exercises using the whole body, including the leg press, leg extension, leg flexion, chest press, shoulder press, and calf raise.

Here's how weight training builds muscle. When you put stress on a muscle by making it work, small tears in the muscle fibers occur. Your body repairs these tears and adds strength and size to the muscle. That makes the muscle bigger and stronger, ready to do even more work next time. This cycle of muscle breakdown and repair explains why you should not lift weights every day.

Enjoy a bevy of benefits. Along with increasing strength and muscle mass, strength training may also improve your balance and help prevent falls. A study of older people living in nursing homes or other facilities found that exercises to strengthen their ankles with elastic resistance bands improved their strength, balance, and mobility in six weeks. They exercised just 15 minutes a day, three times a week, working the muscles you use to point your toes and flex your foot — ankle dorsiflexor and plantar flexor muscles. By the end of the study, they had lowered their risk of a dangerous fall.

Strength training can also keep you from putting on fat as you get older. Finally, adding muscle mass improves your body's ability to use insulin and keep blood sugar stable.

Don't give up. Strength training is good for almost everyone. You can benefit even if you have arthritis, heart disease, or diabetes, whether you're old or young. Be sure to talk to your doctor before you begin, especially if you have high blood pressure or heart problems.

But strength training is not easy. As you get older, exerting your muscles gets harder and harder. That means you have to perform at a greater percentage of your maximum work capacity just to do the same job. In other words, moving the same amount of weight takes more effort. That can be disheartening and make you want to stop, creating a vicious cycle of weakness. But the effort is worth it.

Your program may be as simple as lifting small weights called dumbbells. You can also use weight machines at a health club or try using resistance bands. For a low-budget plan, create your own gym equipment from items you have around the house. A 16-ounce can of pineapple makes a great 1-pound weight, for example, and you can fill up a gallon jug with water for a heavier weight. Look at what you have and be creative.

To start a strength-training program, see *Top 3 exercises to beat arthritis pain* in the *Simple solutions for pain-free living* chapter. For specific exercises, read *Get fit while sitting*. You'll find it in the *Belly fat: easy ways to slenderize and energize* chapter.

One man's fountain of youth

Jack has been exercising since he was a young man. A friend first brought him to a gym and showed him a simple weight-lifting routine. For years, Jack followed the program and enjoyed the look and feel of his muscular physique.

Jack is now 78, and he still lifts weights several times a week. But as he has gotten older, Jack appreciates other fitness benefits.

"In my condo complex, I'm the one called to help carry groceries or hang a heavy picture on the wall," he says. "I'm strong enough to do a lot of the things I've always done. That makes me feel young — even if my driver's license gives away my true age."

Amazing nutrient burns calories while building muscle

Your metabolism will love this. Protein, found in everything from lean meat to black beans, can help you melt away fat and strengthen your muscles without breaking a sweat.

In fact, you could burn up to 200 calories a day simply by eating more protein-rich foods. Your body uses up more energy digesting protein than it does fat or carbohydrates. For every 1 gram (g) of protein you eat, you burn about 1 calorie. Eat 200 g of protein, and you could burn an extra 200 calories. That's a lot of protein. Unfortunately, getting that much may not be safe. It's better to eat protein-rich foods in moderation as part of a balanced diet.

This important nutrient also helps stave off the muscle loss that comes with aging. Older people, in particular, should eat more protein to maintain muscle and remain mobile. Eating just one serving of a high-protein food, like lean beef, boosts your muscle building by 50 percent. What's more, eating it around the time you exercise may give growing muscles even more oomph.

The muscle-building benefits max out at 30 g of protein per meal. That's about 4 ounces of chicken, fish, dairy, or lean beef. A breakfast of one egg along with a glass of milk, cup of yogurt, or handful of nuts would do it, too.

Try to eat 30 g of protein at each meal to keep your muscles strong and healthy. That may mean eating more protein than usual at breakfast and lunch, and less than usual at dinner, says Douglas Paddon-Jones, associate professor at the University of Texas Medical Branch.

"Usually, we eat very little protein at breakfast, eat a bit more at lunch, and then consume a large amount at night. So we're not taking enough protein on board for efficient muscle-building during the day, and at night we're taking in more than we can use. Most of the excess is oxidized and could end up as glucose or fat." It's worse than inefficient — it can also be fattening.

SimpleSOLUTION

Have a hard time getting enough protein from meat and other foods?
Consider protein supplements.

Older women who took daily supplements of essential amino acids —
building blocks of protein — were able to put on more muscle in three
months than women who took only a sugar pill. The supplements contained
15 grams (g) of the specific amino acids your body can't manufacture and
must get from food.

Other research found that 15 g of whey protein may work even better
than amino acid supplements. Whey protein powder is easy to find at
health food stores or supermarkets. Blend up a muscle-building breakfast with your favorite fruit, milk, ice cubes, and 4 tablespoons of whey
protein powder.

Jump-start your workout with a jolt of java

Coffee. It's not just for waking you up anymore. New research shows
the caffeine in a cuppa joe may also help your muscles deal with exercise,
letting you do more with less pain.

Researchers studied young men who rode exercise bikes for a tough
30-minute workout. About an hour before they exercised, the men got
a pill — either caffeine or a placebo. The caffeine booster was equal
to about two or three cups of coffee. Those who had caffeine reported
less pain in their quadriceps — large muscles in the thighs — during
the bike workout.

Interestingly, caffeine had about the same effect on the men whether they typically consumed lots of caffeine, say three or four cups of coffee daily, or next to none.

University of Illinois professor and researcher Robert Motl explains how caffeine can help improve your attitude about exercising.

"If you go to the gym and you exercise and it hurts, you may be prone to stop doing that because pain is an aversive stimulus that tells you to withdraw," Motl points out. "So if we could give people a little caffeine and reduce the amount of pain they're experiencing, maybe that would help them stick with that exercise."

Try black tea or diet cola as your caffeine source if you don't like the taste of coffee. An 8-ounce serving of black tea has about 53 milligrams (mg) of caffeine, while a 12-ounce diet cola has roughly 42 mg.

Caffeine is not the only thing you can consume to help you get the most from your muscles. For more information on what to eat and drink to cut muscle pain, see *Tasty tricks for a pain-free workout* in the *Simple solutions for pain-free living* chapter.

2 simple ways to avoid falls

Don't be felled by frailty. Nasty falls send 8 million people to the emergency room every year. Here are two simple ways to maintain your strength and stay steady on your feet.

Get off the couch. A bit of exercise is the first trick to sidestep falls. Researchers found that men who stay physically fit through aerobic exercise cut their risk of falling. They checked in with people over a period of 20 years, asking how much exercise they got, whether they had fallen, and what they were doing when they fell. The older people who fell when walking were most likely to have low fitness levels.

The results make sense, since your risk of falling is affected by your balance and muscle fitness. Just two hours a week of fun activities, like brisk walking or swimming, can help your leg muscles stay in shape so you can stay on your feet.

Bone up on vitamin D. The sunshine vitamin can help your heart and cut inflammation. Research shows it also helps build strong muscles and may ward off a dangerous fall.

In a new study, older men and women with higher levels of vitamin D did better on tests of physical functioning. Tests included walking as fast as they could for 400 meters — that's one lap around a standard track. They also had to stand up from a chair without using the arms, show their ability to balance, and complete other tests of leg strength. People with more vitamin D at the start of the study also stayed strong, doing better on the tests four years later.

Too little vitamin D is bad news for your muscles in many ways.

- Young women in California with the lowest vitamin D levels also had more fat in their muscle tissue.

- Severe lack of vitamin D is linked to muscle weakness. In the worst cases, the problem can be so severe it mimics amyotrophic lateral sclerosis (ALS), or Lou Gehrig's disease.

- Vitamin D deficiency is linked to pelvic floor muscle disorders, such as urinary incontinence and pelvic organ prolapse, in older women.

- Among people taking statins and suffering from muscle pain, two-thirds also have low levels of vitamin D.

For details on getting enough vitamin D, see *Super vitamin watches over your heart*. You'll find it in the *Natural remedies that pump up your heart* chapter.

QUICK*fix*

You drink ginger tea to calm an upset stomach. You can also harness the healing power of this powerful root to ward off muscle pain.

Two recent studies found that people who ate ginger — 2 grams of either raw or heat-treated ginger — daily for eight days before exercising suffered 25 percent less pain when they over-worked their muscles. Experts don't know exactly why ginger helps, but they think it's the anti-inflammatory and anti-pain properties in gingerols, the active ingredient in ginger.

You'll find fresh ginger in your supermarket's produce section. Peel off the skin and grate the root onto foods, or brew a cup of ginger tea.

Add some pep to your step

Feeling tired and fatigued is not all about sleep. There are many causes of fatigue, from chemical imbalances to blood sugar levels and med-ications. If you're tired of feeling tired all the time, here's how you can put a little zest back into your day.

Make peace with your thyroid. Your muscles tend to feel weak after overexertion — you played a difficult tennis match, or you rode with your grandchildren on a long bike ride. That kind of weakness and fatigue usually goes away within a few days.

But in rare cases, general muscle weakness may be caused by a chemical imbalance, specifically a thyroid problem. That's because your thyroid gland, a little butterfly-shaped gland in your neck, controls how your body uses energy. It can malfunction in two main ways:

- Hypothyroidism, or a low thyroid level, can cause fatigue, weakness, and sluggishness. It can also lead to conditions like weight gain, depression, memory problems, constipation, dry or yellow skin, intolerance to cold, coarse and thinning hair, and brittle nails.

- Hyperthyroidism, or a high thyroid level, can cause symptoms that are similar — or just the opposite — fatigue, weight loss, intolerance to heat, raised heart rate, sweating, irritability, anxiety, muscle weakness, and thyroid enlargement.

See your doctor to get your hormone levels checked if you think your thyroid may be causing problems.

Fuel up regularly. Fatigue can also be caused by shifting blood sugar levels. That's why you should keep your blood sugar steady rather than letting it drop. You can do that by avoiding large meals. Instead, divide your eating into a number of small meals throughout the day. That way your body and your brain receive a more regular supply of energy-boosting fuel.

Most importantly, don't skip breakfast. If you do, you're more likely to be tired and irritable later. But don't reach for a doughnut or other sugary treat. Instead, pick a breakfast that includes complex carbohydrates, protein, and a bit of fat so the fuel will be released gradually, keeping you energized for longer.

Beware of drug side effects. Fatigue can be a side effect of some medications, including antihistamines, blood pressure drugs, steroids, and diuretics.

Even drugs meant to treat the problem may actually be culprits. Sleeping pills might help you get more rest at night, but they can have a cruel aftereffect — daytime drowsiness the next day. This day-after letdown was a problem for more than one-third of sleeping pill users in one survey.

But no matter how certain you are that your drugs are causing your fatigue, don't stop taking them without first talking to your doctor.

Give natural remedies a chance. Here are a few things to try before you run to your doctor.

- Don't shortchange your sleep, but don't overdo it either. If you lie in bed not sleeping, cut back on time in bed and don't nap during the day. These changes may lessen your fatigue, because you'll fall asleep more quickly.

- Don't overextend yourself. An overly full schedule can make you feel stressed, and stress can leave you feeling drained and tired. Banish unnecessary activities from your day as much as possible to avoid feeling anxious.

- Watch your bad habits. First, don't smoke. Nicotine in tobacco is a stimulant, which makes your insomnia worse. Second, pay attention to how much alcohol you drink. It fouls up your sleep patterns at night. Having a drink at lunch can make you feel sleepy during the afternoon. If you drink before bed, alcohol clears your system about four or five hours later. Then you may find yourself wide awake, not getting your full night's rest.

- Be active. Your metabolism is encouraged to slow down when you live the life of a couch potato. That can make you feel sluggish. So get in motion and you'll feel more energized. Skip the common shortcuts of modern life — elevators, escalators, and driving when you could walk or ride your bike.

QUICK *fix*

Lose fat and gain muscle just by changing your oil. Researchers found that overweight, middle-age women who took safflower oil in capsules — the equivalent of roughly 1 2/3 teaspoons of oil daily — gained about 1.6 percent of lean muscle in four months. Even better, they lost about 6.3 percent of their belly fat in that time. The women, all of whom had diabetes, did not exercise or otherwise change their diets. That's a nice trade-off for a little effort.

Experts suggest the benefits come from the polyunsaturated fats in safflower oil. You can buy safflower oil in supplements, or try using a little safflower oil in a vinegar-oil dressing to drizzle on your salads.

Calm cramps with pickle juice

It's an old folk remedy for muscle cramps — drink a shot of pickle juice. Athletes, coaches, and trainers swear by this cure, and now scientists say it works. Research shows the pickle juice cure can cut your muscle cramps — no drugs required.

Muscle cramps can happen any time. Nighttime leg cramps are a sleep-stealing problem for 70 percent of people over age 50. They may be due to muscle fatigue, dehydration, or electrolyte imbalance, or they may be a side effect of your medicine.

Some cramps come on during exercise. Experts are unsure what causes these. They used to blame dehydration, but research shows that may not be the cause. A new theory says cramps occur because you overwork your muscles. Then the nerves that keep your muscles from overcontracting start to misfire, allowing the muscle to tighten up into a cramp.

What about that pickle juice? This remedy was tested with a group of young men while they exercised. Drinking 2.5 ounces of juice — from regular Vlasic dills — helped them get relief from a cramp 37 percent faster than for men who drank water, and 45 percent faster than men who drank nothing.

This test looked at pickle juice with exercise-induced cramps, but the solution may work for your nighttime cramps as well. Consuming mustard, vinegar, or sauerkraut may also work, but pickle juice may be a more pleasing remedy.

Here's another way to find relief. A pine bark extract called pycnogenol may cut cramps and muscle pain, whether at rest or during exercise. This antioxidant supplement is sometimes taken to fight arthritis pain. Experts say it boosts blood flow to your muscles to speed recovery. Pycnogenol may aid the activity of nitric oxide, a blood gas that helps blood flow. In one study, people found relief with four 50-milligram (mg) tablets of pycnogenol daily.

If leg cramps are disturbing your sleep, follow these helpful cramp-prevention tricks.

- Stay hydrated by drinking six to eight glasses of water daily.

- Stretch your muscles throughout the day and at bedtime.

- Don't let your feet and legs be restricted in bed by a tight-fitting sheet or heavy blanket.

- Be sure you get enough calcium, potassium, and vitamin E.

Bathe away muscle pain

A warm, soothing bath can be just the ticket to wash away soreness after you've overworked your muscles. Here's your recipe for relief.

1/4 cup rosemary leaves, fresh or dried

2 tablespoons dried marjoram leaves

12 crushed bay leaves

2 cups sea salt

Blend all ingredients in a coffee grinder, then mix into a tub of warm water and soak for 15 to 20 minutes. Bay leaves and marjoram are known for stimulating circulation and soothing achy muscles.

Beat the heat for exercise comfort

Getting overheated is no joke. New research shows an episode of heatstroke can lead to long-term damage to your kidneys, liver, and brain. That means the old advice to just wait a week or so before you exercise again may not be enough.

Overdoing it in the heat means blood that should be circulating to your muscles to help them work must be rerouted to your skin to cool your body. Up to 25 percent of your body's blood can get rerouted away from muscles or organs.

In severe heat, this rerouting can lead to heat exhaustion — you may collapse and be unable to continue exercising. If it gets worse, it can lead to heatstroke, a dangerous condition that may include delirium or coma.

Experts are starting to understand that heat-related illness includes long-term damage. When your intestines don't get enough blood, they become leaky. That means toxins leak out and result in inflammation and serious damage to other organs, especially your liver and kidneys. That's why some doctors now recommend getting a heat tolerance test before returning to exercise if you've suffered heatstroke.

If you become overheated, cool down immediately with cold towels or an ice water bath. Better yet, take steps to prevent the problem.

Cool your body from the inside out. Believe it or not, you can prepare for exercise in the heat by drinking a slushie — that tasty concoction of crushed ice and syrup. Researchers tested the idea that precooling athletes before a workout might delay their overheating, which normally hampers performance.

Young men in the study drank either a fruit slushie or fruit-flavored water before running on a treadmill in a hot room. Men who drank slushies were able to run for an average of 50 minutes before stopping, while those who drank the flavored water ran for just 40 minutes.

The slushie trick can work for you, too. Precooling provides a fairly short-term benefit, but you may profit from a slushie before a tennis match or a three-mile walk in the heat. Just don't overdo the tasty slushies because they can be high in calories.

Wrap yourself in cool relief. You can also cool your body from the outside in. Try wearing a cooling towel or neck wrap while playing golf on a hot day. These towels cool by evaporation. You wet them with hot or cold water, wring out, and use. They are reusable and washable, made from a superabsorbent material.

Popular brands include Frogg Toggs ChillyPad cooling towel, Sammy Cool 'n Dry towel, and ChillOut evaporative cooling towel. Or look for disposable towels that are ready to cool you down straight out of the package, such as Chill Cooling Towels.

Question & Answer

My friend says getting a massage after running a race helps with her recovery. Is that true?

That's the reason many athletes, from the professional to the leisurely, splurge for a massage after a hard workout or a tough race. For years they've been told massage improves circulation to your muscles and encourages removal of lactic acid and other waste products. But new research suggests that's not true.

Scientists in Canada looked at blood flow after hard exercise, with some athletes getting a massage and others going without. They found massage actually slowed blood flow to muscles, so waste wasn't removed.

If you enjoy a massage because it feels good, go ahead. But don't think you're speeding up healing.

Stretch your way to stronger muscles

Ahh, the feeling of a nice, gentle stretch. It can make you feel more limber, even while it helps you relax after exercising. Now experts say adding stretching to resistance training can help build muscle strength more quickly. But do it the right way.

Challenge your muscles. New research shows stretching can boost weight-lifting gains in muscle strength. A small study of college students compared the benefits of resistance training — weight lifting — with those of weight training plus stretching.

All subjects did the same weight-lifting routine three times a week for eight weeks. But half the students also did 30 minutes of stretching twice a week. Those who added stretching improved their muscle strength more than those who only lifted weights.

Both the resistance exercises and the stretches targeted muscles in the lower body. Experts say stretching challenges your muscles in ways similar to weight lifting, so the double workout helps them grow stronger.

Warm up first. Remember how your school gym teacher made you touch your toes and reach for the sky? That was old-school stretching, done before exercise in an attempt to avoid injury. Sometimes it hurt, but the pain was supposed to be good for your muscles.

But stretching before your muscles are warm may be a mistake. New research shows you can do more harm than good by stretching muscles before a workout, when they're still cold. This may actually encourage your muscles to contract more — tighten up in response to the stretch — which could raise your risk of injury. Instead, do stretches at another time, perhaps right after a workout.

Keep it moving. You still need to warm up before exercise, and dynamic stretches seem to be the way to go.

Some experts say dynamic stretches — such as lunges, which keep you in motion and work more than one muscle group — are better choices than static stretches — the old "touch your toes and hold the pose" routine.

With static stretching, you merely endure the pain of the stretch. With dynamic stretching, all muscles learn to be more flexible while certain muscles are in motion. That's more like what goes on during exercise. Dynamic stretching also provides more benefits in terms of boosting flexibility and performance.

Find dynamic stretches that mimic your sport, like side-to-side squats or deep knee lunges if you're a runner.

Stretch the benefits. Stretching offers advantages in addition to getting you ready for a workout. The right kind of stretch at the right time can:

- improve your flexibility.

- maintain your range of motion so you can do everyday movements, such as turning your head to look behind when you drive.

- prevent muscle cramps.

Besides, stretching the right way just plain feels good while you do it.

QUICK*fix*

Drinking too much soda can make you fat. It can also make you weak. Research shows drinking too many colas can lead to hypokalemia, a condition in which potassium levels fall and muscle function suffers. The problem can range from mild weakness to paralysis. High levels of glucose, fructose, and caffeine in colas bring on the condition.

Other research on mice tested what the large amounts of phosphates in soft drinks do to your body. Phosphates in excess seem to encourage muscle atrophy, skin withering, kidney disease, and even hardening of the arteries. All that adds up to aging.

Stretches for a comfy car trip

Travel comfortably — even during a long ride. Keep your muscles from getting tight and your joints from feeling stiff while you sit still for hours on a plane or in a car. You can do these stretching exercises while seated.

- Neck stretch. Slowly tilt your head toward one shoulder, hold still for a minute, then tilt and hold in the other direction.

- Shoulder stretch. Bend your left arm a bit and bring it across your chest as far as you can. Put your right arm across your left elbow to hold it in place for 10 seconds. Switch arms and repeat.

- Shoulder roll. Roll both shoulders forward in a circling motion several times. Then reverse the circles, rolling both shoulders to the rear.

- Core contraction. Press your lower back into the seat behind you while you tighten the muscles of your belly. Hold for a few seconds.

- Leg extension. Sit with your feet flat on the floor and knees together. Lift your left foot in front of you while you straighten your left leg. Bring it up until the leg is parallel to the floor and your toes point at the sky. Hold, then switch legs.

Even more important, get out of the car or your plane seat and walk around every hour or two to keep from feeling stiff. Periodic movement may also prevent you from developing a blood clot in your leg, a condition called deep vein thrombosis.

Surprising cause of muscle pain

Pain and weakness in your muscles isn't always from overdoing it on the golf course. It may be a drug side effect — if you are taking a statin. Doctors know this, and they check your enzyme levels to see if there's a problem. Yet, that might not be enough to find out if statins are doing you harm.

The standard enzyme test looks for high blood levels of the muscle enzyme creatine phosphokinase (CPK). That's a typical sign of myopathy, or muscle damage. But researchers checked damage to the muscle fibers in people who already knew they had myopathy. Of 44 people, 25 showed structural muscle damage — although only one person had a high level of CPK. That means the CPK test wasn't picking up all the damage.

Muscle damage was found even among people who had stopped taking statins for quite a while. Typically, you expect statin-related muscle pain and weakness to go away within days or weeks of stopping the drugs. These findings surprised researchers, showing that even if your blood enzymes are normal, you could still have muscle damage from your statin.

Some 10 percent of people taking statins report muscle-related side effects. Minor cases are called myositis, pain and inflammation of the muscles that occur when statins cause a buildup of CPK in your blood.

The most serious problem is rhabdomyolysis, in which muscles all over your body become painful and weak. And that's not all — muscle enzymes collect in your kidneys, leading to kidney failure and even death. Because this condition is serious, call your doctor if you're taking a statin and you have unusual or unexplained muscle aches. You should also have periodic blood tests to check for high levels of the liver enzyme transaminase, which is a sign of liver damage.

An early type of statin, cerivastatin (Baycol), was taken off the market after 31 people taking it died of rhabdomyolysis. Today's statins are safer, although these side effects are still possible — even if you've been taking the drugs for years without any problems.

Severe muscle damage is also more common in some situations:

- taking both a statin and certain other drugs, including fibrates and niacin, the immunosuppressant cyclosporine, certain anti-fungal and antibiotic drugs, the antidepressant nefazodone, and the heart drug verapamil

- drinking lots of grapefruit juice — more than a quart daily

- older age, especially over 80 years old

- frailty or having a small body frame

- chronic kidney disease

- having surgery

Other possible side effects of statins include eye disorders, thinking and memory problems, and peripheral neuropathy — numbness or pain in your fingers and toes. Talk to your doctor if you're worried about taking your statin, but don't stop taking it without his approval.

Question & Answer

Will vitamin supplements help me get more out of exercising?

Probably not. In fact, new research shows taking antioxidant vitamins — vitamin C and vitamin E in this case — may actually block some of the benefits of exercise. But antioxidant-rich foods don't have the same effect, so load up on greens, citrus fruits, and other vitamin-rich produce.

Simple solutions for pain-free living

Top 3 activities to beat arthritis pain

People who are fit at midlife double their chances of living to 85 years old. That's a great reason to get up and get active. But the pain of osteoarthritis can get in the way of the exercise regime you've always followed.

Osteoarthritis is pretty common among the silver-haired set. It develops when the cartilage that is supposed to cushion your joints wears away, allowing bones to feel like they're rubbing together painfully. The change can happen because of age, injuries, or simply your family history. Don't let arthritis pain keep you on the couch. Try one of these helpful activities, and find new life in your old joints.

Take a walk. Put one foot in front of the other, and you're on your way to boosting your heart and joint health. People with knee or hip arthritis who started a walking program had less pain and better mobility after just 12 weeks. They walked 3,000 steps, or about 1 1/2 miles, on either three or five days per week. These folks, ages 42 to 73, were also taking glucosamine supplements. They found that combining the walking program with the supplements helped with arthritis pain and stiffness.

Get a pedometer to count your steps so you'll know your total activity for the day — not just during an official walk. Aim for about 10,000 steps per day. Even if you don't reach that goal every day, you will increase your activity and likely decrease pain.

Lift some weights. Researchers at Tufts University found that older people with moderate to severe knee arthritis benefited from a 16-week strength-training program. Along with stronger muscles, decreased disability, and better overall conditioning, the people in the study reported about 43 percent less pain. This type of exercise also helps you as you age by strengthening your bones and helping you avoid falls.

Strength training might include lifting light weights, using weight machines at your gym, or working with elastic resistance bands. Start with light weights, then gradually increase the amount you lift. If you can't lift a weight eight times in a row, it's too heavy for you. Work up to 10 to 15 repetitions for each exercise. It's best to work all your major muscle groups — arms, legs, core — at least two days each week. But don't exercise the same group of muscles two days in a row. Muscles need time to rest and rebuild.

Enjoy a swim. For a no-impact cardio workout that may save your joints, take a dip in the pool. You can get all the benefits of vigorous exercise — no matter your age or health condition — with this one simple activity. It tones your whole body, raises your metabolism, and lowers your blood pressure with absolutely no pain and stress on your body and joints.

Swimming also works great to take off extra pounds, an important change to reduce stress on the joints of your lower body. For every 1 pound of excess weight you lose, you take 4 pounds of stress off your knees. A 154-pound person swimming slow freestyle laps in the pool burns about 255 calories in just 30 minutes. That's more than you burn with the same amount of walking, dancing, or gardening.

SimpleSOLUTION

Going barefoot may be easier on your arthritic knees than wearing fancy stability shoes or even regular walking shoes, say the experts at Rush Medical College.

Of course, no sane person would walk down a city street barefoot, stepping on all sorts of dangerous debris. That's where new types of thin-soled shoes, like Vibram Five Fingers, come in. They aim to protect your feet while giving you a walking experience much closer to being barefoot.

You can learn more about Vibram and other flexible shoes at these store Web sites.

- *www.vibramfivefingers.com*
- *www.feelmax.com*
- *www.terraplana.com*

Natural relief for arthritis woes

Looking for a non-drug treatment for osteoarthritis pain? You're not alone. Know which natural and herbal remedies really work, and you can avoid the confusion and disappointment of trying an impostor.

Have faith in the old standbys. Natural supplements with a good track record of effectiveness include glucosamine and chondroitin, often combined in a single pill. Some research shows they may be as effective as ibuprofen at relieving symptoms of osteoarthritis (OA).

Glucosamine and chondroitin are found in normal healthy cartilage. They bind with water to cushion and protect your joints and may help repair damage. Glucosamine in supplements typically comes from crab shells, while synthetic chondroitin is often made from cow cartilage.

Lots of research has been done to see if these two supplements actually work to slow OA, preserve cartilage, and reduce knee pain. The large GAIT study — Glucosamine/chondroitin Arthritis Intervention Trial — was supposed to decide the question once and for all, but the results were unclear. The two supplements had limited effectiveness overall, but they did work in people with moderate to severe OA pain.

Aside from pills, glucosamine and chondroitin are available in pre-mixed drink form or in a powder that you mix with water to make a fruity drink. Makers of these products say drinkable versions get the ingredients into your body more quickly.

Whichever form you decide to try, aim for about 1,500 milligrams (mg) of glucosamine daily. Be careful if you have diabetes, since glucosamine may raise blood sugar, or if you're allergic to shellfish, the most common source.

Consider other alternatives. If you decide glucosamine and chondroitin are not for you, check out one of these other natural pain and inflammation busters.

- **Willow bark extract.** Some herbal experts recommend willow bark extract as a substitute for aspirin to combat fever, pain, and inflammation. This plant is a traditional source of salicin, the pain reliever in aspirin. In fact, research shows it may be as effective against inflammation as aspirin and certain other pain-fighting drugs. Willow bark extract is safe for most people at doses of 120 to 240 mg salicin, but be careful or avoid this supplement if you have a history of ulcers.

- **SAMe.** Short for S-adenosylmethionine, SAMe is a natural compound that seems to help both arthritis and depression. It's found in all living cells, but you can buy it in supplement form. SAMe fights pain and inflammation, and it may also help build cartilage. Research shows it works as well as some nonsteroidal anti-inflammatory drugs (NSAIDs). You can take up to 800 mg per day, divided into several 200-mg doses.

- **Rose hips.** This fruit that develops from the blossoms of wild roses is a traditional anti-inflammatory herb. Studies showed it helped people with knee and hip OA by cutting pain and boosting joint flexibility. You can buy rose hips in a standardized powder or fruit juice form.

- **Aquamin.** This supplement, made of red algae seaweed from Iceland, contains a mixture of calcium, magnesium, and some 74 other minerals. With such a combination of potentially active ingredients, experts don't know just what is at work, but Aquamin seems to be a natural anti-inflammatory. In one study, people with knee pain found Aquamin worked better than glucosamine or chondroitin, improving their pain and mobility. Look for it in your drugstore or on Web sites like *www.drugstore.com* and *www.amazon.com*.

Talk to your doctor before you begin taking a new supplement, even something called "natural" or "herbal," to avoid an interaction with drugs you already take.

Gum care takes bite out of RA

It's no coincidence that people who suffer from rheumatoid arthritis (RA) may also have problems with their teeth. The inflammation that comes with one condition also goes along with the other. You can kill two birds with one stone by paying attention to your teeth and gums.

Rheumatoid arthritis is an autoimmune condition, which means your body starts attacking itself for an unknown reason. In RA, the lining of your joints is the main target of the attack. This leads to swelling and pain in your joints. You may also have stiffness, weakness, and general fatigue.

Inflammation in both your joints and your mouth is one link between RA and gum disease. Another key factor is that painful hands often have trouble doing the kind of thorough oral hygiene that can slow the development of gum disease. One study found that people with moderate to severe gum disease, or periodontitis, have three times the risk of developing RA than other people. The link goes the other way as well, with another study finding that people with RA are eight times more likely to have gum disease.

So if you already have RA, take these steps to pamper your teeth and gums. The extra effort may also lessen the severity of your arthritis.

Care for your pearly whites. You know the drill — brush with fluoride toothpaste, floss daily, and replace your toothbrush every three months, just like your dentist says. Some dentists suggest adding a daily fluoride rinse for extra protection. If pain in your hands gets in the way of careful brushing, consider options like using an electric toothbrush or a brush with a wide, easy-to-grip handle.

Get friendly with your dentist. The Arthritis Foundation recommends that people with RA go beyond regular dental cleaning to have scaling and root planing done at least twice a year. These treatments go below the gum line to remove debris, pus, bacteria, and tartar from places you can't reach, then smooth the root surfaces to help keep them clean. Your dentist may also place antibiotic gel into your gum pockets to control bacterial growth.

Boost your vitamin D. New research has found that women living in northern states that get little sun — places like New Hampshire, Vermont, and Maine — are more likely to develop RA than those in sunnier climates. The difference may be a lack of vitamin D, which your body makes from sunlight.

Lack of vitamin D is also linked with periodontitis. You need this sunshine vitamin to build and maintain strong bones and teeth. Vitamin D is thought to have anti-inflammatory benefits, which may help reduce swelling and gum bleeding. Other health problems, including osteoporosis, multiple sclerosis, and certain cancers, may also be related to lack of vitamin D.

You can get vitamin D from sunlight, food, or supplements. Spending up to 30 minutes at midday with the sun hitting your face, arms, legs, or back without sunscreen twice a week can give you enough. Otherwise, add vitamin-D fortified foods, like milk, and vitamin-D rich foods, like salmon, mackerel, and tuna. Consider taking supplements if you don't get out in the sun much. If you prefer supplements, aim for 1,000 IU of vitamin D3 a day.

Question & Answer

Can cracking your knuckles lead to arthritis in your fingers?

No. Knuckle cracking will not cause arthritis. But doing it habitually can lead to injuries in the ligaments surrounding the joints or dislocation of the tendons at that joint. Over the years, this habit can lead to a weaker grip compared to people who don't crack their knuckles. If you already have arthritis and you crack your knuckles a lot, you're more likely to get this ligament and tendon damage than other people.

Get a hand around the house

Have a case of fumbly fingers? Arthritis pain and stiffness can do that to you. Before you resort to asking for help with the simple tasks of daily life, get a handle on some of these handy helpers.

- Jar opener. You can find one that mounts under your kitchen cabinet for easy access, or pick a hand-held version that looks like a vise grip. An even simpler solution is a flat, rubber circle that helps you grip a jar lid tightly.

- Fat handles. Find forks, spoons, carrot peelers — even a tooth-brush — with wider handles that are easier to grip.

- Buttoner. This hand-held tool lets you button tiny shirt buttons without overworking your fingers.

- Door opener. You can find the right style to help open door-knobs or flip-up car door handles.

- Spring-action scissors. Squeeze the handles to cut, then release and the scissors spring open with no stress on your hands.

- Reach extender. This tool looks like pinchers on a long stick. It lets you pick up items from the floor without bending over.

- "Arthritis bra." It closes in front with Velcro and large hooks rather than with tiny hooks and eyes.

SimpleSOLUTION

Your joints age, just like the rest of you. But you can avoid increased pain and possibly even joint replacement if you follow these top five tips to keep your joints young and healthy.

- Lose weight if you need to. Excess weight puts more pressure on knees and hips with every step.

- Go low impact for exercise. Keep jogging if you enjoy it, but mix in less jarring exercises like swimming or tai chi on some days.

- Avoid injury. Skip risky activities like that fast-paced basketball or football game.

- Stay fit. Get your muscles in shape to keep joints properly aligned.

- Eat right. Add foods with omega-3 fatty acids, like salmon or tuna, to cut inflammation.

Find relief beyond your doctor's office

Sometimes the best person to treat your pain is not a medical doctor at all. He may be a chiropractor.

The field of chiropractic care involves relationships among your spine, nervous system, and the rest of your body. Sometimes that means getting a spinal manipulation or adjustment — a procedure that puts quick pressure on a joint to mobilize it or increase its range of motion.

A chiropractor, osteopath, or physical therapist can adjust your vertebrae to relieve pain that's caused by poor alignment. If your back pain has lasted less than a month and there's no sign of a spinal nerve root disorder, like herniated disc or spinal stenosis, you may be a good candidate for treatment by spinal manipulation.

Repeated research has shown that chiropractic care and spinal manipulation may help both lower back pain and tension headaches. Even better, chiropractic care may be covered by your health insurance or Medicare.

But certain chiropractors may try to overstep the bounds of their profession, making claims that don't hold water or running up your bill. Beware of these signs of a questionable chiropractor.

- He doesn't do a complete physical exam and take a full medical history before starting treatment, yet he wants to take X-rays of your full spine before he starts.

- He claims the treatment will cure or prevent a disease, like cancer or heart disease, or boost your immunity.

- He tries to get your family members to come in for treatment.

- He or his staff try to sell you vitamin cures, cleansing cures, or homeopathic remedies.

- He won't work with your regular medical doctor or discredits traditional medicine.

- His office requires you to sign a contract for long-term treatment.

You may find a reputable chiropractor by asking your friends and relatives for references and looking for one who's a member of the American Chiropractic Association.

Rarely, complications may occur from chiropractic adjustment, especially in people with conditions like arthritis, brittle-bone disease, bone-softening diseases, clotting disorders, or migraines. Chiropractic adjustment may also be risky if you have an aneurysm or certain circulatory problems, or if you take anticoagulants.

Strengthen core for pain-free days

David spent hours every day hunched over his computer keyboard. He thought he balanced that habit with lifting weights and jogging a bit. But still he suffered from a stiff neck and painful knots in his back and shoulders.

David got advice from a fitness trainer at his health club. The trainer suggested core training, or exercises to strengthen the muscles of David's abdomen, back, and sides — all the way from his shoulders to his hips. Some exercises use a physio ball, like a huge beach ball you balance on.

After a few months, David's shoulders and neck stopped hurting — even though his posture at the computer had not improved. He's still working on that.

Get results with offbeat remedies

Surgery may help your back or joint pain. But then again, it may not — and it will cost you plenty to find out. Before you go under the knife, consider trying one of these cheaper and less-invasive treatments for chronic pain in your knees, back, neck, and elsewhere.

Find healing from within. Prolotherapy involves a series of glucose — a simple sugar — injections to the painful area. The injections trigger your body's inflammatory system, encouraging buildup of extra ligament tissue to stabilize the bones and muscles in a joint. One study found it worked in 32 of 36 people with Achilles tendinosis, allowing them to get back to their previous exercise routines. Other research saw benefits for knee and back pain.

Get a jolt of pain relief. Transcutaneous electrical nerve stimulation (TENS) is a mouthful, but the treatment is simple. The TENS device, which sends out gentle electrical impulses, has small electrodes that attach to your skin at or near the site of pain. Experts think TENS works by stimulating the nerves to change your perception of pain, possibly raising levels of endorphins — natural "feel-good" hormones your body pumps out. Research is mixed on the effectiveness of TENS. Avoid this procedure if you have a pacemaker or implanted heart defibrillator.

Let an expert take a stab. Acupuncture has gone high-tech with electro-acupuncture treatment. It's similar to traditional acupuncture, which places tiny needles at specific points on your body where nerves enter a muscle. But electro-acupuncture includes wires attached to the needles so an electrical current stimulates the release of pain-relieving brain chemicals.

Shine a light on relief. Cold-laser therapy, also called low-level laser therapy, is a fairly new treatment for neck pain, knee pain, and other chronic ills, including pain and morning stiffness caused by rheumatoid arthritis.

This treatment involves using so-called "pure" light of a single wavelength but no heat. It causes chemical reactions in certain target cells to relieve pain and stiffness. Cold-laser therapy has no side effects, so it's quite safe. But benefits seem to wear off after a few months.

Join a group. Meeting with others suffering from the same problems can help. You may be able to share your thoughts about chronic pain, avoiding physical activity, or other issues. One study followed 600 people with back pain, offering them group therapy or standard doctor's treatment including drugs. Just six sessions of group therapy — called cognitive behavioral therapy — provided relief that lasted as long as a year. Group therapy also saved money.

Get a referral from your doctor if you want to try one of these remedies, and be aware health insurance may not pay for alternative therapies.

Question & Answer

I think I can forecast a weather change based on pain in my fingers. Is that possible?

Lots of people believe this, and it might be true. Feeling pain in your joints when the weather is in flux may be due to changing barometric pressure. This variation could cause a pressure change in the synovial fluid that lubricates your joints. But research is unclear on the matter, although one study found changes in barometric pressure and dropping temperatures affected joint pain. The question is still undecided, so don't move to a dry, warm climate in search of healing for your arthritis. There's no guarantee you would find relief.

Break the chain of gout pain

Your gout may let you bypass Parkinson's disease. That could be a silver lining behind this painful condition, marked by excess uric acid in your blood and joints. Experts don't know exactly why people with the most uric acid have a lower risk of Parkinson's. But you can beat back the joint pain with changes to your diet and lifestyle.

Gout attacks occur when uric acid crystals build up around certain joints, especially in your big toe. Uric acid comes from purines, either in the food you eat or made by your body. The problem is most common among men in their 40s and 50s, but women become more prone as they age.

A new drug, febuxostat (Uloric), can help lower uric acid levels. It may be a good choice if you can't take allopurinol (Zyloprim), the old standby drug, or probenecid, which is not appropriate for people with kidney disease. You can also take prescription-strength nonsteroidal anti-inflammatory drugs (NSAIDs) to combat the pain and inflammation of a gout attack until it subsides, usually in about five days. If you can't take NSAIDs, there's still the option of colchicine or a corticosteroid.

Even if you find a medicine that works to lower uric acid, you're not in the clear. Rising or falling uric acid levels can trigger a gout attack. So when you start taking a drug to lower your uric acid levels, the pain may start anew. Many health professionals say to continue taking the medicine and wait out the attacks — probably less than six to 12 months.

The best way to avoid a painful gout flare-up is to pay attention to your diet.

- Avoid purine-rich foods, typically high-protein foods like organ meats and bacon, along with yeast, gravy, and fish such as herring, mackerel, and sardines.

- Don't get dehydrated. Research found that people susceptible to gout who drank more water — five to eight glasses of water daily rather than a single glass — lowered their risk of a gout attack by 40 percent.

- Get enough vitamin C. Research found that men who took vitamin C supplements — just 1,000 milligrams (mg) a day — had less risk of developing gout over 20 years. Experts think vitamin C works by easing inflammation and by lowering uric acid levels. Chow down on foods like bell peppers, strawberries, and citrus fruits.

- Drink milk. Skim milk was found to be helpful in one study. The orotic acid in dairy helps your kidneys pull uric acid out of your body.

- Avoid alcohol, especially beer, and soft drinks. Alcohol contains purines, plus it encourages your body to make uric acid. And drinking as few as one sugar-sweetened soft drink a day raises your risk for gout. Diet soft drinks don't have the same effect, since it's the high-fructose corn syrup in regular sodas that raises uric acid levels in your blood.

- Enjoy your morning brew. Men who drink four or more cups of coffee a day lower their risk of gout by up to 60 percent. Tea or other caffeinated drinks don't do the trick.

- Put cherries on top. Make cherries your vitamin C fruit of choice, and you add the benefits of anthocyanins, natural plant chemicals that give the fruit its color. These little gems cut the inflammation and pain of gout.

You can also reduce your chances of an attack by losing extra pounds. That helps lower blood levels of uric acid.

Take 7 steps away from foot pain

Your tired old tootsies don't need to feel bad. Painful feet are not inevitable as you age. Whether it's from crowded toes or heel impact, your foot pain has a solution.

Pain in your feet can be caused by many things, including changes related to getting older and basic overuse. People tend to be on their feet roughly four hours every day. And with 33 joints, 26 bones, and more than 100 tendons, ligaments, and muscles, your foot is a complex body part with a lot that can go wrong.

Follow these basic rules to avoid unnecessary foot pain.

Keep up with grooming. Avoid painful ingrown toenails by trimming them straight across the top, not rounded at the edges. But keep nails long enough so the edges won't get embedded in your skin. You can also wear sandals or open-toed shoes to put less pressure on your toenails.

Watch for signs of aging. Stay on top of these age-related structural foot changes:

- Hammertoes, also called claw toes. Tightening of ligaments can make your toes turn downward, taking the shape of a claw. Avoid pain by wearing wide shoes with square, boxy toes. You can also try specially designed shields or slings for problem toes.

- Bunions. These bony growths that form at the joint where your toe meets your foot are caused by constant pressure from shoes pushing one toe against the others. To avoid the problem, wear soft, wide, low-heeled leather shoes that lace up. Sandals that leave toes wiggle room may also do the trick.

- Thinning fat pads on the bottom of your feet. This means you have less cushioning, so look for sturdier shoes.

Wear the right shoes. Your feet can grow with age, so check your shoes for fit. Also pick the right shoes for the activity, like wearing running shoes when you go jogging. It's best to avoid wearing high heels. If you feel you must wear them, stick to 2-inch heels or lower, but don't wear them for very long.

Support your arches. Flat feet need the most arch support. If your shoes don't provide support, consider orthotic inserts. You can buy an over-the-counter pair, or get a custom pair for best fit. Custom-made orthotics work well to distribute your weight properly and avoid painful pressure in spots. But they cost around $400 to $600 a pair.

Bathe your tootsies. Enjoying a warm foot bath for about 10 minutes a couple times a week can keep your feet relaxed, ward off foot fatigue, and prevent pain. Mix one-half cup Epsom salts into the water to boost circulation.

Keep your shoes on. Beware of going barefoot. You can probably do it in good weather for short periods — if you don't already have foot problems. But bare feet have higher risks of injury, and you should never go barefoot if you have diabetes.

Stretch out the pain. Plantar fasciitis causes pain on the bottom of your foot and heel. Try these stretches, well known to runners who suffer the pain.

- Sit on the floor with your painful foot stretched out in front of you. Wrap a towel around the bottom of your foot, and hold the two ends of the towel in your hands. Then gently pull back on the towel to stretch your foot.

- Stand about an arm's length away from a wall, and lean against it on your hands. Place the uninjured foot on the floor in front of the injured foot. Raise the heel of your injured foot, and gently stretch the injured leg and foot.

QUICK *fix*

An old wives' tale says if your second toe is longer than your first, you'll be the head of your household. That's debatable, but experts call this condition Morton's toe.

When you walk, your big toe touches the ground before your other toes. In people with Morton's toe, the second toe touches the ground first, but it's not strong enough to withstand the pressure. This changes your body's alignment and causes pain in your feet, legs, and back. You may also notice a callus on the bottom of your foot next to the second toe.

Here's a simple solution. Place a pad of thick tape or moleskin under the first metatarsal — the bone in your foot behind the big toe. Then this part of your foot will push off the ground rather than your second toe.

Pour your heart into migraine relief

The 30 million Americans who suffer from migraines may also be at risk for a heart attack. This finding means these painful headaches, often accompanied by nausea, vomiting, or sensitivity to light and sound, are more than just a nuisance. They may be a sign your heart is in danger.

New research shows that people who have migraines have double the risk of a heart attack compared to other people. The risk is tripled if you suffer from migraines with aura — visual disturbances that can happen right before a migraine. Even so, the real risk of a heart attack is still pretty low, with only around 4 percent of those in the study experiencing heart attacks. If you have migraines, you also have a greater chance of having a stroke — particularly for migraines with aura.

There's more. People who have migraines also tend to have other heart risk factors, including high blood pressure, diabetes, and high cholesterol. The link may be related to weaknesses in the function of your endothelium, the inner lining of blood vessels. Experts also see a connection between migraine and rosacea, the red-face skin condition that is related to blood vessel widening and narrowing.

Your take-home message? If you have migraines, be extra vigilant about your heart health.

Stop the pain naturally. Famous migraineurs, as sufferers are called, include Thomas Jefferson, Sigmund Freud, and Elizabeth Taylor. Obviously, they didn't let the pain keep them from living life to the fullest. Take control, and you can stop letting migraines rule your days.

Certain migraine triggers are not in your control. These include hormones and changing weather. But you may be able to control other factors. Keep a journal, making note of everything you ate and drank, how you slept, and what you did for the 24 hours before the migraine hit. This will help you identify your personal migraine triggers and stay away from them. Often, a combination of triggers can bring on an episode.

- Pay attention to caffeine, especially if you drink a lot of it. Some studies show caffeine brings on headaches, while other studies show it reduces them.

- Watch your intake of common problem foods, like wine, aged cheese, and deli meat, along with food additives like monosodium glutamate (MSG) and nitrates.

- Look out for bright lights, loud noises, and powerful smells. Such strong sensory input can be triggers for some people.

- Get the right amount of sleep — not too much or too little.

- Beware of stress, the biggest trigger. A stress-induced migraine typically occurs after the stress is gone.

You can also try herbal remedies if avoiding your triggers doesn't do the trick. Chewing on leaves of the feverfew plant is a traditional method of warding off migraines. But you will probably prefer to take feverfew in supplement form, since chewing the leaves can cause mouth sores. A review of research found taking feverfew supplements daily may cut frequency of migraines. Butterbur is a second popular preventive herb, although there's only sparse evidence it works. Some herbal experts recommend taking it daily to ward off migraines.

Seek medical help if all else fails. Migraines that can't be stopped can do serious damage to your quality of life. Even if none of these do-it-yourself solutions stops your headaches, you still have hope. Your doctor may prescribe one of several new drugs that can cut short a migraine attack. They're in a class of drugs called triptans, and they include eletriptan (Relpax), sumatriptan (Imitrex), and zolmitriptan (Zomig).

Or your solution may be as simple as taking a large dose of aspirin. A review of research found 50 percent of people with severe migraine pain had relief within two hours after taking 900 to 1,000 milligrams (mg) of aspirin. A regular aspirin tablet is 325 mg. The remedy worked against pain, nausea, vomiting, and sensitivity to light. In fact, one in four people in the study had complete relief. Keep in mind aspirin comes with side effects, like heartburn and gastrointestinal bleeding.

Magnetic box ends migraines

You may soon be able to stop a migraine without taking drugs. Researchers tested a small, hand-held device that releases a magnetic pulse on people who suffer from migraines with aura. The device emits what's called single-pulse transcranial magnetic stimulation (sTMS). It is believed to disrupt electrical events in your brain that cause early symptoms of a migraine. Of about 100 people who used the device at the start of a migraine, some 40 percent were free of pain two hours later, with no serious side effects.

4 ways to stop fibromyalgia pain

Fibro my what? That's fibromyalgia, a kind of chronic pain syndrome that can be hard to diagnose and even harder to treat. It's more common among women, and it can put a real strain on many areas of your life.

People with fibromyalgia have chronic, widespread muscle pain, fatigue, and tender points. This term, used to distinguish between fibromyalgia and other painful conditions, refers to 18 specific spots on your body that can be sensitive to pressure. With fibromyalgia, there's no joint inflammation, so technically it's not arthritis. But the condition is in the group of rheumatic disorders because it causes chronic pain and affects your joints and soft tissues. You may also have morning stiffness, trouble sleeping, memory or concentration problems — sometimes called "fibro fog" — bowel problems, restless leg syndrome, and tingling in your hands and feet.

Nowadays, the symptoms can be treated with drugs. Beyond pain-relieving drugs, certain antidepressants, sleep aids, and muscle relaxants are commonly prescribed.

Try these natural remedies to end the pain and win back your life from fibromyalgia.

Pinpoint your pain. The ancient healing art of acupuncture may do the trick. Researchers found that people suffering from fibromyalgia had relief from pain, anxiety, and fatigue after a series of acupuncture treatments. It seems a natural painkiller called adenosine increased in the area near the acupuncture site.

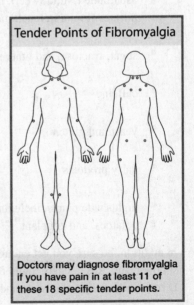

Tender Points of Fibromyalgia

Doctors may diagnose fibromyalgia if you have pain in at least 11 of these 18 specific tender points.

Put nature's healers to work. The herb skullcap is a traditional remedy for fibromyalgia, used to treat these symptoms since the 19th century. It's considered a natural antispasmodic, although there's little scientific evidence to support the use of skullcap.

A newer, natural option may be chlorella, a supplement made from algae. You can find it in capsule form at drugstores and health food stores. One study found taking liquid or tablet forms of chlorella daily reduced tender point pain in people with fibromyalgia. But the study was small and had mixed results, so more testing may be needed to be sure.

Uncover food sensitivities. No single diet exists to deal with the symptoms of fibromyalgia. But sufferers have found relief by making certain changes to the way they eat. Everyone has different sensitivities, but try avoiding these things.

- aspartame (NutraSweet), monosodium glutamate (MSG), and nitrates (found in lunch meats and bacon)

- sugar, fructose, and other simple carbohydrates

- caffeine

- yeast and gluten

- dairy products

- nightshade plants, including tomatoes, chili and bell peppers, potatoes, and eggplant

In addition, be sure you get enough vitamin D from food, sunlight, or supplements. Researchers found that people with low levels of vitamin D had a higher risk of muscle and bone pain, including fibromyalgia.

Stay active — even when it hurts. You may not feel like exercising when the pain of fibromyalgia hits, but research shows both aerobic and resistance exercise can help. Twelve weeks of strength training cut pain and depression, while it boosted the overall well-being of people with fibromyalgia. Moderate aerobic exercise also helped improve symptoms. Other researchers recommended people with the condition do exercises to improve their balance to reduce falls.

Even newer research found that women who are overweight — with a body mass index (BMI) of 25 or more — have a 60 to 70 percent higher chance of developing fibromyalgia than thinner women. Those who exercised less than one hour each week also had a greater risk.

But you don't need to spend hours at the gym. Just 30 minutes a day of "lifestyle physical activity" can help you overcome fibromyalgia pain and disability. Try fitting in the following.

- Take the stairs instead of the elevator.

- Work in your garden.

- Do leg lifts or arm circles while you watch television.

- Use a pedometer to count your steps daily.

- Clean your house vigorously listening to your favorite music.

Get a grip on gluten sensitivity

You may be sensitive to your morning toast and not even know it. A typical person with gluten sensitivity has problems for 11 years before it's diagnosed. That's a long time to live with a condition that can affect your entire body. Even more worrisome, researchers have found that extreme gluten sensitivity, or celiac disease, may be four times as common now than it was just 50 years ago. The do-it-yourself solution — cut gluten from your diet.

Celiac disease is an autoimmune disease, meaning your body attacks itself. In this case, a serious reaction to gluten, a component of wheat and other grains, damages your small intestines. Symptoms include chronic diarrhea, vomiting, constipation, weight loss, and plenty of belly pain. Other symptoms include bone or joint pain, migraines, and mouth sores.

Get the right diagnosis. Doctors identify celiac disease with two tests — a bowel biopsy to find flattened villi, showing your body has been on the attack, and a blood test indicating certain antibodies. The condition is hard to diagnose based on symptoms, since some people don't notice any signs at all. Nowadays, experts admit people can have a low-grade gluten sensitivity that doesn't even show up on blood tests. Some say it's not even a "yes" or "no" diagnosis, but rather a spectrum of more or less gluten sensitivity. That's why you may not meet official diagnostic criteria but still be affected by gluten in the food you eat.

Go gluten-free for gut comfort. If you think you may be sensitive to gluten — even if you don't have a definite diagnosis — you can try a gluten-free diet to see if it helps. Here's how to avoid gluten.

- Check food labels for the symbol "GF" within a circle. This mark indicates the product is certified gluten-free.

- Read food labels to see if the item contains wheat, rye, barley, malt, or oats. Although oats are actually gluten-free, they can be contaminated if they are processed in the same plant with other grains. That means most foods made from grains — breads, pasta, crackers, cookies — are off limits.

- Look for gluten-free alternatives to your favorite foods, like pasta made from brown rice, corn, or quinoa.

- Beware of gluten from unexpected sources, like communion wafers, medicine, lipstick, canned foods, luncheon meats, candy, and ice cream.

Untreated celiac disease can lead to long-term health problems, like osteoporosis, vitamin D and calcium deficiencies, damage to your tooth

Prolotherapy helps joints heal themselves

Paul enjoyed staying fit by riding his bicycle, but as he got older, he couldn't put in the same miles every day. When he tried to keep up with younger cyclists, he ended up with a knee injury from overuse. That took him off the road for several months.

Paul's doctor suggested prolotherapy, a series of glucose injections to the joint. Paul had three injections to his painful knee over the next two months, spending about $125 for each treatment. Six months later, he was back on his bike and keeping up with his buddies.

"Prolotherapy was cheaper in the long run than surgery would have been," Paul said. "It really worked great for me."

enamel, and possibly neurological problems. Total gluten elimination is not easy, but it seems to reverse symptoms and let your intestines start healing themselves. You may notice an improvement within a few days of changing your diet. It works for 95 percent of people with gluten sensitivity, but you'll need to stick with the plan for life.

Strike back at gallstone attack

You lost a lot of weight on one of those quick diets, but now your body is giving you a painful payback. The sharp pains in your midsection start near your rib cage and radiate toward your back. It could be a sign you have gallstones.

Losing weight quickly, or losing a lot of weight and gaining it back, often comes before a gallstone attack. That's because your liver reacts to the change by pumping out more cholesterol, a main ingredient in one type of stone.

Your gallbladder, a small organ near the liver, is a storage tank for bile, which helps your body break down fats in the food you eat. When bile sits in your gallbladder too long, it can become concentrated and form stones. Some gallstones that pass through the bile duct don't cause pain, but for many people, they are excruciating — like a golf ball being pushed through a straw. You might have a bout of pain right after eating a large meal, or the pain could wake you up at night hours later.

Gallbladder problems are common, with more than 800,000 people in the United States needing gallbladder removal every year. Many more have gallstones but don't need their gallbladders removed. Today, it's common to have your gallbladder removed through laparoscopic — also called keyhole — surgery, which is safer and requires smaller incisions and less recovery time than conventional surgery.

Take these steps to cut your risk of painful gallstones.

Enjoy your morning brew. If you drink coffee, don't stop the habit. Research is mixed about whether coffee prevents gallstones. Some reports say it does, while others say no. The most recent study found that women who drank coffee were less likely to have had their gallbladders removed because of stones.

Overall, experts think drinking coffee may lower your risk for both gallstones and kidney stones. The caffeine in coffee encourages your gallbladder to contract to release bile, cutting down on the development of stones.

Eat more fruits and veggies. Researchers studied women who took part in the Nurses' Health Study, following them for 16 years. Women who ate more fruits and vegetables — especially green leafies, cruciferous veggies, citrus fruits and other fruits and vegetables high in vitamin C — were less likely to develop gallbladder disease. Thus, the produce lovers kept their gallbladders more often than those who ate less produce. Protective ingredients include minerals like magnesium, antioxidants such as vitamin C, and fiber, which speeds up movement of food through your intestines and changes the makeup of bile.

Avoid HRT pills. If you're a woman thinking about hormone-replacement therapy (HRT), consider using a patch or cream form rather than a pill. One study found a lower risk of gallstones among women taking HRT through the skin rather than oral therapy.

Oral HRT may raise your risk of gallstones because the hormones are broken down in your liver before they enter your bloodstream. In contrast, hormones you absorb through your skin move directly into your blood, avoiding this "first-pass metabolism" in the liver. Experts say for every 140 women who choose patch or cream HRT over pills for five years, one gallbladder removal is avoided.

See about statins. To reduce the risk of gallstones that need surgery, ask your doctor about taking a statin — especially if you have high cholesterol or other risk factors for heart disease.

Researchers in England found that middle-age people who took a statin for at least a year had a lower risk of gallstones needing surgery. Similarly, women in the Nurses' Health Study who took cholesterol-lowering drugs — mostly statins — had less risk of gallbladder removal.

What's the connection? Statins keep your liver from making too much cholesterol, and gallstones are made of either bilirubin or cholesterol. Less cholesterol in your system means less cholesterol that can be made into gallstones.

Take warning from your aching lower back

Lower back pain may be a sign your heart is at risk. Experts reviewed research on heart disease and back problems. They found links between fatty buildup in the aorta — the main artery that supplies blood to the body — and breakdown of disks in the spine. They also noticed a link between blocked arteries to the lower back and back pain. People with high cholesterol and those who smoke also had more back pain.

The problem may be that heart disease causes blockage of blood vessels to your lower back and spine. Take your lower back pain seriously and see your doctor.

Good news for shingles sufferers

Call it chicken pox 2.0 — that nasty childhood disease come back to haunt you in your golden years. That's what it can feel like when a bout of shingles appears, with its red rash and stinging pain. But a new capsaicin patch may block the pain's hold on your life.

Know the signs. If you had chicken pox as a child, you're at risk for shingles later on. That's because the virus hides out in your body for years, waiting for a chance to come alive in the form of shingles. Half of people who reach age 85 experience it. You may notice a red rash along one side of your body. It can spread to your face and cause blindness if an optical nerve is affected.

Even after the shingles rash is gone, the pain of postherpetic neuralgia (PHN) can be horrible, easily lasting three months. Almost half of people over age 70 suffer with PHN for more than a year, unable to work, play, or enjoy life. The pain can be so bad you need large amounts of painkilling drugs or epidural injections. If you think you may be developing shingles, see your doctor for an antiviral drug. These work best if given within 48 hours of the start of the rash.

Put a patch on the problem. The U.S. Food and Drug Administration (FDA) recently approved Qutenza, a patch containing synthetic capsaicin. That's the chemical in hot peppers that makes your tongue burn. It's used in some pain-relieving creams to desensitize your skin and lower the amount of substance P, a natural compound that transmits pain signals to your brain.

Qutenza is a prescription patch that you wear for about an hour. Your doctor first applies topical anesthetic to your skin, then puts on the patch. The procedure hurts a bit, even with anesthetic, and it may make your blood pressure rise while it's working. But people seem to think it's well worth the short-term discomfort to avoid long-term PHN pain.

Take steps to avoid shingles. The best way to deal with shingles may be to avoid it altogether. First, ask your doctor about getting the shingles vaccine, Zostavax, when you turn 60 years old. Research shows it may protect you from this very painful condition. But even if you get shingles after you've had the vaccine, your pain will likely be less severe.

You can also boost your immunity and avoid shingles by learning the ancient art of tai chi. Researchers in California found that seniors who took classes in tai chi chih — a westernized version of the martial art — three times a week boosted their immunity as much as if they had gotten the shingles vaccine. Even better, those who took the classes and got the vaccine boosted their immunity to twice the level of seniors who only received the vaccine.

In addition, the research showed that seniors who took tai chi classes improved their ability to do everyday tasks, like walking up stairs and carrying packages. Other research has found that tai chi classes may help you sleep. Just 25 weeks of tai chi classes helped seniors sleep better so they were less drowsy during the day and better able to concentrate.

Question & Answer

The older I get, the more trouble I have feeling stiff after sitting for a while. Why is this?

As you get older, your ligaments, tendons, and cartilage — the cushioning tissue in joints — change, and you have less lubricating fluid in those joints. After you sit for a while, the fluid is not evenly distributed within joint spaces. It can be worse if you suffer from osteoarthritis. Then when you stand up, there's less lubrication to keep cartilage from rubbing together. But as you move around, the fluid also moves around and you feel less stiff.

Tell your doctor exactly when the problem happens, and she may help diagnose a specific joint problem.

Break the itch-scratch-itch cycle

When you have an itch, you want to scratch it. But sometimes scratching just makes the itch worse. It's called the itch-scratch-itch cycle, and it can make you forget about everything except the annoying sensation.

Itching, or pruritus, is related to pain — both happen at the skin and are relayed to your brain along the same nerve pathways. But constant itching that you can't stop with scratching can be more uncomfortable than pain. In fact, some people scratch so hard they bring on pain, finding that easier to handle than the itch.

The best remedy depends on what's causing the itch.

Dry skin. For dry skin or chronic eczema, use a good moisturizer and stay away from extremes of hot and cold, like hot baths. Also avoid skin irritants like wearing itchy wool or scrubbing your skin.

Colloidal oatmeal in the form of a bath or lotion may help. Certain proteins and polysaccharides in oatmeal form a barrier to shield your skin, protecting and moisturizing it. You can make your own bath mixture by combining two cups of oatmeal with four cups of water. Boil the mixture, then add to a tub of warm water and soak. Be careful when you step in, since the tub will be slippery. You can buy lotions and other skin-care products that contain colloidal oatmeal, such as the Aveeno line of products.

Acupuncture also seems to work for people with atopic eczema by urging your body to produce natural pain-blocking chemicals.

Bites and blisters. For itching caused by bug bites or poison ivy, you might start with a cold compress or an over-the-counter steroid cream. But see your doctor if swelling and inflammation expand beyond the original location of the bite or blister. You may need oral antihistamines or corticosteroids.

No clear cause. If you have ongoing itching with no rash or other visible sign, you may have a serious condition like anemia, thyroid or liver disease, or even an internal cancer. See your doctor if it doesn't go away.

QUICK*fix*

Don't blame exercise for your lower back pain. The problem may be poor posture after your workout is done.

Physical therapist Robin McKenzie says pain that doesn't start until after you're done running — or cycling or golfing — is likely not due to overexertion. Instead, pain after sports often occurs because people tend to slouch or slump when they are done working out.

Maybe it's in the car on the way home, or maybe it's in your chair at the country club. That bad posture can cause damage to joints in your spine. Stop the slouch, stop the pain. But keep exercising. If pain begins while you're exercising, McKenzie says, get checked for injury.

Tasty tricks for a pain-free workout

You've made the resolution to start an exercise program, but you are not looking forward to sore muscles and achy joints. Don't fret — getting fit doesn't have to hurt. Follow these steps before, during, and after each workout to avoid post-exercise pain.

Before: Drink cherry juice. Researchers found that tart cherry juice had the anti-inflammatory power to cut post-exercise pain in a group of runners. The athletes drank about 10.5 ounces of cherry juice twice a day for seven days before a long-distance relay event. They also enjoyed a glass on the day of the race. Juice drinkers reported less pain and muscle soreness after the run than athletes who didn't drink the juice. Experts believe anthocyanins, antioxidant compounds in cherry juice that give it color, get the credit for cutting inflammation. Benefit to you? Less pain.

During: Exercise wisely. Put wisdom to your advantage and avoid "boomeritis." That's a new nickname for injuries and aches that can happen when you overtrain or do the same workout every day for years and years. Once you pass age 50, you can't continue training exactly like you did when you were younger. The results would be overuse injuries like tendinitis, bursitis, and stress fractures. Make these changes to your routine to avoid this trap.

- Warm up and cool down to avoid injuring cold muscles. Do this by pedaling in a low gear, for example, or walking in place for a few minutes before your workout. Do the same thing after you exercise until your breathing and heart rate return to normal.

- Learn how to stretch. Joints, muscles, and tendons become less flexible as you age, so they benefit from a gentle stretch after you have warmed up. Hold that stretch for at least 30 seconds.

- Cross train, or switch activities, so you don't perform the same exercises every day. If you have been riding your bike for years for aerobic exercise, work on your swimming strokes. Or if you spend your weekends on the golf course, try fitting in some tennis for a change.

- Listen to your body. Take a day off when you feel an ache. Don't try to push through the pain as your younger self might have done. You're old enough to know better.

After: Enjoy a chocolate milk chaser. This tasty beverage lets you load up on protein, calcium, energy from the chocolate, and vitamin D.

Researchers showed that athletes who drank chocolate milk after both aerobic and resistance exercise enjoyed better recovery. In one study, cyclists who drank chocolate milk after a hard workout were able to perform better during a second workout than those who drank a typical fruity sports drink. Another study on weight lifters showed how proteins in milk help your body rebuild muscle that gets broken down during resistance training.

And don't forget that low-fat milk — even chocolate milk — helps you rehydrate your body after exercise, replacing fluid lost to sweating. Who needs more reasons to enjoy a little chocolate pick-me-up?

Hot and cold relief for achy joints

Pro football players sometimes soak in a hot tub after a game to relieve their sore muscles. This trick may work just as well for you. Both heat and cold can help relieve the pain of joints damaged by osteoarthritis, letting you exercise in comfort.

Heat relaxes muscles around a stiff joint, relieving arthritis pain. You benefit from applying heat both before and after exercise. But don't use heat for more than 15 minutes at a time, and follow product safety instructions to avoid a burn. Here are some heat-treatment options.

- Enjoy moist heat from a hot tub; warm, steamy shower; or heated wet towel.

- Apply dry heat using a heating pad, mitt, or heat lamp. Try a microwaveable heating pad that stays warm for hours.

- Dip your hands in warm paraffin wax for a heat treatment that keeps on working on achy fingers.

Cold helps your joints because it reduces swelling, while it distracts you from the pain. You can safely apply treatment with a cold pack that's stored in the freezer. Homemade treatments include applying a plastic bag of ice cubes, a wet towel dipped in ice water, or a bag of frozen vegetables.

Never apply ice directly to your skin. To avoid frostbite, put a hand towel on your skin before applying the icy treatment. Don't use cold therapy for more than 15 to 20 minutes at a time. You may find the best relief from alternating between hot and cold applications.

The trouble with X-rays

Pay attention to your pain — even after an X-ray shows you're fine. It may be missing something. Research shows X-rays of an injured hip or pelvis don't always show a fracture. But a scan called magnetic resonance imaging (MRI) is more sensitive.

In the study, researchers used MRI to retest 92 people with suspicious pain. All had been seen in an emergency room, where X-rays found no sign of broken bones. But MRIs found 35 fractures.

If you have continuing pain after a fall or accident, talk to your doctor about whether you need an MRI to be sure. It's best to diagnose and treat a broken bone quickly.

The healing power of touch

Try the simple touch cure that may help many of your health problems. The right type of massage can boost your immunity, ease pain, reduce fatigue, and even lower your blood pressure. New research shows it works.

Generally speaking, massaging your muscles relaxes them and boosts blood circulation. That can help warm your muscles and cut pain. Massage may even block pain signals to your brain.

Smooth out your knots. A treatment called trigger point massage can help ease pain. Also known as pressure point massage, it involves a massage therapist applying deep, focused pressure on myofascial trigger points — or "knots" — that can form in your muscles. Pressing on these trigger points causes pain, and they can cause pain and other symptoms elsewhere in your body.

Try this trick to battle ongoing back pain. Tape together two old tennis balls. Then lie on your back with the balls centered under your spine. Make sure they are parallel to your waist, slightly above your lower back. Raise your arms to the ceiling. Then lower them one at a time, first to the sides and then above your head. This movement forces the tennis balls to give you a back massage.

If neck pain and stiffness bother you, check out this maneuver. On the back of your hand, imagine a triangle having equal sides with corners at the knuckles of your index and ring fingers and one toward your wrist. Massage the third corner of the triangle with your other hand. While you massage, stretch your neck and feel the stiffness and pain dissolve away.

Pump up immunity. Some say massage can even boost your immune response. It's true massage may increase the flow of lymph, a fluid that circulates through your body's lymphatic system. Lymph carries cells that fight disease and gather waste for removal. Some people believe massage boosts lymph system drainage, getting fluid and immune cells moving.

Renew your vitality. Beyond relaxation, you can battle tiredness using self-massage on certain secret anti-fatigue points.

University of Michigan researchers studied a group of college students taking a boring daylong class. The students were taught to use two types of acupressure on themselves — one to relax and another to stimulate. Sure enough, pressing the "alertness" or stimulating points in between long periods of sitting made the students feel more awake.

Try these five stimulation points to wake up fast. Stimulate each spot, starting at your head and working your way down. For the crown, tap it gently for three minutes. For all other spots, rub them clockwise and counterclockwise for three minutes with your thumb or fingers.

- Put your fingers on your crown, the point in the center of the top of your head.

- Find the two bony ridges at the base of your skull. Go down 1 inch lower, then move 1.5 inches closer to the left ear on one side and the right ear on the other.

- Press into the web of each hand, in between your thumb and index finger.

- Locate the spot below each knee cap. Go four finger-widths lower, then move half an inch to the outside.

- Find the spot where your second and third toes join, then press there on the bottom of your foot, just below the ball.

Lower blood pressure. If high blood pressure is your problem, pick the right kind of massage — traditional Swedish massage.

There's no single cause for high blood pressure, but health professionals think long-term stress is a factor. Stress is also related to pain, so a massage may work on both problems at once. Research has shown Swedish massage — long strokes and kneading of muscles — lowered blood pressure in people with high blood pressure.

A new study found Swedish massage lowered both systolic and diastolic blood pressure in men, while trigger point therapy and sports massage increased systolic blood pressure — the first number in a blood pressure reading. Experts say the difference is that these two types of massage can cause pain and an increase in sympathetic nerve activity, which results in a rise in blood pressure.

Know when to get help

Everyone has aches and pains. Keep this checklist handy so you'll know when it's time to get help.

Body part in pain	See a doctor if ...
head	pain is severe and comes on suddenly. it goes on for days or months. you also have fever, rash, or neck stiffness. pain is accompanied by vomiting, memory problems, seizures, or personality changes.
chest	you have any pain at all. It could be anything from heartburn to a serious heart attack.
stomach	pain is so severe you can't move without making it worse. you also have other signs of trouble like chest pain or bloody diarrhea.
back	you also have numbness, tingling, or weakness, or you had a fall or injury.
neck	pain lasts longer than two weeks. you also have headache, fever, weight loss, clumsiness, or tingling in your arms or legs.
knee	pain from exercise gets worse or continues during rest or at night. your joint locks up, or you have swelling or bruises nearby. pain is so bad it keeps you from doing your usual activities.
teeth	pain lasts more than a few days. you also have a fever. pain keeps you from swallowing or breathing normally.

5 risky pain-relief mistakes

Your prescription or over-the-counter pain reliever works. That's
great. You still must be vigilant to steer clear of dangerous interactions
and overdoses. Avoid these common pain-reliever errors.

Doubling up on drugs. If your doctor gives you a prescription nonsteroidal anti-inflammatory drug (NSAID) like celecoxib (Celebrex),
you can't continue taking your over-the-counter NSAID. That means
drugs like naproxen (Aleve), ibuprofen (Advil), and aspirin are out of
bounds. You don't want to double your NSAID intake.

Using an NSAID patch and pill together. Using a patch or cream
form of an NSAID still puts that drug into your blood. That means
you may be double dosing if you also take an NSAID in pill form. So
be cautious if you use topical NSAIDs, like the Flector patch or
diclofenac (Voltaren) gel.

Mixing baby aspirin with other NSAIDs. Your doctor may prescribe
a certain NSAID, like Celebrex, to protect you from the gastrointestinal
(GI) problems caused by some pain medications. But if you continue
taking a baby aspirin every day to protect your heart, you lose the
stomach protection you got from taking that particular NSAID. Ask
your doctor if you should continue aspirin therapy.

Taking NSAIDs long term. In most cases, people age 75 and older
shouldn't take NSAIDs long term for chronic pain. Experts say the
risks are too great as you age, especially for GI bleeding, heart attack,
stroke, or interactions with other drugs. It's actually safer to take an
opiate like codeine or morphine — or preferably acetaminophen —
for long-term use.

Combining pain relief with blood thinning. Warfarin (Coumadin)
is a common blood thinner, often taken by people with the heart
arrhythmia atrial fibrillation. It takes a few weeks once you start taking
warfarin for your blood levels to stabilize. Look out for these two
possible problems if you begin taking an NSAID during this time.

- It may thin your blood too much. If you start taking an NSAID like naproxen, celecoxib, or others, it will bind to the same protein receptor in your blood that warfarin would attach to. In fact, the NSAID wins, pushing off warfarin so it floats freely in your blood. That means a greater risk of bleeding.

- It may cause a bleeding stomach ulcer. NSAIDs raise your risk of an ulcer, and if you get one while you're on warfarin, it tends to bleed more.

Question & Answer

My friend says I should try a new treatment for my chronic back pain, but there's no proof it works. Is it worth trying?

Yes. Sometimes remedies that really shouldn't work actually do. Think about the sugar pills researchers use to test a new drug. Typically, for nearly one-third of people, the sugar pill is effective. That's the placebo effect.

The placebo effect is not "all in your head." Rather, when you expect a treatment to work, your body sometimes reacts with an actual biological change, producing certain chemicals or stress hormones that signal pain or pleasure. Result? The sugar pill does the job. So if you think a treatment might work, give it a try.

Index

Injury, preventing 55
Insoluble fiber 169, 303
Insomnia
    avoiding 213, 219-220
    belly fat and 205
    bladder problems and 205-206
    eating and 210
    exercise for 216
    health problems from 203-204
    heat and 231-232
    memory loss and 254-255
    natural remedies for 227-229
    technology and 212
    worrying about 221-222
Insulin resistance 66, 68-69
Insulin, cooling 107
Interesterified fat 159
Intermittent claudication 138
Internet 248
    calculator 38
Iron, vegetarian diet and 42
Irritable bowel syndrome (IBS)
    302-303

J

Jar opener, for arthritis 332
Jaw pain 300
Joint pain 333, 337, 354, 358.
    See also Arthritis
Journal
    gratitude 189
    stress 275
Juice 19
    cherry 356
    cranberry 124
    lemon 73, 183
    pickle 315-316

K

Kava 290
Ketosis 33
Kidney problems 33
Knuckles, cracking 331
Kukoamines 142

L

L-carnitine 59
Lacto-vegetarian 41
Lactobacillus 303
Laughter, and heart 287
Lavender 291
LDL (low density liproprotein)
    cholesterol 156. *See also*
    Cholesterol
Leg cramps 234, 315-316. *See
    also* Restless Legs Syndrome
    (RLS)
Legs, strengthening 57
Lemon juice, and blood sugar 73,
    83
Lentils 16
Lettuce 143
Life, simplifying 292
Lifespan, and weight 6
Light box, for SAD 200
Limbic system 287
Liver damage, from kava 290
Loneliness 171-172
    Internet and 200
    pets for 175
    religion and 191
Lou Gehrig's disease 311
Low blood sugar. *See*
    Hypoglycemia
Low-carb diet 265

Lutein 155
Lychee 67
Lycopene 155-156

M

Magnesium 67
  metabolic syndrome and 137
Magnetic resonance imaging
  (MRI) 359
Massage 292-294, 359-361
  exercise and 319
Maximum Weight Limit (MWL)
  5
Meals, planning 81
Meat, processed 69, 160
Medicines. *See* Drugs
Mediterranean diet 36-38, 84,
  195, 265
Melatonin 177, 194, 211, 219,
  228
Memory
  exercise for 242
  foods for 261-263
  puzzles for 237
  sleep and 224
  tai chi and 283
  techniques 249-251
  vitamin B12 for 262, 269
Memory loss
  drugs and 257-258
  education and 251
  insomnia and 254-255
  preventing 238
  socializing and 252-254
  soy and 260
  stress and 255-256
Menopause 2, 116
Mental health care 201-202
Mental Health Parity Law 201
Menus, online 161

Mercury, in fish 163
Message, eternal 187-188
Metabolic syndrome 36, 137, 155
  insomnia and 204
Metabolism 1-3, 21-22, 46-47,
  52-54, 144, 308, 314
Metamucil 124, 303
Meter, for blood sugar. *See*
  Glucose monitor
Middle-age spread, stopping 205
Migraine 342-344
Milk, chocolate, and exercise 357
Minerals, for high blood pressure
  136-138
Mitochondria 25
Mnemonics 250
Molasses 86
Monitor, glucose 98, 105-106
Monosodium glutamate (MSG)
  19, 343, 346
Monounsaturated fatty acid
  (MUFA) 23, 37
Mood
  alcohol and 178-180
  books for 190
  carbohydrates and 34, 193
  characteristics 173
  dieting and 192-193
  drugs and 180
  exercise and 280-281
  foods for 194-195
  hormones and 177
  tracking 275
Morton's toe 342
Mouth guard 208
Muscles
  drugs and 323-324
  massage and 293
  pain, soothing 317
  protein for 308
  relaxing 286

Social worker 176
Socializing, to prevent memory
loss 252-254
Sodium 267
Soluble fiber 169, 303
Sour cream, substitute for 46
Soy
cholesterol and 156
diabetes and 74
for menopause 178
memory loss and 260
Spastic colon. See Irritable bowel
syndrome (IBS)
Spices 164-166
Spinal manipulation 334
Spirituality, benefits of 190-192
Splenda 88
St. John's wort 196
Stairs, climbing 134
Starch, resistant 27-28, 82, 142,
154
Static stretches 320
Statins
diabetes and 109
for gallstones 352
heart disease and 122
muscle damage and 323-324
Strength training. See Weight
training
Stress
aging and 288
aromatherapy for 291
clutter and 294-296
controlling 72, 104, 275-276
creativity and 296-298
deep breathing and 285-286
diabetes and 102-104
digestive system and 302
foods and 271-272
herbs for 289-290
immune system and 285

irritable bowel syndrome and
302-303
journal 275
massage for 292-294
memory loss and 255-256
migraine and 343
nail biting and 273
prayer and 191
weight and 14, 279-281
Stress hormones. See Cortisol;
Catecholamines
Stretches, types of 320
Strips, for blood sugar. See
Glucose monitor
Stroke
antidepressants and 198
aspirin and 129
B vitamins and 150-152
body fat and 132-134
vitamin D and 135
Sugar, substitute for 46, 87-88
Supplements
detoxifying 29
exercise and 324
fat burning 59-60
fish oil 164
for diabetes 100-102
for osteoarthritis 327-329
protein 309
Swedish massage 293, 361
Sweeteners, artificial 18, 86-88
Swimming, benefits of 326

T

Tai chi 216, 243, 282-284, 354
Tea
diabetes and 66, 74
for stress 273-274
ginger 312
green 21-22

Vitamin D (*continued*)
  rheumatoid arthritis and 331
  vegan diet and 42
Vitamin K 66, 143
Volunteering 185, 253

W

Walking 51-52, 70, 93, 131, 138, 281
Walnuts 74, 157, 263
Warfarin 102, 166, 363-364
Water 22
Weather, and joint pain 337
Weight
  cholesterol and 125
  diabetes and 64, 70
  fibromyalgia and 347
  gallstones and 350-352
  holidays and 44-46
  joints and 333
  lifespan and 6
  metabolism and 29
  nuts and 158
  stress and 14, 279-281
Weight loss 5-6
  Alzheimer's disease and 267
  Amish and 50-51
  body fat and 133-134
  breakfast and 143-144
  calories and 10-11, 29-30
  dairy for 26
  diabetes and 84-85
  diet pills and 60
  exercise and 13
  foods for 15-17
  goal 8-9
  snacks and 20-21

snoring and 230
tips for 7, 13-14
video games and 58
whole grains for 148
Weight training 53-54, 94-95, 243, 306-307, 326
Whey protein 309
White flour, substitute for 46
White noise, and sleep 220
Whole grains, benefits of 25-26, 75-76, 147-149
Wii 58, 288
Willow bark extract 328
Women, and heart disease 119-121
Worry. *See* Anxiety
Worry break 298
Wounds, and blood sugar 62

X

X-ray 359

Y

Yawning, to relieve stress 282
Yoga 243, 281, 304
Yogurt 18

Z

Zeaxanthin 155
Zero trans fats 159
Zinc, and exercise 185
Zostavax, for shingles 354